Of Manners Gentle

This book is the first in a series published jointly by Oxford University Press and the Australian Institute of Criminology. The series relates to matters of practical and theoretical criminology.

Of Manners Gentle

ENFORCEMENT STRATEGIES OF AUSTRALIAN BUSINESS REGULATORY AGENCIES

Peter Grabosky
Australian Institute of Criminology

John Braithwaite
Australian National University

Melbourne
Oxford University Press
Oxford   Auckland   New York
in association with
Australian Institute of Criminology

OXFORD UNIVERSITY PRESS

Oxford, New York, Toronto, Delhi, Bombay, Calcutta, Madras, Karachi, Singapore, Hong Kong, Tokyo, Nairobi, Dar es Salaam, Cape Town, Melbourne, Auckland, and associates in Beirut, Berlin, Ibadan, Nicosia.

National Library of Australia
Cataloguing-in-Publication data:
Grabosky, Peter N. (Peter Nils), 1945–
Of Manners Gentle.

Bibliography.
Includes index.
ISBN 0 19 554691 1.
ISBN 0 19 554690 3 (pbk.).

1. Administrative agencies – Australia. 2. Industry and state – Australia. I. Braithwaite, John, 1951–   . II. Australian Institute of Criminology. III. Title.

354.940082.

Edited by Leona Jorgensen
Jacket Designed by Guy Mirabella
Typeset by Kerri Rowley, Sue Thompson
Printed by Impact Printing, Melbourne
Published by Oxford University Press, 7 Bowen Crescent, Melbourne
OXFORD is a trademark of Oxford University Press.

Contents

Acknowledgements

This book could not have been written without the assistance of almost a thousand people. They know who they are, and we are sure they understand that if we sent them all a free copy of the book, we would have lost half our market! First and foremost, we express our deepest gratitude to the executives of the 111 commonwealth, state, and local government agencies who kindly consented to lengthy interviews with us, and who provided us with often very detailed criticisms of draft chapters.

We also wish to thank the Australian Institute of Criminology and the Australian National University for institutional support throughout the course of the project. In addition, we wish to acknowledge the financial support of the Commonwealth Department of Employment and Industrial Relations, which facilitated specifically our research on occupational health and safety policy.

The staff of the J.V. Barry Memorial Library at the Institute were of great assistance in conducting bibliographic searches, arranging interlibrary loans, and generally facilitating our access to various diverse bodies of literature. We are grateful to Nikki Rizsko, Gael Parr, Kristina Klop and Anna Davie for their efforts on our behalf.

A number of colleagues kindly read and commented upon various chapters within their areas of expertise. We wish to thank: Ellen Baar, Michael Barker, Gerry Bates, Stephen Churches, David Cole, Des Connell, Ross Cranston, Rob Fowler, Peter Hanks, Andrew Hopkins, Ralph Jacobi, Jocelyn McGirr, Garth Nettheim, Nadia Potas, Neil Rees, Jocelynne Scutt, and Roman Tomasic.

David Biles, Brent Fisse, Richard Harding, Peter Loof, and Terry Speed read the manuscript in its entirety.

Twenty different people laboured long hours transcribing interview tapes and preparing various drafts of the manuscript. We wish specially to acknowledge the contributions of Diane Grant and Lavinia Hill in this regard.

Advice and assistance in data analysis were kindly provided by Valerie Braithwaite, Terry Speed, and John Walker; a special note of thanks must go to Debra Rickwood for her patience and tolerance, as well as for her enthusiasm and efficiency in undertaking a variety of computing tasks. We also benefited from research assistance by Michelle Robertson.

Leona Jorgensen did the copy editing, Judy Iltis of the J.V. Barry Memorial Library prepared the index, and Kerri Rowley did the typesetting. For overall publishing supervision we thank Jack Sandry of the Institute and Ev Beissbarth of Oxford University Press. Our deepest appreciation goes to all these people. We assume responsibility for any errors which may have persisted despite their scrutiny.

Peter Grabosky
John Braithwaite
October 1985

1
Introduction

Business regulation is a fashionable topic. As is the case with most fashionable topics, much discussion of business regulation tends to generate more heat than light. To some business spokespeople, government interference in the marketplace is regarded as the embodiment of evil. Others adopt a more flexible approach, objecting strenuously to some forms of regulation, but tolerating, indeed, embracing, those forms of government involvement which happen to foster their own business interests. Some members of the public, on the other hand, regard government regulation as the last line of defence against unscrupulous or otherwise predatory corporate conduct. In this book, we do not seek to generate heat on either the 'pro' or 'anti' sides of the regulation debate, but rather shed light on enforcement strategies as expressed by top management of the major business regulatory agencies in Australia.

Our concern is not with the content of business regulation, the rights and wrongs of whether particular regulations ought to exist, but with what agencies do to enforce the regulations they have. We seek to portray the variation which exists across the enforcement strategies of Australian regulatory agencies, and to explain the basis for the differences which we identify. Is there a style of regulation which is unique to Queensland or to the commonwealth, or do regulatory similarities appear in all states in specific areas such as occupational health and safety or consumer affairs? Do agencies responsible for regulating a small number of firms in one industry (e.g. mining) behave differently from those which oversee a large number of diverse firms? These are among the questions which we hope to answer.

This book shows in a systematic way that Australian business regulatory agencies are of manners gentle. Not only is this reflected in the attitudes of the regulators, it also characterizes their policies and regulatory outcomes such as prosecutions, licence suspensions, plant shutdowns, injunctions, or the informal use of adverse publicity. Litigation or any kind of adversarial encounter with industry is commonly undertaken only as a last resort.

We will show that the benign nature of business regulation in Australia is not determined by any inadequacy of powers at their disposal. Indeed, the majority of agencies we studied are vested with statutory powers of entry, search, seizure, and investigation which would make them the envy of Australian police forces. However, these powers are rarely, if ever, used. In fact, some regulatory executives expressed embarrassment at their very existence. We show that when it is big business that is being regulated, the propensity to non-adversarial regulation is especially pronounced. These findings would appear to render much of the big business rhetoric about the onerous burdens of business regulation shallow indeed.

In traversing the patchwork of Australian business regulation in the pages that follow, readers will undoubtedly be as struck as we were by what a fragmented, unco-ordinated melange of overlapping commonwealth, state, and local government agencies it is. Fragmentation makes passing the buck to other institutional domains a standard operating procedure among many Australian regulatory agencies. The only systematic policy of some commonwealth agencies is to defer to state agencies, and the common practice of some state agencies is to push responsibility for the really difficult problems onto the commonwealth or local governments. We will see that it is very rare for Australian regulatory agencies to have explicit policies for limiting the risk of capture by the interests they are supposed to be regulating. Although corruption allegations had been directed at nineteen of the agencies we visited, it was extremely rare for agencies to have standard procedures for guarding against corruption. Even written enforcement policies were very rare. This book, therefore, shows that not only are Australian regulatory agencies characterized by gentle manners, they are also characterized by *ad hoc* administration. In some ways, the subtitle of this book is a misrepresentation because so many Australian regulatory agencies are basically lacking in strategy. Rather, their conduct tends to take the form of:

1 Platitudinous appeals to industry to act responsibly;
2 Token enforcement targeted in a manner which bears no necessary relationship to failures to heed those platitudinous appeals;
3 Keeping the lid on problems which could blow up into scandals; and
4 Passing the buck to another agency within the labyrinth of Australian federalism when the lid cannot be kept on a scandal.

The Agencies

This book is based on interviews which we conducted with senior officers of ninety-six commonwealth, state, and local government agencies involved in business regulation. In total, we approached 101 organizations which met our definition of a regulatory agency. A business regulatory agency was defined as a government department, a subunit of a government department, a statutory authority, or commission, established independently of the corporate sector, with significant responsibilities for regulating activities of commercial corporations which might run counter to what the legislature determines to be broader community interests. 'Commercial corporations' encompass government-owned organizations which sell products or services, such as Telecom or TAA, but exclude government bodies which do not engage in commerce. A distinguishing characteristic of all our agencies is that they administer legislation which empowers them or their minister to prosecute business offenders. The only exception to this is the Office of Road Safety in the Commonwealth Department of Transport.

This office is a unique federal agency which includes among its primary responsibilities the safe design of motor vehicles for the Australian market. The office answers to the Australian Transport Advisory Council, which consists of all transport ministers. Each state and territory minister for transport has the power to enforce compliance with the Australian Design Rules monitored by the Office of Road Safety. The power to prosecute, therefore, is one stage removed from the office itself. Although all of the other agencies have the power to prosecute, either directly or through their political masters, a third had not used the power in the three years preceding our visit.

The 101 organizations meeting this definition were approached on the basis that they were the major regulatory agencies in Australia. These are listed in the appendix. The list includes each of the state, territory, and commonwealth agencies responsible for corporate affairs, consumer affairs, environmental protection, food standards, combating discrimination, and occupational health and safety (including mine safety). These are the areas where there are many agencies covering the same field of regulation in different jurisdictions. Of course, there are many other domains where there is one major agency responsible. The reasons why all of these agencies are of major significance, we hope is clear from the book. Where we may deserve criticism is for the agencies omitted. For example, there is only a token representation of six local government agencies, when hundreds could have been included. These six were not chosen randomly, but were selected because we judged them to be those with the most substantial regulatory responsibilities: they were chosen from the largest local government authorities in the country.

There is also one regional authority responsible to state government: the Metropolitan Waste Disposal Authority in Sydney. This is one of a handful of agencies to which state governments have handed responsibility for regulating problems like waste disposal across combined local government jurisdictions. The Metropolitan Waste Disposal Authority is the most significant authority of this kind.

While local government agencies have not been accorded systematic coverage, the study does fairly systematically address commonwealth, state, and territory regulation. We feel the most important agencies excluded are those responsible for regulating nursing homes. With more resources, this would have been the next area covered.

Some might criticize the sample for the exclusion of primary produce marketing boards. However, regulation here, as in regulation of pesticide use, is not primarily directed at companies, but at individual farmers. Moreover, bodies like the Australian Wheat Board or state egg marketing boards, even though they initiate prosecutions for selling black market produce, are primarily trading rather than regulatory bodies. State fisheries and forestry departments are the closest approximations to business regulatory agencies in the primary industry sector, though even these are somewhat ambiguous examples of regulatory agencies as defined here. Two state fisheries departments were included in the sample to provide some insight into how these may differ from more traditional regulatory agencies.

Beyond primary production, there are bodies like the Steel and Automotive Industry Authorities, but these are more in the nature of consultative bodies on which industry is itself represented rather than government regulatory bodies; they have no power to prosecute.

In addition to the semi-structured interviews with the ninety-six organizations listed in the appendix, we did conduct an additional fifteen unstructured interviews at what might be called quasi-regulatory agencies. These were government bodies which did not directly enforce the law against companies, but which were nevertheless vital to understanding how the total regulatory system works in Australia. For example, the food standards area in the Commonwealth Department of Health does not enforce food standards, but does have an important role in the development of uniform food standards, the co-ordination of national recalls of hazardous food products, and in liaison with state and local authorities over the quarantine of hazardous food imports. For similar reasons we spoke with occupational health authorities in all state and territory health departments; the National Occupational Health and Safety Commission; the Australian Atomic Energy Commission, and its regulatory bureau, the Environmental Contaminants Division; and the Assessment Branch of the Commonwealth Department of Arts, Heritage, and the Environment; the Queensland Department of Harbours and Marine; and the Western Australian Department of Conservation and Environment. These interviews were not coded for the purpose of any of the quantitative analysis in the book.

Securing the Interviews

The Director of the Australian Institute of Criminology wrote on behalf of the authors to heads of government departments responsible for the 116 regulatory and quasi-regulatory agencies. The letter was sent about six weeks in advance of our requested date of interview and enclosed a list of the questions we intended to ask. This meant that by the time of our arrival, the respondent had ascertained answers to questions beyond his or her direct experience from relevant parts of the organization. In many cases, when we arrived a senior officer gave us written answers to the questions which had been prepared by a variety of more junior officers.

The letter requested a three hour interview, but where written answers were provided, two hours were generally sufficient. In the minority of cases where preparatory work had not been done, some visits lasted for four hours initially and required a follow-up visit, telephone calls, or correspondence. In fact, at least some follow-up correspondence to tidy up details which had not been resolved in the interview was required in most cases.

Both researchers were present for all interviews. The reasons for having two interviewers for this kind of research have been detailed elsewhere (Braithwaite, 1985). They include superior rapport, facilitation of note taking, improved coverage of topics with a semi-structured schedule, and data reliability. All coding for purposes of quantitative analysis was also done by the authors; eleven interviews were coded by both authors to ensure reliability. Rarely were we confronted with only one respondent. In some cases senior respondents surrounded themselves with as many as seven more junior officers to assist with answering questions. Our initial inclination was to accept interviews only with the head of the agency. We soon learned that this was a misguided intention. In almost half of the interviews we did secure an interview with the head of the agency, but we felt that these were generally not as successful as the remaining interviews which were dominated by an officer on the second most senior level in the agency. These latter officers were generally better prepared and more familiar with the middle-range policy issues which were the focus of our questions. Even when the head of the agency was present, it was often his or her deputies who did most of the talking.

We failed to secure interviews at five of the agencies contacted. The Northern Territory Registrar-General's Office (responsible for corporate affairs) was happy to co-operate with the research, but at the time we visited Darwin, there were no senior staff of the office in town! Subsequent correspondence and telephone conversations did occur with this agency. The Queensland Corporate Affairs Commission declined a face-to-face interview, but did provide some written answers to our questions. The data from both these agencies were useful but of insufficient quality to justify inclusion in our quantitative analysis.

Outright refusal to co-operate with the research was the response of only the New South Wales Department of Industrial Relations, and Queensland's Water Quality Council, and the Queensland Air Pollution Council at the instruction of their minister, Mr Russ Hinze.

Thus, the response rate was 95 per cent. At the beginning of each interview respondents were asked if they had any objection to our taping the discussions. Over 90 per cent of respondents consented. Tapes were transcribed for each interview. To minimize respondents' inhibitions, we strongly encouraged them to ask us to turn the recorder off whenever they wanted to say something off the record. Practically all respondents followed our suggestion, and had the machine off for part of the interview. This, we feel, gave us the best of both worlds: the superior attention to detail from having a transcript, and the frankness which could only be obtained off the record for sensitive matters. We did not feel that the tape recorder inhibited discussion; most of our questions covered basic descriptive issues, with the more sensitive matters ordered towards the end of the interview.

One respondent explicitly requested at the outset that we not quote him verbatim. Another requested the right to edit any quotations attributed to her. We have honoured both of these requests. No such conditions were imposed by other respondents; therefore, we have felt free to quote them directly to illustrate various points. Where quotations are in smaller type in the text without any other citation, they are taken from our interview transcripts.

Draft chapters were sent to each agency we visited, as well as to others knowledgeable in the areas of regulation concerned, for criticism and updating. Not all respondents were pleased with our analysis. Whilst we regret any discomfort which we may have caused, it is our strongly held view that the interests of the Australian public can best be served by a frank and robust discussion of the regulatory process.

Interviews for this book were conducted throughout 1984, with some follow-up in early 1985. Unfortunately, our task of depicting the current state of regulatory activity within ninety-six separate agencies was thwarted in part by those changes which inevitably occur with the passage of time.

After we had concluded our interviews, indeed as our concluding chapter was being written, the commonwealth government embarked upon a fundamental change of direction with regard to the detection and control of medical benefits abuses. Shortly before, responsibility for the control of water quality in the Northern Territory was transferred from the Department of Transport and Works to the Department of Mines and Energy. It appears inevitable that before, or at least soon after, this book is published, some references will become of historical rather than current value. We can, however, say with some confidence that the pages below reflect regulatory reality as at 1 May 1985.

A Note on Statistics

Unless otherwise noted, the enforcement statistics presented in the tables throughout this book relate to successful prosecutions (convictions) to the exclusion of unsuccessful proceedings launched. Where we were able to ascertain that a number of closely related charges were laid at the same point in time against the same defendant, we counted these as one case. Where both a company and an individual were convicted for the same offence, we counted these as separate defendants and separate convictions.

Australian Studies of the Regulatory Process

The study of business regulation in Australia is still in its infancy. To be sure, there exist a number of government documents and journalistic accounts dealing with specific regulatory regimes. Some of the more noteworthy of these publications are cited in the chapters which follow.

General reviews of the regulatory process are fewer in number. These have tended to be commissioned by state governments with a view toward rationalizing regulatory legislation (Gayler, 1980; Victoria, Legal and Constitutional Committee, 1984). One important exception is the work of Tomasic (1984), a collection of articles addressing general regulatory issues accompanied by a set of case studies of specific Australian regulatory regimes. Systematic comparative analyses which seek to describe and explain variations in Australian regulatory activity are non-existent. The present book is the first of this kind.

Regulatory Research Abroad

Overseas efforts to characterize regulatory strategies have emphasized the specification of ideal types. These lie at either ends of a continuum of formality suggested by the more general work of Black (1976). The more formal style of regulation, for which Reiss (1984) uses the term 'deterrence' and Hawkins (1984), the term 'sanctioning', is based essentially upon a penal response to a regulatory violation. The general concern is the application of punishment for corporate misconduct, for retributive and deterrent purposes. A harmful or potentially harmful act in breach of the law deserves punishment. The infliction of such punishment is intended to discourage the specific offender from committing further violations, and to discourage prospective offenders in general from breaching regulatory standards. Deterrence or sanctioning strategies seek to identify and detect breaches of law through patrol and inspection; they then seek to develop a case for the courts through investigation.

What both Reiss and Hawkins refer to as 'compliance' strategies represent an informal style of regulation. Recourse to the legal process occurs rarely, and then only as a last resort. Compliance with regulatory standards is sought not by threat or coercion, but by negotiation or conciliation. These compliance strategies seek to minimize opportunities for breaches of law through consultation, diagnosis, and persuasion, or through the provision of technical assistance. For example, in his seminal study of British consumer agencies, Cranston (1979) found that only a small percentage of known offences were prosecuted, with simple cautions or inaction being the most common regulatory response. In summarizing thirty-five studies of regulatory agencies, Hawkins concluded that compliance strategies were by far the most common, at least in Britain and North America (Hawkins, 1984, 3).

In much the same manner as Reiss and Hawkins, Bardach and Kagan (1982) also perceive two basic models of regulation. At one extreme is the style of enforcement typified by the title of their study: *Going by the Book*. They see this style as essentially unreasonable and excessively legalistic, involving the strict imposition of standards which are, in short, unrealistic. The polar opposite of such 'regulatory unreasonableness' is a more tolerant, flexible regime in which enforcement authorities are discriminating and pragmatic in their application of law. The basic goal of 'reasonable regulation' is to achieve compliance without invoking the formal legal process. In contrast to Hawkins, Bardach and Kagan regard the unreasonable, legalistic model as the predominant style of enforcement in the United States, at least at the beginning of the 1980s before the deregulatory initiatives of the Reagan administration began to take hold.

Frank (1984) proposes yet another typology of regulatory activity: in essence a refinement of the compliance–deterrence distinction. Intersecting the prosecution–persuasion continuum is one which differentiates between centralized and decentralized administrative control. Some enforcement organizations are characterized by a highly developed formal bureaucracy, with centralized authority, and close monitoring of enforcement practice by senior management. In others, the dominant feature is the informal culture of the organization, and a lesser degree of central control.

In Chapter 16, we assess how these typologies square with the empirical realities of the diversity of Australian regulatory agencies. To be sure, the dominant characteristic of Australian regulatory agencies is the compliance model. The manners of Australian regulatory officials are gentle indeed. But there are some which have more of a deterrence orientation. More importantly, there are basic variations on the deterrence–compliance dimension, variations which are essentially unrelated to an agency's organizational characteristics.

Our data are uniquely placed for building a typology of regulatory agencies. No study has ever before attempted to summarize the entire range of major regulatory bodies in one country. Until now, the emphasis in the literature has quite rightly been on historical analyses, or on intensive studies of particular agencies. However, the time has come to begin to locate these case studies on a broader canvas of regulatory patterns. Our broad-brush, comparative approach is neither superior nor inferior to intensive studies of single agencies over time. Rather, we hope our findings will complement those of a more traditional genre.

Plan of the Book

Chapters 2-13 will review the most important substantive areas of regulatory activity in Australia. Each of these chapters will seek to identify the characteristics which distinguish that particular area of regulation from the others, and will seek to identify important differences between regulatory agencies with an otherwise similar mission.

The three concluding chapters will attempt a general explanation of variations in regulatory behaviour, and to develop a typology of regulatory agencies.

References and Recommended Reading*

Bardach, E. and Kagan, R. (1982), *Going by the Book: The Problem of Regulatory Unreasonableness*, Temple University Press, Philadelphia.

Black, D. (1976), *The Behavior of Law*, Academic Press, New York.

Braithwaite, J. (1985), 'Corporate Crime Research: Why Two Interviewers are Needed', *Sociology*, 19, 136-8.

Cranston, R. (1979), *Regulating Business: Law and Consumer Agencies*, Macmillan, London.

Frank, N. (1984), 'Policing Corporate Crime: A Typology of Enforcement Styles', *Justice Quarterly*, 1, 235-51.

Gayler, D. (1980), *Deregulation: A Plan of Action to Rationalise South Australian Legislation*, Government Printer, Adelaide.

*Hawkins, K. (1984), *Environment and Enforcement: Regulation and the Social Definition of Pollution*, Oxford University Press, New York.

*Reiss, A. (1984), 'Selecting Strategies of Social Control Over Organisational Life', in K. Hawkins and J. Thomas (eds), *Enforcing Regulation*, Kluwer-Nijhoff, Boston, 23-36.

*Tomasic, R. (ed.) (1984), *Business Regulation in Australia*, CCH Australia, Sydney.

Victoria, Legal and Constitutional Committee (1984), *A Report to the Parliament on the Subordinate Legislation [Deregulation] Bill, 1983*, Government Printer, Melbourne.

2
Corporate Affairs

Introduction

The past twenty years have seen dramatic examples of the development and refinement of companies as vehicles for crime in Australia. Perhaps the most notorious, the 'bottom of the harbour' schemes, involved the wide scale use of the company structure for the purpose of tax evasion. The mining boom of the late 1960s saw wild fluctuations in the prices of shares inspired by fabricated information. There have also been countless variations on the classic bankruptcy fraud, where companies incur debts which their management have no prospect, or indeed intention, of paying. Tantalizing assurances of astronomical profits have tempted unwitting investors to purchase submerged blocks of land, or to part with their money for some vaguely described, and ultimately mythical, investment scheme.

No attempt has been made to total systematically the direct costs incurred by taxpayers, investors, and creditors as a result of the above activities. The sum, no doubt, would be staggering. Of equal, if not greater significance, however, are the indirect costs to the economy as a whole. Investors who perceive a rigged sharemarket will withhold or withdraw their funds, thus making it more difficult for companies to acquire capital. A general suspicion that the business world is largely populated by predators can have a chilling effect on commerce and may ultimately lead to economic stagnation. All but the most extreme exponents of *laissez-faire* economics would advocate some degree of state intervention as preferable to the Hobbesian world of a corporate jungle. The task of finding the optimal point at which commerce might thrive and predation be kept to a minimum is one which has challenged Australian governments in recent years. The goal has proved to be an elusive one, as, in most instances, the requisite political will remains lacking. Corporate affairs regulation in Australia today is characterized by severe understaffing, massive backlogs, and political interference.

The Development of Uniformity
in Australian Company Law

As is the case with many aspects of Australian legal culture, company law derived from the English law; in this case, mainly from the Companies Act 1862. This consolidated the law regarding incorporation; prior to the nineteenth century, the privilege of forming a company was conferred by the crown or parliament on a case by case basis.

The purpose of facilitating the establishment of companies, and of limiting the liability of shareholders to the amount of their contribution, is to encourage the process of capital formation. Economic growth and economic well being depend upon the ability of companies to raise capital. Few people would place their entire personal worth at risk, but many would be willing to balance the possibility of a finite specified loss against the possibility of a gain.

English company law was adopted in each of the Australian colonies, with local variations, and evolved idiosyncratically through the nineteenth century. After federation, the regulation of companies operating within the various states was left to state parliaments. However, as the Australian economy developed during the twentieth century, it became increasingly apparent that the web of commerce often transcended state boundaries. While the smallest companies might operate entirely within a state, a growing number of companies, and particularly the larger ones, sought to do business in more than one jurisdiction, and were thus required to register with, and conform to, the specific legislation of each. The costs of conducting affairs on a national scale were substantial.

As the inconvenience imposed by this decentralized scheme touched an increasing number of companies, pressures intensified for national uniformity in companies regulation. Conferences between commonwealth and state authorities led to a uniform Companies Act in the early 1960s, based largely on the Victorian act of 1958. Further developments were inspired by the reports of the Company Law Advisory Committee (1971), chaired by Mr Justice Eggleston, and by the intention of the Whitlam government, before its dismissal, to enact national companies legislation in federal parliament. Whilst the power of the commonwealth to legislate in the area of company law had hitherto been constitutionally questionable, a 1971 decision in the High Court of Australia appeared to weaken existing impediments (*Strickland* v *Rocla Concrete Pipes* (1971) 45 ALJR 485).

Following the dramatic share market fluctuations of the late 1960s, which saw fortunes won, and lost, with stunning suddenness, a senate select committee on securities and exchange with Senator Peter Rae in the chair, held an inquiry into Australian securities markets and their regulation (Australia, Senate, 1974). The Rae report drew attention to incompetence, malpractice, and improper conduct on the part of financial journalists, sharebrokers, and directors of public companies. Noting that a number of major frauds involved transactions across state jurisdictions, the report recommended the establishment of a national regulatory body.

The demise of the Whitlam government reduced the momentum of commonwealth dominance in the companies and securities field, but pressures toward uniformity and centralization persisted. Extensive consultations between commonwealth and state governments culminated in the formal agreement of December 1978 to establish a national co-operative scheme of companies and securities regulation. It is this attempt at uniformity of law and standardization of practice which is the most distinctive characteristic of the corporate affairs domain.

The National Co-operative Scheme

Overall responsibility for the administration of the scheme resides in the Ministerial Council for Companies and Securities, a body comprised of state and commonwealth ministers responsible for company law and securities industry regulation. The National Companies and Securities Commission (NCSC) was created under the *National Companies and Securities Commission Act* 1979. Accountable to the ministerial council, its prime function is to administer the three basic codes of the co-operative scheme: the companies code (*Companies Act* 1981), the securities industry code (*Securities Industry Act* 1980), and the takeovers code (*Companies (Acquisition of Shares) Act* 1980). Essential uniformity of codes was achieved through the states adopting commonwealth legislation previously endorsed and approved by the ministerial council. The NCSC is funded jointly: 50 per cent by the commonwealth, and 50 per cent by the states, on a per capita basis.

The corporate affairs commissions of the states and the Australian Capital Territory have been designated as delegates of the national commission. An important proviso of the relationship, however, is the requirement that the commission 'have regard to the principle of maximum development of a decentralized capacity to interpret and promulgate the uniform policy and administration of the scheme'. In mid-1984 the NCSC had a staff of only sixty-two, in contrast to the more than 1,300 officers of the delegate commissions.

In effect, this means that the NCSC's direct regulatory role is limited. The NCSC has delegated the majority of its functions relating to administration of companies and securities legislation to the state agencies. Whilst the NCSC provides direction and policy guidelines, refers cases to the state and Australian Capital Territory commissions for investigation, and has prepared detailed operations manuals to encourage uniformity of administration, the commission has no control over the allocation of resources within or between delegate agencies. Having delegated the power to initiate prosecutions, it does not have the capacity to direct the conduct of enforcement activity at state level.

Relations between the NCSC and the state agencies have been characterized as poor (Warren, 1984). The co-operative scheme is co-operative in name only; the states are not prepared to support it fully, and are reluctant to relinquish their former independence (Frith, 1984). In fact, senior NCSC officials expressed to us considerable frustration at the inability, for whatever reason, of state agencies to act in a number of instances.

We send what we think are good cases to the states because we don't have the resources to do them ourselves. In fact, most time is spent on sending good stuff we've picked up and two or three years later we're still writing letters begging them to reply as to what they've done.

In very few cases we have resources to go in and say look, get off your butts, give us a report on that. We want a report. The report then comes over and they say there is no case to answer. One of the very first ones I had to do with, they said there was no case to answer, and you could go through this report and their interviews and there was a *prima facie* case there. You could go in and prosecute them on the documents.

Lack of state support is apparent in financial terms as well. Additional funds necessary to appoint new staff have been resisted by most of the state treasuries.

The NCSC, nevertheless, plays a more active role in the administration of the companies (acquisition of shares) legislation. Under the takeovers code, one may acquire up to 20 per cent of a company's shares without restrictions. Beyond this, one may acquire no more than 3 per cent every six months unless one makes a formal offer to all shareholders, or an announcement on the floor of the exchange to purchase all shares offered at a specified price. A particularly significant aspect of this NCSC regulatory regime is its legislative flexibility. The code vests the NCSC with wide discretionary powers. For example, section 57 empowers the commission to grant exemptions from compliance with the code; under the provisions of section 58, the commission may declare the code as if modified; and section 60 gives the commission power to declare an acquisition or related conduct to be unacceptable.

The justification for governmental involvement in a company takeover is to ensure that shareholders in the target company possess sufficient information to exercise their rights. It is also desirable from a general economic standpoint that share markets operate efficiently, and that settlement, ownership and transfer of shares be effected quickly and at low cost.

Within the regulatory role which it has forged for itself, the NCSC has developed a distinctive strategy. Most significant, perhaps, is its rejection of the criminal sanction in favour of various civil remedies. The reasons for the choice lie in the fact that the civil remedies available to the NCSC are formidable, may be imposed without delay, and, in financial terms, would almost always exceed the amount of fines which members of the judiciary are willing to impose on businesspersons following conviction in a criminal court.

Among the regulatory tools available to the NCSC are the power to influence the conduct of a takeover, to freeze trading in the shares of a particular company, to cancel all trade, and to reverse trading in specified shares. All of these can impose significantly greater financial burdens upon a company than would the prevailing level of fines.

By way of illustration, the NCSC cited a recent case involving Endeavour Resources, a company associated with Perth businessman Alan Bond, which breached a provision of the takeovers code while seeking to gain control of Northern Mining. The NCSC forced Endeavour to make a full takeover, thus costing millions of dollars more than it had originally intended to spend in order to obtain control of the target company. As it happened, Bond was prosecuted concurrently by the Victorian Corporate Affairs Commission. He was fined a mere $500 and that was reduced on appeal to a bond. However, costs of approximately $45,000 were awarded against the defendant.

Another justification for the NCSC's use of civil, as opposed to criminal remedies is that civil avenues do not inhibit the use of publicity before and during proceedings to the extent that the criminal process does.

The NCSC is empowered to hold hearings of an investigative nature in private. Witnesses may be examined under oath, and their testimony is admissible in civil proceedings. Respondents, however, are not automatically entitled to be present throughout the hearing, or to cross-examine witnesses (Kluver and Woellner, 1983, 209-45). Public hearings can also be held, but these are infrequent, and are normally used for such purposes as airing law reform proposals.

In light of the inadequate resources available to Australian regulatory agencies in the companies and securities domain, some degree of self-regulation would seem inevitable. The flexibility, indeed elasticity, of accountancy standards has posed problems for years. Increased public pressure called for company accounts to be based upon verifiable data, to be presented in a form that would reflect real values to creditors and to regulatory authorities, as well as to members of the accountancy profession. Rather than impose such standards from above, the NCSC and its delegates urged the creation of the Accounting Standards Review Board to develop basic common principles on behalf of the profession.

Whilst the Securities Industry Act gives the NCSC power to license and to discipline securities dealers and investment advisors, the licensing power has largely been delegated to state agencies. In relation to dealers and their representatives, who are members of stock exchanges, disciplinary functions are performed by the stock exchanges themselves. Similarly, state offices register auditors and liquidators, but disciplinary power is vested in state and territory companies' auditors and liquidators disciplinary boards.

The NCSC has placed great emphasis on the self-regulation of certain industries, subject to regulatory oversight by relevant government authorities. This philosophy of co-regulation, as it is described, is exemplified by the NCSC's approach to the role of stock exchanges. The NCSC meets with the stock exchanges regularly.

We ask them how they are going, what they're doing. We ask them what resources they've put in, how they're enforcing their rules, what sort of monitoring they have, why they give waivers to their rules, whether they make that information public, and provided they seem to be accountable and efficient, we would virtually do no work in that industry at all other than very peripheral monitoring.

In addition, the NCSC itself monitors share markets regularly, watching for unanticipated fluctuations of share prices and for transfers of large numbers of shares. It is also empowered to suspend trading, and to cancel previous transactions.

An example of such a situation occurred early in 1984 when the release of false information to the Perth Stock Exchange resulted in a sharp increase in the price of shares in an oil exploration firm. The NCSC obtained orders which reversed these transactions.

Self-regulation of stock exchanges, though, is not viewed with universal satisfaction. As one senior corporate affairs official told us:

The stock exchanges here have had self-regulation for years, and it just doesn't work. Any organization that self-regulates leaves itself open to problems . . . Some of these people should be very severely dealt with. But they [the stock exchanges] don't want any adverse publicity, so if they can, they hush it up in their own ranks and say justice has been done.

Meetings of the NCSC are closed to the public, and, except where the NCSC determines otherwise, all information in its possession is restricted. It is thus not surprising that a larger proportion of its staff resources are devoted to processing requests under the Freedom of Information Act rather than to investigative tasks.

The various state corporate affairs offices or commissions have two major functions: registration and investigation. Registration is the basis of company regulation in Australia, and all registered companies are required to lodge annual returns with the corporate affairs body in their state or territory. Under the uniform scheme, companies lodging documents need do so in only one corporate affairs office.

The availability of company records is essential to enable potential investors or creditors to exercise their rights intelligently in relation to a company. As one senior South Australian official told us, insufficient attention to the registration function greatly facilitates the use of the company as an instrument of crime.

These bottom of the harbour frauds, they absolutely blossomed because compliance with straight out simple statutory obligations – strict liability offences – were not enforced. There was not proper enforcement to ensure that returns of directors were promptly put in, returns as to allotments to shareholders, returns as to registered offices, and it's absolutely certain that that provided the environment in which these guys operated to send the companies to the bottom of the harbour.

The investigative and enforcement role of corporate affairs agencies arises when some evidence of wrongdoing comes to the attention of the office or commission. This only rarely arises as the result of patrolling or monitoring activities by the commission, but in some instances, a commission's attention may be drawn by complaints from members of the public, or from other government agencies. Most commonly, malpractice is called to the agency's attention by liquidators, who are required to notify the government of offences they uncover, and when any failed company is unable to repay its creditors more than fifty cents in the dollar.

In addition to standard investigation of affairs of companies, provisions exist in legislation for special investigations. These may be instigated by the relevant minister or by the ministerial council. The powers of special investigators are extremely broad, and, in many respects, are comparable to those of a royal commission.

Despite the existence of uniform legislation and a co-operative scheme ostensibly dedicated to consistency and standardization in the administration of companies and securities law, one sees substantial variation in the exercise of this function across the states and territories of Australia. An overview of commonwealth and state corporate affairs agencies is provided in Table 1. In comparing the various corporate affairs agencies, one is immediately struck by the lack of staff resources at their disposal, relative to the number of registered companies in the jurisdiction. Complaints of inadequate staff became a familiar refrain as we visited the various agencies, and similar observations have been made by such disinterested observers as counsel assisting the Costigan Royal Commission (Meagher, 1983, 44), and the Special Prosecutor (Redlich, 1984).

Interstate Differences in Corporate Affairs Regulation

The manner in which the various corporate affairs commissions manage their common problem of resource constraint, however, leads to significant differences in regulatory behaviour.

Victoria

For a number of years the Victorian Corporate Affairs Office did not pursue enforcement of registration requirements, having prosecuted on a very limited basis for failure to lodge documents between 1979 and 1982, because of resource constraints and 'inadequacies in a computer program'. The risks inherent in such a *laissez-faire* approach were made apparent when Victorian investigators discovered extensive use of dummy companies for the purposes of tax evasion (McCabe and La Franchi, 1982). In 1983 the Victorian office embarked upon a vigorous programme of identifying those companies which were delinquent in submitting annual returns, and of prosecuting for persistent non-compliance. Victoria, however, does not check or confirm the contents of those returns which are lodged. The former commissioner has opposed a more proactive posture, saying:

Table 1
Commonwealth and State Corporate Affairs Agencies: Resource and Conviction Data

Agency	Total Staff (1.7.84)	Staff Engaged in Investigations (1.7.84)	Annual Expenditure (1984-85) $	Number of Registered Companies in Jurisdiction (30.6.84)	Number of Convictions and Average Fines 1982-84 Financial Years				Prison Sentences
					Failure to Lodge Returns		Other Matters		
					Convictions	Av. Fine $	Convictions	Av. Fine $	
National Companies and Securities Commission	62	6	4,900,000	—	—	—	—	—	—
New South Wales Corporate Affairs Commission	500	108	19,410,000	224,303	2,044	—	483	—	14
Victoria Corporate Affairs Office	293	48	7,150,560	173,359	9,380	—	251	—	21
Queensland Corporate Affairs Commission	220	17	—	84,967	2,966	183	19	723	1
South Australia Corporate Affairs Commission	85	14	2,081,000	41,036	932	97	48	507	4
Western Australia Corporate Affairs Office	119	23	3,211,026	52,162	52	—	74	—	1
Tasmania Corporate Affairs Office	22	3	—	8,933	0	—	1	—	1
Northern Territory Registrar-Generals Office	5	3	—	9,500	450	65	0	—	0
Australian Capital Territory Corporate Affairs Commission	70	14	—	16,903	689	129	6	271	0

Sources: Corporate Affairs Commissions, National Companies and Securities Commission

... if it were the function of corporate affairs offices to check and confirm all information lodged with them, they would rapidly become the largest government department in Australia (Wade, 1984, 46).

In certain areas of company regulation, the Victorian office plays a more active role than its counterparts in the other states. Its investigation staff routinely monitor radio, television, and newspaper advertisements with a view to identifying investment schemes which could be in breach of the companies code.

Victorian authorities claim to be also distinctive in their use of test case litigation as an instrument of company law reform. The case of *Commissioner for Corporate Affairs* v. *Peter William Harvey* [1981] VR 669 established new criteria for the appointment and conduct of liquidators, while *Wade* v. *A Home Away Pty Ltd* [1981] VR 475 upheld restrictions on the promotion of time sharing schemes.

One area in which the Victorian Corporate Affairs Office has expressed interest recently is that of investor education. Greed and gullibility are no less characteristic of Australians than of citizens of other western industrial societies, and the proliferation of investment schemes, both licit and illicit, has seen many pitfalls to confront the unwitting.

Australia's continued affluence has produced a growing number of small investors, many of whom are fairly naive. Since consumer affairs agencies tend not to regard investors as consumers, investor education remains an area of potential corporate affairs involvement. The Victorian office sought funds for this purpose, but without success. This concern is not shared by officials in other jurisdictions, however. An official in another state told us that 'there are a thousand ways to separate a fool from his money, but I don't see that as my responsibility'.

New South Wales

The New South Wales commission, the largest of the state corporate affairs agencies, prosecutes proportionately fewer companies for failure to lodge returns than do most of its counterparts, but it has devoted more resources to large special investigations than any of the other corporate affairs bodies. This has been a distinguishing characteristic of New South Wales corporate affairs regulation for at least two decades (Adby, 1985). Whilst Victorian authorities attribute this to the fact that Sydney has a disproportionate share of corporate predators, it became apparent to us that the New South Wales commission has quite intentionally used the well publicized showcase investigation as a regulatory tool. As a senior officer told us:

I think we rely upon the fact that a prosecution out of an investigation is not necessarily the only positive result. We take the view that our presence in the field in investigating a matter that comes to the attention of the commission is of itself a positive result even though it may not be possible to discover sufficient evidence of criminal misconduct.

I would say that the mere presence in the general commercial area — and it's known that inquiries are being undertaken — it's known that if certain conduct is pursued that an investigation by the commission is likely because of our past activity. And I would suggest that that activity of itself would be a deterrent to the commission of conduct of that kind.

Early in 1985, the newly appointed New South Wales Attorney-General announced a reorganization of the Corporate Affairs Commission, involving a merger of the commission's legal and investigation divisions. This integration is said to be designed to facilitate the development of prosecutions. In a manner reminiscent of his predecessors, the minister heralded this as the opening round of a crackdown on corporate offenders:

There has to be a big move to wrap up all the major company conspiracies in this state. It's no use just charging these people with having failed to pay their payroll tax or having failed to lodge their annual company returns (Wilson, 1985).

To assist in making its presence felt in the commercial community, the commission has its own public relations office. They do not, however, issue press releases in criminal cases until a matter has been finalized.

We wouldn't want to be in contempt of court for a start, and because we're the prosecuting authority, I would suggest we would not be the appropriate authority to start issuing press releases during the course of a matter.

The commission does seek publicity once a conviction has been obtained, however. In addition, the office tends to alert journalists to forthcoming events, and to provide background material to assist in the coverage of hearings. Indeed, the subjects of some special investigations by the New South Wales commission have become household words: Nugan Hand, Cambridge Credit, and the Barton Group are three of the more prominent. Other targets, such as Harry M. Miller, and companies associated with the leader of the state opposition, were already highly visible and politically prominent.

The immense complexity which characterizes some corporate affairs matters has often posed significant problems for the judicial process. It has been argued by some that long and complex trials are beyond the competence of many jurors, in addition to being very costly. One innovation intended to overcome such difficulty is the streamlining of the criminal process in New South Wales by the Supreme Court (Summary Jurisdiction) Act. This legislation permits the accused to opt for trial before a Supreme Court judge, instead of before a jury. Defendants, however, appear to see some strategic advantage in jury trials. At the time of our interview, only one defendant had waived his right to trial by jury in this manner. He was found guilty.

Queensland

Our efforts to learn about corporate affairs in Queensland met with some resistance. A letter to the Commissioner for Corporate Affairs

requesting an interview elicited a response from the Under Secretary for
Justice which advised:

It is not the Commissioner's role to discuss matters of Government Policy with
organisations such as your own and accordingly, I am unable to accede to your
request in this instance (Correspondence, 1 June 1984).

An invitation to pose questions of fact, in writing, was gratefully
accepted, but the term 'government policy' was construed so widely
that we could be told little more than staffing levels and qualification
requirements for investigators. A request for a copy of the commission's
annual report met with the response that none was published.

Data obtained ultimately from the Queensland Department of
Justice revealed a very modest reliance on criminal sanctions in
Queensland, especially with regard to more complex matters involving
serious breaches.

Other informants suggested that the Queensland Corporate Affairs
Commission places a higher priority on the registration function than
upon the investigation of alleged misconduct. This was corroborated by
the abovementioned prosecution statistics and by staff allocation data
which revealed that less than 10 per cent of corporate affairs staff are
involved in investigative work.

Western Australia

As is typical of other jurisdictions, regulatory policy in Western
Australia takes the interest of the victim into account, particularly in respect of the enforcement of the 'prescribed interests' provisions of the
companies code.

Where a substantial public interest is involved in such investment
schemes as 'time sharing', 'franchising' and other schemes where offer
or issue of interests to the public are involved which appear to be in
breach of the code, efforts are directed towards compliance rather than
prosecution in the first instance.

In many cases, prosecution, depending on the quality of the defence,
may only attract a nominal fine. However, the resultant publicity would
in most cases be disastrous for the continuity of the scheme, resulting in
large withdrawals of investors' funds with the inevitable collapse of
the scheme.

Nevertheless, a scheme operating within the provisions of the law,
and able to negotiate short term finance if necessary, has a good chance
of success, to the benefit of the promoters and the average investor in the
street.

So you investigate, but try to keep the publicity down as low as possible. If there's
a big institution going down the tube, you don't just rush out and say we're going
to take you to court, irrespective. You've got to weigh the pros and cons.

An earlier study of the New South Wales commission revealed some
reluctance to prosecute where such action would threaten the interests

of creditors (Sutton, 1983, 179). It was also apparent that authorities in Western Australia, as in New South Wales and in Victoria prior to 1983, devoted very little energy to prosecuting companies for failing to lodge annual returns. This was attributed to 'difficulties associated with the application of new legislation, insufficient staff resources, and the development of computerized compliance systems'.

Three months after our interviews in Perth, the Western Australian government moved to restructure corporate affairs as a separate department with increased resources. Whether this heralds any change in policy remains uncertain: the press release announcing the change noted cryptically that the 'state government hopes to attract new business' (*West Australian*, 9 October 1984, 16).

South Australia

The year 1984 appeared to mark a major policy shift in South Australia, as prosecutions for failure to lodge returns ceased almost entirely, whilst prosecutions for more complex matters almost trebled.

The South Australian Corporate Affairs Commission placed great importance on bringing the full weight of the criminal process to bear against corporate offenders. As the commission's senior solicitor told us:

One of the things about which I have a very strong conviction, having pros-ecuted a lot of corporate criminals, both summarily and by indictment, I can say this without exception, there has been an absolute fear in the minds of defend-ants of going to jail. One of getting the conviction, that's the first thing they fight like crazy to avoid, because of the stigma and the consequences that flow from it, and secondly the prospect of going to jail. The fine's not that much of a worry because they've plenty of money in the bin, but the fear of going to jail is paramount in their minds, and I'm sure, absolutely certain, that with the right sort of publicity to jail sentences for convictions in this area, it does have an educational effect or a deterrent effect.
Most of these guys lead a pretty good life. You know, the wine, women, and song mentality. They are pretty high flyers: $50 for lunch here, and take this lady out tonight, and flit off to Sydney to see this. That sort of lifestyle. But it's the trauma in terms of their change in lifestyle which I think they fear. I know that you just sense, at every stage of the trial, that that's what they fear.

Tasmania

As we were told by the Tasmanian Corporate Affairs Commissioner 'It's a very different world down here'. The Tasmanian capital market is very small, and thus probably attracts proportionately fewer predators. The office had not registered a prospectus in ten years. Unlike the larger commissions, the Tasmanian agency regards law enforcement as a less important function. Its use of prosecution has been negligible, whether for routine or complex matters. Indeed, the commission did not have an investigation section prior to 1983. Previously, major company failures were intermittent and relatively rare. When they occurred they had political overtones, and there were special investigators appointed. Allegations that the son of the Lord Mayor of Launceston had departed Australia with $2.5 million belonging to numerous would-be investors, however, inspired the establishment of a permanent investigative body.

Australian Capital Territory

The Australian Capital Territory Corporate Affairs Commission is primarily concerned with the registration function. Like Tasmania, and unlike the larger corporate affairs agencies, the Australian Capital Territory commission does not regard law enforcement as its primary function. The commissioner told us 'I've never considered prosecution as having an educational function', a view which contrasts sharply with that of the South Australian office quoted above.

Nevertheless, it consistently prosecutes companies for failure to lodge returns, and shows a high rate of convictions in proportion to the number of registered companies.

The commission has chosen to keep a low profile, 'We are not treating prosecutions or investigations as an educational activity... We don't like to run showcases'. It should be noted that reports of corporate affairs convictions have appeared with increasing regularity in the *Canberra Times*.

The Australian Capital Territory commission has a higher ratio of staff to number of registered companies than any other corporate affairs body. One official whom we interviewed, a person with a broad national perspective on corporate affairs regulation, described it as 'grossly overstaffed'. Because of this relative resource advantage, the Australian Capital Territory commission is unique in its ability to check, thoroughly and systematically, the accuracy of most annual returns.

The commissioner still argues that staff resources are inadequate, and maintains that many investigations and possible prosecutions must be foregone for want of resources. A clue to the commission's problems may lie in the commissioner's admission in mid-1984 that 'We have no computer facilities at all . . . We haven't even got a word processor yet'.

Northern Territory

The Northern Territory differs from its counterparts in corporate affairs regulation in that it is not a member of the co-operative scheme, though members of the ministerial council which had previously blocked its membership have now agreed to its admission. Because of its size, and the fact that it has only one public company, the territory plays a more modest regulatory role; the registration function predominates. There have not been any prosecutions under companies legislation for indictable matters since the territory was granted self-government in 1978, although approximately 150 companies are prosecuted each year for failure to lodge annual returns. The Registrar-General's Office randomly selects 10 to 15 per cent of returns each year for in-depth examination.

The territory Registrar-General does use the press to encourage timely lodgement of returns. Public advertisements are placed in territory newspapers reminding companies to file returns by a specified date. Shortly after the deadline, a press release is drafted reading '(500) companies are listed for prosecution for failure to lodge annual returns'. Publication of this message combined with personalized warning letters tends to evoke a compliant response from many companies.

On one occasion, the Registrar-General used his power to shut down a Queensland company operating illegally. The company, without a prospectus, was offering interests in a jojoba bean plantation by public advertisement. The Registrar-General walked into the company's shop-front office and ordered it closed forthwith.

In a jurisdiction as small as the Northern Territory, large investigations are extremely rare. In 1984, however, the Registrar-General's office engaged in a lengthy investigation, and subsequent prolonged court hearing, into improper conduct on the part of a liquidator under section 278 of the territory's Companies Ordinance. Judgement was in favour of the Registrar-General.

Who Prosecutes?

Substantial differences exist from state to state in the extent to which corporate affairs commissions rely on their own staff to conduct prosecutions, or whether they brief officers of the state crown law department. At one extreme sit the corporate affairs offices in Victoria and South Australia which conduct all of their own prosecutions. Officials of the two agencies strongly believed that this was the best way to operate. The South Australian official whom we interviewed spoke of the convenience of having prosecutors working in the same office as the investigators. The New South Wales commission conducts its own summary prosecutions, and briefs barristers specially commissioned to prosecute indictable matters.

At the other extreme are the Western Australian and Tasmanian agencies, which do not handle any of their own cases. Western Australian officials expressed some concern at the delays which their cases experienced, and at the lack of specialized expertise on the part of some of the crown solicitors acting on their behalf.

Common Constraints on Corporate Affairs Regulation

The concern that the commonwealth and state governments might publicly express about the importance of companies and securities regulation do not appear to be reflected in either the resources or in the political support they accord the corporate affairs agencies around Australia. At the time of our visit, information storage and retrieval systems were at least fifteen years out of date, and there is neither a national data base nor comparability across the delegate commissions. With the exception of the Australian Capital Territory, no agency has the human resources to exercise a proper registration function. Meanwhile, monitoring of company activity remains an unattainable ideal. As the Australian Capital Territory commissioner wistfully told us:

If we were able to inspect every registered office of every company, say once a year, just march in and inspect . . . We've got the legal right, but what we haven't got is the manpower. If we were able to do that once a year with each of our 20,000 companies, we would be able to prevent an awful lot of wrongdoing.

The senior solicitor of the South Australian commission expressed more modest aspirations of simply being able to visit the offices of companies which had failed to lodge returns:

Now the chances are that you'd find their registered office had changed, that all their directors had changed around, the chances are that you'd get there and you'd find that there weren't proper books of account, or there weren't any at all, or what there was was an absolute mess, or when you got there your instinct would tell you that there was something crook going on, and you'd be in at the ground floor.

With the exception of New South Wales, which monitors press advertisements relating to investment schemes, and Victoria, which is significantly involved in investigation of securities violations, the investigative resources of corporate affairs commissions are mobilized by liquidators' reports: they tend to focus on 'dead' companies. Rather than preventing wrongdoing or responding to corporate crime as it occurs, corporate affairs investigators are more akin to homicide detectives, with their work commencing when a 'corpse' is discovered. As a general principle, enforcement against living and breathing companies is found to be either too complex or too politically sensitive.

Even within this limited role as corporate undertakers, the corporate affairs commissions which we visited were hopelessly backlogged. They were able to investigate only a fraction of those cases where serious wrongdoing had been called to their attention.

A few months before our interview, the Victorian office dropped over 500 matters from its investigative files, leaving it with a backlog of 150 cases. An officer of the New South Wales commission, in describing the serious allegations which are referred to its investigation division, said:

I would dare say that the majority of them would warrant investigation . . . In excess of 50 per cent are not set aside for investigation because there's been no reasonable prospect of us being able to get to them, and of those that are set aside for investigation, I would say that there would be a further 20 per cent culled out.

An earlier New South Wales government study showed that even these estimates may be conservative. More than two thirds of 1,168 matters referred to the investigation division in 1975 were accorded no further action beyond the initial intake. Of the 344 matters which were investigated by mid-1977 only twenty-four matters had reached court, with only sixty-nine additional matters still under investigation. The remaining matters had been dropped (New South Wales Bureau of Crime Statistics and Research, 1978, 20-2).

The South Australian commission referred to its backlog as 'massive', and noted in July 1984 that they were still investigating cases arising from offences occurring in 1979.

A Western Australian officer also commented on the backlog in his jurisdiction and said:

We have a substantial backlog of insolvency files which is steadily increasing due to an increase in liquidations over the past few years and existing budget restraints on staff numbers. We're like the boy and the dyke most of the time: plugging the finger in the hole just to keep going.

Even the relatively well endowed Australian Capital Territory commission is unable to handle all of its business:

Every now and then Pete has to write off a case of some substance. We have to write off some work simply because we can't devote enough resources to it. We have many complex cases that on occasion, because of other priorities, we can't handle.

Skeletal resources may also indicate a lack of political will to regulate corporate affairs. One respondent advised that a recently appointed Labor Attorney-General told him not to 'rock the boat'. In response to requests for more resources, more than one minister has replied: 'The more resources you have, the more matters you will find to investigate'.

In June 1985, the Victorian Corporate Affairs Commissioner, who had repeatedly sought additional investigative staff, was removed. The Attorney-General, seeking to 'maintain deregulatory momentum', replaced her with an appointee who saw his role as that of a 'business facilitator rather than a policeman' (Bacon, 1985, 19-20).

One respondent with a broad national perspective on corporate affairs regulation advised us that interference from both sides of politics characterized companies and securities enforcement. Very heavy pressure has been brought to bear upon various agencies from the highest quarters, urging them to overlook certain matters.

State ministers are able to quash prosecutions quite readily, and have done so. In one celebrated case, we were told that a minister saw to it that evidence was destroyed at the request of a knight of the realm.

In the light of the constraints under which they labour, the degree of frustration expressed in private by corporate affairs officials is more than understandable.

References and Recommended Reading*

Adby, K. (1985), *White Collar Crime: The Special Investigation as a Method of Enforcement of Company Law*, Criminology Research Council, Canberra.

Australia, Senate (1974), *Report of the Select Committee on Securities and Exchange: Australian Securities Markets and their Regulation*, Australian Government Publishing Service, Canberra.

Bacon, W. (1985), 'The Company Probes Row that Unseated Jan Wade', *National Times*, 2-8 August, 19-20.

Company Law Advisory Committee (1971), *First Interim Report, October 1970, on the Control of Fund Raising, Share Capital and Debentures*, Australian Government Publishing Service, Canberra.

Frith, B. (1984), 'Federal Companies Law Support', *Australian*, 26 September, 14.

Kluver, J. and Woellner, R. (1983), *Powers of Investigation in Revenue, Companies and Trade Practices Law*, Butterworths, Sydney.

McCabe, P. and La Franchi, D. (1982), *Report of Inspectors Appointed to Investigate the Particular Affairs of Navillus Pty Ltd and 922 Other Companies*, Government Printer, Melbourne.

Meagher, D. (1983), 'The Business Practice of Organised Crime', in D. Meagher (ed.), *Organised Crime: Papers presented to the 53rd ANZAAS Congress, Perth, Western Australia 16-20 May 1983*, Australian Government Publishing Service, Canberra, 23-54.

*New South Wales Bureau of Crime Statistics and Research (1978), *Company Investigations: 1975-1977*, Government Printer, Sydney.

Redlich, R. (1984), *Annual Report of the Special Prosecutor 1983-84*, Australian Government Publishing Service, Canberra.

*Sutton, A. (1983), Company Crime in New South Wales: A Sociological Perspective, PhD Thesis, School of Sociology, University of New South Wales.

Tomasic, R. (1984), 'Business Regulation and the Administrative State', in R. Tomasic (ed.), *Business Regulation in Australia*, CCH Australia, Sydney, 43-67.

Wade, J. (1984), 'Corporate Affairs Office — Victoria', *Companies and Securities Law Journal*, 2, 1, 40-6.

Warren, R. (1984), 'The National Companies and Securities Commission: A View from the Marketplace', *Corporate Affairs and the Future*, Northern Territory Development Commission, Darwin, 45-62.

Wilson, M. (1985), 'Sheahan Promises Corporate Crackdown with CAC Revamp', *Sydney Morning Herald*, 24 January, 32.

3
Environmental Protection

Introduction

Australia has not experienced such dramatic events as London's killer smog, which brought about the deaths of 4,000 people in 1952, or the destruction of literally thousands of lakes by acid rain in Europe and North America. Nevertheless, Australia has experienced significant environmental damage, with consequent cost to human health, considerable financial loss, and visible reduction of the quality of life.

There is increasing recognition that the costs of pollution are great, despite the many Australians who remain nonchalant about matters of environmental quality. Air pollution in Australia contributes to respiratory disease, and to a reduction of the quality and yield of commercial crops (Bilger, 1974; Venn, 1981); offensive or excessive noise contributes to a variety of stress related diseases (South Australia, 1972, 67); and soil erosion, a much greater problem in Australia than in most countries, significantly detracts from agricultural productivity (Woods, 1983; Wells, Wood, and Laut, 1984). There are also instances where salinity of inland waterways threatens the water supplies of farms and cities (Commonwealth Department of Resources and Energy, 1983), and the release of toxic substances into air or water contributes to miscarriages and birth defects, to genetic damage, and to cancer (House of Representatives Standing Committee on Environment and Conservation, 1982).

Pollution also takes a toll in aesthetic terms. The stately Norfolk Island pines which once lined Sydney's beaches are now but a memory, and bathers in Port Phillip Bay not infrequently encounter dead fish. The dramatic reduction of wildlife — in many cases the endangerment and even the extinction of species — has also resulted from abuse of the Australian environment: a drive across Southern Tasmania takes one from the Derwent, notorious for heavy metal concentration, through the hills of Queenstown, denuded of vegetation by air pollution, to the Gordon River, where the decimated Huon pine will take millennia to replace.

In the light of overseas environmental disasters, public and government awareness of the importance of protecting the environment developed in Australia during the late 1960s. As individuals and industries persisted in ecologically harmful practices, governments in all Australian jurisdictions came to play a more active role in environmental protection.

The Administrative Framework

General reviews of environmental law and policy in Australia are provided by Bates (1983), Fowler (1984), Fisher (1980), and Gilpin (1980). Prior to 1970, laws relating to air and water quality tended to be enforced by various state and local authorities, in furtherance of health, sewerage, and water supply functions, with noise control largely the responsibility of the police. Hence, no agencies were explicitly accorded the task of environmental protection.

As the Australian Constitution does not make any reference to environmental protection, jurisdiction is reserved for the states. Recent developments in constitutional law, however, have significantly enhanced the commonwealth role. Commonwealth power to influence environmental regulation derives from the power to regulate foreign investment in Australia, to regulate exports, to legislate on matters of Aboriginal cultural heritage, and to implement Australia's international obligations.

The refusal of the commonwealth government to grant an export licence for the export of mineral sands effectively stopped the mining of these sands on Fraser Island, Queensland. This exercise of the export power was upheld by the High Court of Australia in the *Murphyores* case (1976) 136 CLR 1. Commonwealth exercise of its power to regulate the non-trading activities of domestic trading corporations (so long as these are ultimately linked to trading activities), and its use of the foreign affairs power, prevented the Tasmanian government from constructing the controversial dam in south-west Tasmania, an area which had been designated a world heritage area pursuant to international agreement. This too was upheld by the High Court (*Commonwealth* v. *Tasmania* (1983) 57 ALJR 450; 46 ALR 65). We were, nevertheless, advised that the Queensland government maintains the view that the commonwealth does not have any power in relation to the environment.

There exists considerable variation in the number and structure of environmental regulatory agencies across the states and territories of Australia, and no two states are organizationally similar. These differences reflect historical and political distinctions as well as fundamental variations in the geography, climate, and economic activity which characterize the respective jurisdictions. For example, in the days before the development of widespread environmental consciousness, pollution was regarded as primarily a public health issue. And, in states where water supplies were scarce, one agency oversaw both the quantity and quality of water resources; in mid-1984, this was still the case in Western Australia, South Australia, and the Northern Territory.

A descriptive profile of agencies responsible for environmental protection is provided in Table 1.

In no state are all regulatory functions relating to the environment entrusted to a single agency. Centralization of function is greatest in Victoria, Tasmania, and in New South Wales, where the Environment Protection Authority, the Department of the Environment, and the State Pollution Control Commission, respectively, bear primary responsibility for the major functions of air quality, water quality, and noise control. The Australian Capital Territory also has a relatively centralized (albeit small) environment protection section in the Commonwealth Department of Territories.

The remaining states and territories are characterized by considerable diffusion of responsibility. In Queensland, water quality is overseen by a water quality section attached to the Department of Local Government, whilst air quality and noise control are the responsibility of separate organizations attached to the Department of Mapping and Surveying. Overall co-ordination of environmental management in Queensland is provided by the Co-ordinator-General, in the Premier's Department.

South Australia's water quality is regulated by the Engineering and Water Supply Department, whereas air quality and noise control are the responsibility of the Department of Environment and Planning. In South Australia, as in New South Wales, a separate Waste Management Authority has been created.

Although a consolidation of environmental regulatory functions in Western Australia is under way, at the time of our visit, the Department of Health and Medical Services bore responsibility for air quality and noise control, while water quality was regulated by the Public Works Department, and by the Waterways Commission in the case of estuarine waters. The role of the Department of Conservation and Environment was limited to an educational and advisory capacity, and to the conduct of environmental studies.

The Northern Territory remains perhaps the most unusual jurisdiction with regard to the organization of pollution control. At the time of our visit in June 1984, there were no laws in existence relating to air quality, apart from specialized provisions governing uranium mining in the Alligator Rivers Region. Water quality was primarily the responsibility of the Water Division of the Department of Transport and Works, although the Department of Mines and Energy had major responsibility for regulating the operation of uranium mining as it affected water quality. In December 1984, the Department of Mines and Energy assumed full responsibility for water quality throughout the Northern Territory. The Department of Mines and Energy's regulation of water quality in the vicinity of uranium mines is subject to commonwealth

Table 1
Government Departments Exercising Responsibility
for Environmental Regulation

	NSW	VIC	QLD	SA
AIR QUALITY	State Pollution Control Commission	Environment Protection Authority	Department of Mapping and Surveying, Air Pollution Council	Department of Environment and Planning
WATER QUALITY	State Pollution Control Commission	Environment Protection Authority	Department of Local Government, Water Quality Council	Department of Engineering and Water Supply
NOISE CONTROL	State Pollution Control Commission	Environment Protection Authority	Department of Mapping and Surveying, Noise Abatement Authority	Department of Environment and Planning
TOXIC WASTE MANAGE-MENT	Metropolitan Waste Disposal Authority (Sydney area); Local Councils; State Pollution Control Commission	Environment Protection Authority	Local Authorities; Health Department	Waste Management Commission
MARINE POLLUTION	Maritime Services Board	Local Port Authorities; Ministry of Transport; Environment Protection Authority	Local Port Authorities; Department of Harbours and Marine; Department of Local Government, Water Quality Control	Department of Marine and Harbours
LAND USE PLANNING	Department of Environment and Planning	Ministry for Planning and Environment	Local Authorities; Department of Local Government	Department of Environment and Planning
IMPACT ASSESSMENT	Department of Environment and Planning	Ministry for Planning and Environment	Premier's Department (Co-ordinator General)	Department of Environment and Planning

Table 1 (Cont.)
Government Departments Exercising Responsibility
for Environmental Regulation

	WA	TAS	NT	ACT
AIR QUALITY	Department of Health and Medical Services	Department of Environment	—	Commonwealth Department of Territories, Environment Protection Section
WATER QUALITY	Public Works Department; Waterways Commission	Department of Environment	Department of Transport and Works, Water Division, (to 21.12.84); Department of Mines and Energy, Water Resources Division	Commonwealth Department of Territories, Environment Protection Section
NOISE CONTROL	Department of Health and Medical Services	Department of Environment	Department of Health	Commonwealth Department of Territories, Environment Protection Section
TOXIC WASTE MANAGE-MENT	Local Government	Department of Environment; Local Government	Department of Mines and Energy	Commonwealth Department of Territories, Environment Protection Section
MARINE POLLUTION	Department of Marine and Harbours; Local Port Authorities	Department of Environment; Local Port Authorities	Department of Transport and Works, Marine Office	Commonwealth Department of Territories, Environment Protection Section
LAND USE PLANNING	Department of Environment and Conservation	Department of Environment; Local Government	Conservation Commission; Department of Lands	National Capital Development Commission
IMPACT ASSESSMENT	Department of Environment and Conservation	Department of Environment	Conservation Commission	Commonwealth Department of Arts, Heritage and Environment Impact Assessment Branch

supervision, as noted below. The Northern Territory Conservation Commission was limited to an educational and advisory role with regard to environmental affairs generally; it also administered environmental impact assessment legislation.

The unique circumstances surrounding uranium mining in the Northern Territory have given rise to substantial commonwealth involvement in the regulatory process. Whilst uranium had been mined at Radium Hill in South Australia in the 1950s, at Mary Kathleen, Queensland, and at Rum Jungle, in the Northern Territory, in the 1960s, considerable debate arose regarding the desirability of mining the rich deposits subsequently discovered in the Alligator Rivers Region. Because the Northern Territory had yet to attain self-government, the decision rested with the commonwealth.

The issue was complex. The threat of nuclear weapons proliferation and international problems of radioactive waste disposal loomed large. In addition, the Alligator Rivers Region encompassed Aboriginal land, and a stunningly rich, but equally fragile, aquatic environment. Previous uranium mining in the Northern Territory, at Rum Jungle, had left a legacy of tailings and significant damage to the Finniss River. In order to weigh the advantages and disadvantages of uranium mining in the Alligator Rivers Region, the Fraser government commissioned a judicial inquiry.

Following the recommendations of the inquiry, chaired by Mr Justice Fox, the commonwealth chose to allow uranium mining to take place, regulated to the maximum extent possible through the laws of the Northern Territory. The Office of the Supervising Scientist and the Co-ordinating Committee for the Alligator Rivers Region were established by the *Environment Protection (Alligator Rivers Region) Act* 1978. Under this act the Supervising Scientist has a supervisory, co-ordinating, and research role in the protection of the region from the effects of uranium mining operations, and is directed to report regularly to parliament. The office is a statutory authority within the portfolio of the Minister for Arts, Heritage, and Environment.

Under current arrangements, the issuing and administration of licences, approvals, and authorizations relating to the environmental aspects of the mining and milling of uranium in the territory is largely the responsibility of the Northern Territory minister and the Department of Mines and Energy, with the Supervising Scientist exercising an overseer role. The statutory provisions for regulating uranium mining in the Northern Territory are complex; a review of the relevant legislation has been provided by the Supervising Scientist's annual report (1979).

The uniqueness of the Northern Territory situation is underscored by the absence of similar commonwealth involvement in the mining of uranium at Roxby Downs, South Australia.

Another example of joint commonwealth–state involvement in the regulatory process may be seen in the Great Barrier Reef Marine Park, a vast area off the coast of Queensland. The Great Barrier Reef Marine Park Authority, a commonwealth body, engages in planning, policy development, and review of management. The actual day to day running of the park, and hence any exercise of regulatory powers, is the responsibility of the Queensland National Parks and Wildlife Service. These powers are exercised subject to the authority and within agreed guidelines developed jointly by Queensland and commonwealth agencies.

Australia is a party to the International Convention for the Prevention of Pollution of the Sea by Oil, 1954. Pursuant to the 1979 Offshore Constitutional Settlement — an agreement between the commonwealth and the states — responsibility for controlling discharges of oil to the marine environment is shared. State jurisdiction extends over territorial waters, while the Commonwealth Department of Transport oversees the open ocean. Similar co-operative arrangements are being developed with regard to the discharge of other pollutants to the marine environment.

Regulation of marine oil pollution in the states is organizationally separate from other environmental control agencies. In New South Wales and South Australia, it resides with the Maritime Services Board and the Department of Marine and Harbours respectively. In Queensland, it is administered by the Department of Harbours and Marine, which delegates control to local port and waterways authorities. In the other states, it remains the province of local port authorities or is shared between them and a central marine and/or environmental body.

Varieties of Regulatory Conduct

With the exception of highly toxic materials and marine oil pollution, state and territory pollution control policies strive toward minimizing ecosystem damage by means of planned abatement of emissions and prevention of accidental discharges, rather than strict prohibition of any release to the environment.

To achieve these goals of minimal discharge consistent with the best practicable technology, environmental agencies have at their disposal a number of regulatory strategies.

These range from strict formality to a more relaxed collegial approach. The methods are not mutually exclusive; indeed, most agencies resort to a mix, depending upon the industry in question, and its immediate circumstances. In addition to those methods common to other areas of regulation, such as negotiation, the provision of technical assistance, and the use of adverse publicity, environmental agencies employ a variety of more distinctive tools.

Impact Assessment
One method of environmental regulation common to all Australian jurisdictions is that of environmental impact assessment. Government

agencies may require prospective developers to provide a detailed statement of the anticipated nett effects which their projects would have on the environment. Such an obligation is intended to raise the level of environmental consciousness on the part of industry, to permit governmental scrutiny of anticipated environmental effects, and to allow members of the public an opportunity to review and comment upon development proposals. Public review of impact assessments is an entitlement generally conferred by legislation. In Tasmania and Queensland, however, no such guarantees exist. In Queensland, environmental impact statements may be made public at the discretion of the proponent!

Licensing

Perhaps the most common instrument of environmental regulation is the licence. Works approvals are also used in Victoria and New South Wales. One aspect of these controls which most distinguishes the environment from other areas of regulation is their individualistic implementation. Rather than defining a harm and then forbidding it, the law grants works approvals requiring pollution controls and licences to discharge, within specified limits. Required for industries which generate significant emissions, often referred to by statute as 'scheduled premises', these works approvals and licences may vary in terms and conditions. New works which will result in emissions, or modifications to works which may influence emissions, will require approvals for proposed pollution controls.

Licences may require certain abatement measures to be implemented, or certain reductions in emissions to be achieved, by a specified date. They may require that an industry engage in systematic monitoring of meteorological conditions and/or discharge levels, and submit data routinely to the relevant regulatory authority. Non-compliance with the terms and conditions of a licence may lead to its suspension or revocation, as has occurred in New South Wales, Victoria, and Western Australia, or to prosecution.

In all jurisdictions, industries may be declared exempt from licensing requirements either at the discretion of the relevant regulatory authority, by regulation, or by the responsible minister. Such exemptions can be granted in cases of economic exigency, and may be granted on a temporary basis. The most widespread use of exemptions occurs in Tasmania, where they have been granted to many, if not most, of the state's major industries! (Tasmania, Department of the Environment, 1980, 24).

State Agreements

One regulatory device, frequently used in conjunction with large scale development projects, is the state agreement, franchise agreement, or indenture (MacDonald, 1977; Warnick, 1982 and 1983). These agreements, almost always ratified by act of parliament, detail the respective obligations of government and developer. The government, for example, may undertake to supply power and water and to build roads to the development site, whereas the developer may be required to pay a defined royalty, to adhere to a specified timetable, and to comply with certain environmental standards.

Agreements are most common to South Australia, Western Australia, and Queensland. Examples include the *Roxby Downs (Indenture Ratification) Act* 1982 (SA), an agreement between the South Australian government and BP Australia/Western Mining to permit the establishment of a uranium mining complex; the *Laporte Industrial Factory Agreement* 1961 (WA), to permit the establishment of a titanium dioxide plant in Western Australia, and the *Greenvale Agreement Act* 1970-71 (Qld), to facilitate the development of nickel mining in Queensland.

Agreements have the advantage of permitting flexible regulation, tailor made to a particular set of environmental contingencies. Along with the variable requirements of licences, they can thus avoid the irrationality of universal laws which can impose excessive costs on some developments where they may not be justified.

State agreements, however, are double-edged swords. Just as the terms of an agreement may require a certain standard of corporate conduct with regard to environmental matters, so too agreements often absolve signatories from any responsibility for emission control.

Self-Monitoring and Mandatory Self-Reporting
Some firms engage in voluntary post-project appraisal to record the extent of impacts which were predicted in the environmental impact statement, or to detect impacts not previously foreshadowed (McLaren and Cole, 1984). In a number of environmental regulatory regimes, companies are required to monitor their own emissions systematically to ensure that they remain below a specified threshhold. These data may then be audited periodically by a regulatory agency. In some instances, this may be encouraged by explicit or implicit immunity from prosecution. Where discharges are prohibited altogether, such as marine oil spills and certain emissions from uranium mines, companies are required to report the incident to the regulatory authority. Failure to report may carry a further penalty. Self-monitoring, of course, relieves the regulatory agency of responsibilities for frequent surveillance, and permits a more economical allocation of resources. Queensland air pollution authorities, for example, leave the task of monitoring at Mount Isa to Mount Isa Mines. Mandatory self-reporting is designed to permit prompt response to potentially serious incidents. There have, however, been no prosecutions in any jurisdiction for failure to report incidents, so there can be little guarantee that companies will not be persuaded that a cover-up is to their advantage.

Public Involvement in the Regulatory Process

Most environmental agencies provide for some type of consultative framework to cater for public participation in the regulatory process. The Co-ordinating Committee for the Alligator Rivers Region, for example, contains representatives of the uranium mining companies, the Federated Miscellaneous Workers Union and the Northern Land Council, in addition to a variety of commonwealth and territory government departments.

The *South Australian Clean Air Act* 1984 provides for a Clean Air Advisory Committee, comprised *inter alia* of persons with various technical qualifications, representatives of the Chamber of Commerce and Industry, the Trades and Labor Council, and a conservation group.

Members of the Queenland Water Quality Council include representatives of primary and secondary industry, the sugar industry, and local universities; however, citizens' environmental groups are unrepresented.

Not only may public participation in environmental policy making be severely limited, but secrecy provisions further narrow public awareness and understanding of the policy process. Proceedings of the Queensland Water Quality Council, for example, are confidential. Secrecy provisions of the *Environment Protection (Alligator Rivers Region) Act* 1978 are so stringent that the Supervising Scientist commented adversely on them in an annual report (Supervising Scientist, 1983, 10-11). By contrast, Victoria's *Freedom of Information Act* 1982 allows public access to information held by the Environment Protection Authority; any decision to deny access is subject to appeal.

With few exceptions, members of the public are restricted in their access to the courts for relief against breaches of environmental legislation. Unlike some overseas jurisdictions, most notably the United States, Australian litigants must show a special interest in a matter in order to be entitled to sue for the enforcement of law. This limitation on 'standing' was determined by the High Court of Australia when it held that the Australian Conservation Foundation lacked sufficient interest to challenge a decision of the commonwealth government relating to environmental impact assessment (*Australian Conservation Foundation* v. *Commonwealth* (1979) 28 ALR 257; see also Australian Law Reform Commission, 1978).

Three exceptions to this general limitation on access to the courts are worthy of note. Under the *Environment Protection (Northern Territory Supreme Court) Act* 1978 (C'th), the Northern Land Council may sue in the Northern Territory Supreme Court to enforce laws relating to protection of the environment in the Alligator Rivers Region.

In New South Wales, third parties have standing in the Land and Environment Court to challenge decisions taken under the Environmental Planning and Assessment Act, and the Heritage Act. It should be noted that neither of these provisions have given rise to vexatious litigation or to excessive court case loads, nor have they been the subject of hostile criticism from regulatory agencies themselves.

In Tasmania and Victoria, third parties may object to decisions under environment protection acts. Third parties in Victoria do not need to show any financial or other direct interest before they can appeal against Environment Protection Authority actions. In Tasmania they are required to post a $250 bond, but, by contrast, it is Victorian government policy to provide legal aid for disadvantaged litigants in environmental cases, although no such case had arisen at the time of writing.

Three additional examples of public involvement in the regulatory process involve the encouragement by environmental agencies of volunteer monitoring by private citizens. The Queensland Beach Protection Authority established a Coastal Observation Programme — Engineering, in the early 1970s. Participants in the programme, residents along Queensland's coast, take regular measurements of the beach, and forward them to headquarters in Brisbane. Similarly, the Western Australian Department of Fisheries and Wildlife has appointed a number of honorary fisheries officers to assist in general surveillance, and the South Australian Department of Environment and Planning has appointed seventy volunteer wardens to monitor historic shipwrecks.

In addition, pilots of civil and military aircraft are required to notify the commonwealth government if they detect evidence of marine pollution.

Effluent Charges
Environmental authorities have been the only agencies which, in their policy deliberations, have given any serious consideration to charges (or taxes on harm) as a regulatory strategy. Instead of defining pollution as an offence, and punishing it whenever it occurs, companies can be required to pay an effluent tax in proportion to the amount of discharge or emission in question. Alternatively, the agency can define an acceptable total amount of pollution for a region, and then sell rights to the highest bidder to discharge up to that level, but no more (Barker, 1984).

Reversing the coin, partial subsidies can be provided to industry for introduction of abatement technology. Alternatively, regulators could devise more flexible licensing systems which would allow polluters latitude in offsetting new abatement measures against continuing emissions, in a manner most economically advantageous to the firm.

While Australian environmental agencies have given greater or lesser consideration to regulation by contriving market incentives, every one of them has rejected it as impracticable. The reason most commonly given in our interviews for the rejection was the logistic impossibility of auditing honest measurement of emissions on which charges would be based.

Interstate Differences in Regulatory Practice

Australian environmental agencies vary widely in terms of the regulatory strategies which they employ. Indeed, environmental regulation is marked by a greater diversity of regulatory behaviour than any other of the areas reviewed in the course of our research.

Victoria

The two most adversarial agencies, those characterized by regulatory strategies of moderately strict enforcement, are the Victorian EPA and the New South Wales State Pollution Control Commission. The *Environment Protection Act* 1970 (Vic.), inspired to a significant degree by United States environmental legislation, formally provides for the establishment of state environment protection policies, and prohibits individual administrative actions inconsistent with these broader aims. Victorian legislation and policy thus appear directed more toward the goal of preventing pollution rather than toward mere abatement. The chairman told us that prosecution was an important part of EPA's activity. Although strict law enforcement, in the narrow sense including prosecution, usually follows co-operative persuasion, EPA management and staff subscribe to the view that prosecution is an important deterrent. This applies particularly to corporations which have proved very sensitive to public exposure in this way. Such an approach is reflected in EPA's use of adverse publicity. Offenders are named in EPA newsletters and annual reports, and press releases routinely follow successful prosecutions and the service of pollution abatement and noise control notices. EPA is one of the only three environmental agencies actually using suspension and revocation of licences as a regulatory tool.

Of all environmental regulators interviewed, only the Victorian EPA chairman said that he placed a great degree of importance on enforcement as part of overall pollution control strategy, that enforcement received more of EPA's resources than education, and that he would be concerned if the number of prosecutions brought by EPA were to decline. EPA directives specify that 'except where the solicitor believes there is insufficient evidence, no obstacle shall be placed in the way of any officer who puts forward a proposal for prosecution'.

Victoria is the only jurisdiction in Australia where a pledge to undertake more prosecutions for environmental offences (or any other kinds of business offences) has been made in an election campaign. It was made in 1982 by the then opposition and subsequently fulfilled by the Cain Labor government.

Fines imposed under the Victorian act are higher than penalties for environmental offences in any other Australian jurisdiction. A summary of Victorian environmental prosecutions is provided in Table 2. Over 96 per cent resulted in conviction on at least one charge.

New South Wales

The State Pollution Control Commission (SPCC) in New South Wales

Table 2
Victoria: Environmental Prosecutions by Originating Agency 1974-84

		Environment Protection Authority		Melbourne and Metropolitan Board of Works	State Rivers and Water Supply Commission/Rural Water Commission	Dandenong Valley Authority	Latrobe Valley Water and Sewerage Board
	Total	Motor Vehicle Noise*	Other				
1973-74	7	—	6	—	—	1	—
1974-75	28	—	13	—	6	7	2
1975-76	42	—	14	5	10	12	1
1976-77	33	—	9	7	9	6	2
1977-78	40	—	4	22	7	6	1
1978-79	63	14	6	19	14	9	1
1979-80	62	25	14	7	9	3	4
1980-81	62	24	8	8	10	8	4
1981-82	62	22	25	4	7	3	1
1982-83	121	60	38	7	13	3	—
1983-84	156	109	35	4	3	2	3

* Involving mostly individual, not corporate, offenders

Source: Environment Protection Authority

professes to take a somewhat less adversarial stance than does its Victorian counterpart, even though it brings nearly twice the number of prosecutions against corporate offenders each year as does the EPA. The legislation which it administers is cast more in the British tradition of pollution management by the best practicable means. The director referred to prosecution as a 'last alternative', expressing the view that the provision of technical advice and assistance in upgrading pollution control practices are more important functions. He told us that conciliation took precedence, 'We are not basically a prosecution organization'. The SPCC also uses publicity as a regulatory tool, naming offenders in press releases and in annual reports. Unlike most of its counterpart agencies, it also suspends and revokes licences.

Whilst the Metropolitan Waste Disposal Authority (MWDA) has undertaken a small number of prosecutions in recent years, its main function is the actual provision and management of waste disposal operations. In the words of its director, it is basically a 'doing' body. The authority has, however, engaged in campaigns to prosecute intractably non-co-operative transporters of toxic wastes. In addition, it has established a system for the accountability of dangerous wastes which reduces the likelihood of unauthorized disposal. Occupiers of premises on which hazardous wastes are generated are licensed, as are transporters of wastes and depots receiving wastes. Generators of selected liquid industrial and grease trap wastes complete a document in quadruplicate, retaining one copy, sending one to MWDA offices, and providing two to the transporter. Upon receipt of the waste shipment and accompanying dockets, the receiving depot forwards one copy to MWDA offices, for matching with the original. Such accountability systems exist only in metropolitan Sydney and in Victoria, although at the time of writing one was being developed by the Brisbane City Council.

The New South Wales Department of Environment and Planning is concerned with planning and assessment matters, and has not sought to play an inspectorial or prosecutorial role; its main influence is through guiding the regulatory activities of local governments.

Table 3 reviews the prosecutorial activities of the major New South Wales environmental regulatory authorities over the past ten years.

Tasmania
Tasmania's environmental protection policy is one of education before enforcement. Since 1977 the Department of the Environment has launched an average of four prosecutions per year against polluting companies, but tends to be tolerant of polluting activity, particularly when a polluter pleads financial constraint. The following passage from a recent annual report is illustrative:

The generally depressed state of the meat industry in the period under review has had a significant effect on the ability of some operators of abattoirs and rendering plants in the state to continue with programmes to ensure that all

Table 3
New South Wales: Convictions for Environmental Offences
by Originating Agency, 1974-84

| | State Pollution Control Commission | | | | | | Maritime Services Board (Oil Pollution Prosecutions) | | Metropolitan Waste Disposal Authority | |
| | Clean Air Act* | | Clean Waters Act | | Noise Control Act | | | | | |
	No.	Av. Fine $	No.	Av. Fine $	No.	Av. Fine $	No.	Av. Fine $	No.	Av. Fine $
1973-74	4	262	9	2,544	—	—	—	—	—	—
1974-75	17	310	14	322	—	—	24	249	—	—
1975-76	6	291	4	622	—	—	29	276	0	—
1976-77	43	559	44	540	—	—	16	291	0	—
1977-78	51	530	42	1,335	1	250	23	735	0	—
1978-79	55	484	38	655	3	433	19	329	0	—
1979-80	34	373	15	737	2	225	14	559	1	360
1980-81	36	673	21	967	7	269	7	321	0	—
1981-82	45	549	23	1,007	2	1,200	3	1,033	3	833
1982-83	47	629	12	2,557	4	200	0	—	0	—
1983-84	12	2,321	16	1,043	9	289	4	375	2	850

* Excluding prosecutions of individuals for motor vehicle emitting smoke

Sources: State Pollution Control Commission
Maritime Services Board
Metropolitan Waste Disposal Authority

emissions into the environment will comply with the prescribed standards. This aspect will be closely monitored by the department in the following year (Tasmania, Department of the Environment, 1980, 12).

Moreover, the opportunity exists in Tasmania, as in other states, to bypass the conventional regulatory regime entirely by obtaining a ministerial exemption. Ministerial exemptions in Tasmania fall into two categories. Under section 35 of the act, the minister may exempt an operator of a scheduled premises from the obligation to hold a licence. This does not in any way exempt the operator from the need to maintain compliance with the provisions of the act and its regulations. In fact, only those premises that have been identified as complying with the act, and not being the subject of complaints or problems, are granted exemption. This is regarded as a useful tool for introducing flexibility into an otherwise rigid system.

Under sections 15, 16, 17, and 21 of the act 'The Minister may . . . exempt any person from the operation of this section in respect of any specified act or course of action'. Exemptions granted under these sections are specific in nature. For example, a discharge may be allowed to contain a particular pollutant in concentrations greater than the maximum specified in the regulations, and in most cases the maximum concentrations permitted will be specified in the exemption.

Tasmanian authorities make considerable use of these options. Prior to 1981, they were published in the department's annual reports. During the 1984 financial year, seventy-one exemptions were in force, half of which applied to municipalities or state authorities. Corporations whose operations were exempt included Australian Newsprint Mills, Comalco, EZ Industries, Cadbury Schweppes, Tioxide Australia, and Mt Lyell Mining. Moreover, the Tasmanian government has recently moved to reclassify several hundred small businesses previously defined as scheduled premises. This will relieve them of the responsibility to hold a licence to discharge waste under the Environment Protection Act, in effect granting a blanket exemption.

The Tasmanian Department of Mines bears some responsibility for environmental matters as affected by mining operations. All exploration licences and mining leases issued in Tasmania contain conditions designed to protect the physical environment. Compliance with these conditions is policed by officers of the Department of Mines. The department, however, is primarily concerned with fostering the mining industry.

In response to a letter from the director of the Tasmanian Conservation Trust requesting that the department encourage a company to commission a botanical survey prior to mineral exploration, the director of Mines replied:

I consider your request to be of the utmost impertinence and would remind you that the function of the Department of Mines and exploration companies is to explore and discover our rare and unique mineral deposits and not to engage in botanical surveys.

The Department is happy to co-operate with you in matters of genuine environmental control and concern. However, I would remind you that we have an important function to carry out with regard to the State's economy and I refuse to be frustrated by such unreasonable requests. My policy is to assist wherever I can but I must advise you that correspondence of this nature is a total waste of time and I intend ignoring it in future (Director, Department of Mines, correspondence, 26 July 1982).

The prosecutorial activity of the Tasmanian Department of the Environment is summarised in Table 4.

Table 4
Tasmania: Department of the Environment
Prosecutions under the Environment Protection Act 1973-84

	Prosecutions	Convictions	Av. Fine
			$
1973-74	0	—	—
1974-75	0	—	—
1975-76	0	—	—
1976-77	19	15	287
1977-78	3	3	633
1978-79	6	6	225
1979-80	5	na	na
1980-81	2	2	270
1981-82	2	2	250
1982-83	5	5	312
1983-84	12	12	331

Source: Department of the Environment

Queensland
The major agencies in Queensland dedicated to environmental regulation differ dramatically in their approaches from those of their counterparts in New South Wales and Victoria. Here one sees an explicit avoidance of prosecution in favour of a tolerant, conciliatory approach. The Air Pollution Council, which undertook seven prosecutions (resulting in five convictions) in its first decade, does so only in extreme situations. It has, however, named defendants in annual reports. The Noise Abatement Authority has reported only one prosecution in its annual report since it came into existence, without naming the accused.

The Surveyor-General of Queensland, in a letter refusing our request for interviews with the council and with the Noise Abatement Authority wrote:

In Queensland, government philosophy concerning the control of air pollution and noise is based on co-operation with industry. Overall, the degree of co-operation has been very good and prosecutions are only considered as a last resort (Surveyor-General, correspondence, 18 May 1984).

The Water Quality Council has never in its entire history taken a polluter to court. In Queensland, ministerial consent is required for a prosecution to go forward. In the few cases where the council has recommended prosecution, the responsible minister has directed that the cases not proceed.

Executives of industries which are experiencing difficulty in complying with prescribed water quality control standards are asked to appear before the council or the minister to explain their position, and to explain why further action should not be taken. The council keeps a low profile, and adverse publicity is used sparingly.

Prosecutorial activity by the three main environment agencies in Queensland is summarized in Table 5.

Table 5
Queensland: Convictions for Environmental Offences
by Originating Agency 1974-84

	Air Pollution Council		Water Quality Council		Noise Abatement Authority	
	No.	Av. Fine $	No.	Av. Fine $	No.	Av. Fine $
1974-75	0	—	0	—	—	—
1975-76	0	—	0	—	—	—
1976-77	0	—	0	—	—	—
1977-78	1	10,000*	0	—	—	—
1978-79	0	—	0	—	0	—
1979-80	0	—	0	—	0	—
1980-81	0	—	0	—	0	—
1981-82	4	188	0	—	0	—
1982-83	0	—	0	—	0	—
1983-84	0	—	0	—	0	—

* Subsequently reduced to $500 on appeal.
Sources: Air Pollution Council
            Water Quality Council
            Noise Abatement Authority

South Australia
The South Australian approach to environmental regulation is similar. We were advised that the premier had made it clear in his briefings with permanent heads that he desires the government to have a partnership relationship with industry. The director-general of the department told us that 'Our objective is to assist industry in achieving environmentally sound development . . .'. Prosecution is thus used rarely, and strategies of advice and negotiation prevail. The Engineering and Water Supply Department, responsible for water quality, also regards prosecution as a last resort, having prosecuted no more than ten companies over the past eight years. A previous water resources minister had, in at least one instance, directed that a prosecution not proceed.

Indenture agreements have also been used in South Australia to pre-empt environmental legislation. Consider, for example, the *Broken Hill Proprietary Company's Steel Works Indenture Act* 1958, section 7:

The company and any subsidiary company as defined in the Indenture shall not be liable for discharging, from its works at or near Whyalla, effluent into the sea or smoke, dust or gas into the atmosphere or for creating noise, smoke, dust or gas at such works, if such discharge or creation is necessary for the efficient operation of the works of the Company or subsidiary company and is not due to negligence on the part of the Company or subsidiary company as the case may be.

Prosecution activity by South Australian agencies is summarized in Table 6.

Table 6
South Australia: Convictions for Environmental Offences
by Originating Agency 1974-84

	South Australian Health Commission		Department of Environment and Planning			
	Clean Air Act		Clean Air Act		Noise Control Act*	
	No.	Av. Fine $	No.	Av. Fine $	No.	Av. Fine $
1974-75	1	324	1	300	—	—
1975-76	0	—	0	—	—	—
1976-77	0	—	0	—	—	—
1977-78	3	789	3	650	—	—
1978-79	0	—	0	—	—	—
1979-80	0	—	0	—	—	—
1980-81	2	495	2	259	—	—
1981-82	0	—	0	—	—	—
1982-83	0	—	0	—	—	—
1983-84	0	—	0	—	1	400

* Excluding domestic noise
Sources: South Australian Health Commission
Department of Environment and Planning

Western Australia
The various agencies in Western Australia responsible for environmental control also tend towards education and conciliation in their general strategies. The chairman of the Environment Protection Authority referred to it as 'an educational rather than an enforcement agency' (Western Australia, Environmental Protection Authority, 1983, 4). There have not been any prosecutions by either the Public Works Department or the Waterways Commission for pollution of inland waters.

In the three most recent years for which data were available, there were a total of fifteen prosecutions brought by the Department of Health and Medical Services under the Clean Air Act, and none under the Noise Abatement Act.

Western Australian authorities, however, have employed alternative regulatory approaches. The Department of Health and Medical Services issues press releases following successful prosecutions. The department has also suspended licences under the Clean Air Act. In

September 1983 the renewal of an effluent disposal licence for Chemical Industries Kwinana was refused by the Water Resources Minister. The publication of a pollution survey of Cockburn Sound which identified those firms contributing to a decline in water quality was followed by the implementation of abatement measures by the companies responsible.

Reliance on private agreement acts or indentures in Western Australia has inhibited environmental regulation to a significant extent. The *Laporte Industrial Factory Agreement* 1961, section 10, provides that 'the State shall, during the term of this agreement assume total responsibility for the disposal of all effluent including cooling water from the Company's works . . .'. Twenty-two years after the enactment of the agreement, the chairman of the Environmental Protection Authority noted the chronic problem of acid iron wastes from Laporte's titanium dioxide manufacturing plant and conceded that 'the agreement between the State and Laporte inhibits environmental management devised to provide the most logical solutions' (Western Australia, Environmental Protection Authority, 1983, 17).

The Clean Air Section of the Western Australian Department of Health and Medical Services sees itself as having a regulatory approach rather similar to air pollution control in Queensland. There is a strong emphasis on co-operative relationships with industry, and on flexibility and gradualism. The philosophy is that 'each year you increase the standards, so over a twenty year period you bring emission levels down . . . so it's no sudden shock to industry'. In other words, it is a negotiated approach to gradual improvement, where prosecution is only threatened against intransigent firms who threaten to reverse the trend toward lower air pollution levels.

Northern Territory
The Northern Territory government adheres to a strategy of consultation and negotiation regarding environmental matters. As noted earlier, the territory has no air quality legislation. A senior officer of the Department of Transport and Works, Water Division told us:

I think in terms of the government's approach with these things we would certainly be required to resolve everything possible by talking directly, eyeball to eyeball, with the person rather than pursue things along formal lines and resort to the legislation, which would be a last stage in the process.

The territory agency primarily concerned with environmental affairs — the Conservation Commission — has very little power to compel substantive behaviour, but rather acts in an advisory capacity to those authorities such as the Department of Mines and Energy, which do have specific regulatory powers. The commission may, however, prosecute for failure to comply with impact assessment procedures. No prosecutions have been initiated for corporate offences against the environment in the territory.

Australian Capital Territory

The task of environmental protection in the Australian Capital Territory differs from that confronting other jurisdictions, in that the major polluters are not drawn from private industry, but rather tend to be commonwealth instrumentalities. At the time of our interview in mid-1984, responsibility for pollution control in the Australian Capital Territory resided with four officers of the Department of Territories. At that time, a number of minor ordinances, carrying very modest penalties, related to pollution control (Barker, 1983). Activities of the section were hitherto limited to policy development and technical assistance, rather than prosecution.

Major legislation, with penalties of up to $50,000 for corporate offenders, was proclaimed in late 1984. Officers with whom we spoke envisaged enforcement strategies patterned after those of the New South Wales State Pollution Control Commission. They heralded the use of random inspections, and of adverse publicity against offenders, whether corporate or governmental.

The system of crown leases in the Australian Capital Territory enables the Department of Territories to attach pollution control notices as conditions to a lease. Such specifications include instructions regarding storage of waste oils, air emissions, and, in the case of a local quarry, vibrations from blasting.

The general strategy of the department is to achieve compliance through persuasion and technical assistance, but not to hesitate to prosecute if gentler methods fail.

If you don't (prosecute) you very quickly run out of steam. If people realize that their chances of being taken to court are low then the move to compliance could be very slow indeed.

Overview

It should be noted that despite the wide variations across Australia in policies relating to prosecution, environmental regulators invariably seek co-operative relationships with industry. All respondents except the Supervising Scientist, the Northern Territory Conservation Commission, and the Australian Capital Territory Environment Protection Section claimed in the interview that negotiating agreements with industry is an important part of their regulatory system; all except the Australian Capital Territory and the South Australian water quality officers said they encouraged companies to do better than the minimum required by law; all except the New South Wales Department of Environment and Planning claimed that encouraging self-regulation had an important place in their regulatory administration.

The degree of autonomy enjoyed by environmental regulatory agencies also differs significantly. The Victorian Environment Protection Act gives the EPA the latitude to pursue a strong enforcement

Table 7
Environmental Regulatory Agencies
Resource and Conviction Data, 1984

Agency	Size of Staff	Per cent of Staff Engaged in Investigation/ Enforcement	Annual Expenditure $	Number of Convictions Most Recent Three Years (Corporate defendants)	Av. Fine $
NSW Dept of Environment and Planning	523	0	42,600,000	1	1
NSW State Pollution Control Commission	251	25	7,999,519	170	786
NSW Metropolitan Waste Disposal Authority	77	3	17,515,000	5	840
Vic. Environment Protection Authority	300	44	9,532,515	92	2,007
Qld Air Pollution Council	36	31	1,298,000	4	188
Qld Water Quality Council	41	30	1,817,000	0	—
Qld Noise Abatement Authority	21	30	607,000	0	—
Qld Beach Protection Authority	20	10	1,618,104	0	—
SA Dept of Environment and Planning (Pollution Management Division)	34	35	1,404,000	1	400
SA Dept of Engineering and Water Supply (Water Quality Section)	8	15	692,000	3	290
WA Dept of Environment and Conservation	70	0	2,859,077	0	—
WA Dept of Health and Medical Services (Clean Air Section)	13	50	574,000	15	313
Tas. Dept of Environment	36	67	961,230	19	317
NT Dept of Transport and Works (Water Division) to 21.12.84	350	3	—	0	—
NT Dept of Mines and Energy (Water Resources Division)	290	3	—	0	—
NT Conservation Commission	476	7	—	0	—
C'th Dept of Territories (ACT Environment Protection Section)	4	25	264,000	0	—
C'th Office of Supervising Scientist	70	10	5,981,970	0	—
C'th Great Barrier Reef Marine Park Authority	77	29	4,379,000	0	—

policy. The EPA can mount prosecutions without reference to the minister or without his approval. By contrast, ministers in Queensland and South Australia have prevented prosecutions from going forward, and in Tasmania, ministers have exempted industries from criminal liability altogether.

Table 7 provides a descriptive profile of the agencies under review, their staff levels and resources, and their prosecutorial activity. It should also be noted that no environmental regulatory agency prosecutes more than a tiny fraction of matters coming to its attention. In addition to offences detected in the course of inspectorial activity, authorities in New South Wales receive upwards of 6,000 complaints per year, while nearly 5,500 are received by the Victorian EPA. Complaints to the three major agencies in Queensland total over 1,500, and the South Australian Department of Environment and Planning receives a total of about 1,000 complaints per year regarding air and noise pollution.

Marine Oil Pollution

As noted above, under present arrangements, the states bear responsibility for marine pollution control in the territorial waters of Australia. As most oil spills occur in and around harbours, and since the detection of spills and collection of evidence is considerably more difficult in the open ocean, the role of the commonwealth is more supportive than regulatory. The Commonwealth Department of Transport, for example, has developed, and provides logistical support for, a national plan to combat pollution. In furtherance of this contingency plan to respond promptly and efficiently to oil spills, the commonwealth purchases and stockpiles abatement equipment which is stored in strategic locations around Australia. The commonwealth also bears the cost of cleaning up oil spills in those instances when polluters are not detected and prosecuted, as well as supporting regular surveillance flights off the Australian coast.

Regulatory responsibility in the states tends to rest primarily with marine rather than environmental authorities. Responsibility rests with one centralized authority in New South Wales and South Australia, but is shared amongst numerous local port authorities in other jurisdictions. In Victoria responsibility is shared by port authorities and the Environment Protection Authority under agreed administrative procedures. Although both have statutory powers, navigable waters legislation has been used more in practice because of its simpler prosecution procedures and its uniformity with the legislation of other states. It has been suggested that smaller port authorities are less capable of an efficient cleanup, as well as having greater difficulty in preparing cases for prosecution. Data in Table 8 suggest, in any event, that decentralized authorities appear no less inclined to prosecute than statewide organizations.

Table 8
Convictions and Average Fines for Pollution of Territorial Waters (Oil Spills) States and Territories of Australia, 1979-83

	NSW		VIC		QLD		SA		WA		TAS		NT		ACT	
	No.	Av. Fine $	No.	Av. Fine $	No.	Av. Fine $	No.	Av. Fine $	No.	Av. Fine $	No.	Av. Fine $	No.	Av. Fine $	No.	Av. Fine $
1979	9	233	9	1,289	0	—	2	0	4	0	0	—	0	—	0	—
1980	2	200	8	756	2	1,550	1	500	5	470	0	—	0	—	0	—
1981	2	200	9	856	2	1,500	1	2,000	3	500	2	350	0	—	0	—
1982	5	500	10	965	2	375	6	244	2	2,000	0	—	0	—	0	—
1983	6	225	5	963	4	250	1	10,000	2	0	0	—	0	—	0	—
Total 1979-83	24	281	40	971	10	785	11	1,118	16	491	2	350	0	—	0	—

Source: Commonwealth Department of Transport

It is generally regarded that the specialized nature of marine operations is such that port authorities are best equipped to oversee the prevention and response to oil spills. Harbour masters and their officers maintain a constant presence in Australian ports. Moreover, it is also the case that marine authorities, by virtue of their control over such operations as berthing and servicing, have a large number of administrative or informal sanctions available to them which could not be used by other regulatory authorities.

Statistics provided by the Commonwealth Department of Transport reveal that the use of prosecution in response to marine oil pollution varies markedly state by state, but in a manner quite different from prosecution for air, water and noise pollution. As Table 8 indicates, Victoria's various port authorities account for the largest number of convictions. Despite growing concern about the frequency of oil spills in Botany Bay, the New South Wales Maritime Services Board has prosecuted much less frequently in the 1980s than it did in the 1970s. Nevertheless, penalties for oil pollution were doubled to $100,000 in 1985. In contrast to the lack of prosecution for pollution of inland waters in Queensland and Western Australia, local port authorities in each of those states have brought an average of two to three cases per year to court. The use of prosecution in Tasmania is infrequent, as it has been in South Australia with the exception of 1982, when six prosecutions were recorded. Neither the Northern Territory nor the commonwealth government reported any prosecutions for oil spills in recent years.

Environmental Contaminants

At the time of our research, administrative arrangements for the regulation of hazardous chemicals in Australia were in the process of significant change. There was no commonwealth control over industrial chemicals other than a voluntary notification scheme introduced in 1982, and controls in various states were not uniform. Existing procedures for the regulation of pesticides, for example, were largely the responsibility of state departments of agriculture, based on a state–federal clearance process under the auspices of the Technical Committee on Agricultural Chemicals of the Australian Agricultural Council. This process is assisted by input on health matters from committees of the National Health and Medical Research Council. It should be noted that this scheme has resulted in the availability in Australia of agricultural chemicals which are banned or severely restricted in the United States and other home countries of transnational chemical companies. Similarly, Australian authorities are very reluctant to classify as suspected or accepted human carcinogens many agricultural chemicals so classified in the United States.

A 1982 commonwealth parliamentary inquiry was very critical of the lax regulation of hazardous chemicals (House of Representatives Standing Committee on Environment and Conservation, 1982). Legislation is being prepared to establish a national chemicals notification and assessment scheme, under the auspices of the National Occupational Health and Safety Commission with assistance provided by the Commonwealth Departments of Health, and Arts, Heritage, and the Environment. The scheme will require assessment of all new industrial chemicals to be introduced into Australia, including their effects upon human health and the environment. It remains unclear whether agricultural chemicals would be included in this scheme. Also, certain hazardous substances currently in use would be subject to the same screening procedures. Prescribed substances, in addition, would be subject to a follow-up review. It is envisaged that the scheme will be implemented by means of complementary legislation in each state and territory.

References and Recommended Reading*

*Australian Environment Council (1983), *Management and Disposal of Hazardous Industrial Wastes*, Australian Government Publishing Service, Canberra.

Australian Law Reform Commission (1978), *Access to the Courts I Standing: Public Interest Suits*, Australian Government Publishing Service, Canberra.

Barker, M. (1983), *Conservation Law in the A.C.T.*, Academy Books, Canberra

*—— (1984), 'Environmental Quality Control: Regulation or Incentives', *Environment and Planning Law Journal*, 1, 3, 222-32.

*Bates, G. (1983), *Environmental Law in Australia*, Butterworths, Sydney.

Bilger, R. (1974), 'The War Against Exhaust Pollution', in R. Dempsey (ed.), *The Politics of Finding Out: Environmental Problems in Australia*, Cheshire, Melbourne.

Commonwealth Department of Resources and Energy (1983), *Water 2000: Consultants Report No. 8 'Salinity issues'*, Australian Government Publishing Service, Canberra.

Fisher, D. (1980), *Environmental Law in Australia*, University of Queensland Press, St Lucia.

*Fowler, R. (1984), 'Environmental Law and its Administration in Australia', *Environment and Planning Law Journal*, 10-49.

Gilpin, A. (1980), *Environment Policy in Australia*, University of Queensland Press, St Lucia.

House of Representatives Standing Committee on Environment and Conservation (1982), *Hazardous Chemicals: Second Report on the Inquiry into Hazardous Chemicals,* Australian Government Publishing Service, Canberra.

MacDonald, K. (1977), 'The Negotiation and Enforcement of Agreements with State Governments Relating to the Development of Mineral Ventures', *Australian Mining and Petroleum Law Journal*, 1, 29.

McLaren, N. and Cole, D. (1984), *Santos Ltd Liquids Project: A Case Study of Environmental Audit and Monitoring*, Social and Ecological Assessments, Adelaide.

Queensland Water Quality Council (1981), *Annual Report for the Year 1980-81*, Government Printer, Brisbane.

—— (1983), *Annual Report for the Year 1982-83*, Government Printer, Brisbane.

—— (1984), *Annual Report for the Year 1983-84*, Government Printer, Brisbane.

South Australia (1972), *Report of the Committee on Environment: The Environment in South Australia*, Government Printer, Adelaide.

Supervising Scientist for the Alligator Rivers Region (1979), *Annual Report 1978-79*, Australian Government Publishing Service, Canberra.

—— (1983), *Annual Report 1982-83*, Australian Government Publishing Service, Canberra.

Tasmania, Department of the Environment (1980), *Report for the Year 1979-80*, Government Printer, Hobart.

Venn, F. (1981), 'Farms Choking on Industrial Fallout', *National Farmer*, 9 July, 10.

Warnick, L. (1982), 'State Agreements — The Legal Effect of Statutory Endorsement', *Australian Mining and Petroleum Law Journal*, 4, 1-54.

—— (1983), 'The Roxby Downs Indenture', *Australian Mining and Petroleum Law Association Yearbook, 1983,* 33-84.

Wells, F.K., Wood, N.H., and Laut, P. (1984), 'Loss of Forests and Woodlands in Australia. A Summary by State, Based on Rural Local Government Areas', *CSIRO Tech. Memo 84/4*, Institute of Biological Resources, Canberra.

Western Australia, Environmental Protection Authority and Conservation and Environmental Council (1983), *Annual Report 1982-83*, Government Printer, Perth.

Woods, L.E. (1983), *Land Degradation in Australia*, Australian Government Publishing Service, Canberra.

4
Occupational Health and Safety Regulation

The Problem

Accidents at work and occupational disease are staggering burdens on the Australian economy. In its final report, the Interim National Occupational Health and Safety Commission (1984, 1) concluded that 'conservative estimates put the financial cost to the community at more than $6 billion per year: double the more widely publicized road accident figure, an estimated $3 billion'.

The cost to the hospitals system of coping with 2.5 million bed days per year resulting from workplace injuries is an enormous fiscal burden (Rann, 1983, 3). In July 1984, the then chairman of the Australian Law Reform Commission, relying on a review of the evidence by Gunningham (1984) has perhaps most powerfully posed the magnitude of the problem:

- a million working days a year are lost because of accidents at work;
- almost half a million people suffer incapacitating work injuries in such accidents;
- over 300 die from work-related injuries and this is almost certainly an under-estimate when it is remembered that probably a third of all cancer cases are work-related, directly or indirectly;
- in most years, the numbers of days lost from occupational injury and disease is almost twice the number lost as a result of strike action, which captures so much media, political, and public attention;
- for every Australian injured on the roads, about five are injured at work (Kirby, 1984, 1-2).

The chemical disaster in Bhopal, India, in 1984, which killed more people than any previous industrial disaster in human history, showed what a mistake it is to assume that the situation is improving. The International Labour Organization recently reported that work safety in the world is deteriorating because of new technology and the introduction of up to 1,000 new chemicals a year (*Canberra Times*, 10 January 1985, 4).

The Administrative Framework

Occupational health and safety enforcement in Australia has been, and is likely to continue to be, primarily a state responsibility. Nevertheless, commonwealth involvement, particularly in the domains of standard setting, research, and education, is likely to increase with the advent of the National Occupational Health and Safety Commission. So too will the commonwealth embark upon a more active enforcement role in the Australian Capital Territory and among commonwealth employees throughout the country.

At the state level, occupational health and safety enforcement is extremely fragmented. A recent survey in Western Australia found that nineteen government departments in that state had some types of occupational health and safety responsibilities. The single most important area is the traditional factories inspectorate generally found in state departments of labour and industry. These include machinery inspectorates, inspectorates for lifts and scaffolding, boilers and pressure vessels, explosives, construction safety, and general factories and shops inspectorates. Queensland, Tasmania, Western Australia, and South Australia have polyglot appendages whose responsibility is to check compliance with occupational health laws (e.g., lead and asbestos exposures); occupational safety laws not covered by other more specialized inspectorates; arbitration inspection, to ensure payment of award wages; workers' welfare inspection (e.g., shearers' accommodation standards); and shop trading hours enforcement.

Beyond the general occupational health and safety inspectorates found in labour and industry departments, the second most important areas are mines inspectorates. Queensland and New South Wales have separate inspectorates for coal and metalliferous mines, while Victoria and Western Australia, with their substantial oil industries, have separate inspectorates which have special expertise in the technology of off-shore oil production and exploration.

Health departments are the third major type of bureaucratic participant in workplace safety. In most states they provide a service to the factories and mines inspectorates, conducting occupational hygiene surveys, testing workers for evidence of exposure to occupational carcinogens, and the like. Secondly, in all states, health departments retain direct enforcement responsibility for radiation safety, as will be discussed in the next chapter.

In all jurisdictions except the Northern Territory and Tasmania, a rationalization of occupational health and safety under a single authority is being considered. These developments are most advanced in New South Wales where the Department of Industrial Relations has already taken over two major areas from the Department of Health (except radiation control) and the Department of Mines. In all other states, mines departments seem to be successfully resisting a takeover of their safety responsibilities. In the Northern Territory, the Department of

Table 1
States and Territories of Australia
Occupational Health and Safety Inspectors (1984) by Jurisdiction

	General Health and Safety Inspectors	Mine Safety Inspectors	Total Inspectors	Workforce in Full-time Employment	Workers per Inspector	Manufacturing Establishments	Manufacturing Establishments Per General Health and Safety Inspector†	Mining Employees#	Mining Employees Per Mine Inspector
NSW	222	19	241	1,804,300	7,487	10,477	47	30,600	1,611
VIC	177	14	191	1,414,800	7,407	8,393	47	6,900	493
QLD	178	33	211	827,500	3,922	3,438	19	18,200	552
SA	53	15	68	440,600	6,479	2,102	40	6,000	400
WA	81	38	119	469,100	3,942	2,499	31	25,200	663
TAS	34	8	42	139,500	3,321	528	16	3,900	488
ACT	9	0	9	91,800	10,200	150	17	—	—
NT	25	27	52	51,700	994	118	5	3,800	141
TOTAL	779	154	933	5,239,400	5,616	27,705	36	94,800	616

* Australian Bureau of Statistics, *The Labour Force, Australia*, Canberra, October 1983, 13.

† Excludes establishments with fewer than four persons. Australian Bureau of Statistics, *Manufacturing Establishments. Summary of Operations by Industry Class, 1982-83*, 20.

\# Australian Bureau of Statistics, *Civilian Employees*, February 1980.

Mines and Energy oversees health and safety not only in mines, but in all workplaces.

Inspectorial Resources of the Agencies

Table 1 shows that there is wide variation in the resources currently available for occupational health and safety enforcement across jurisdictions. The Northern Territory is by far the best resourced jurisdiction. If general occupational health and safety and mine safety inspectors are combined, the territory has far fewer workers per inspector than any of the states. It also has far fewer manufacturing establishments per general occupational health and safety inspector, and fewer miners per mine safety inspector than any other jurisdiction. Actually, the latter situation is understated by the existence of an effective commonwealth duplication of some local mine inspection resources in the form of the staff of the Office of the Supervising Scientist for the Alligator Rivers Region. The latter monitors the safety and environmental impact of uranium mining in the Northern Territory.

The worst resourced is the Australian Capital Territory, where there are 10,200 workers per inspector. This, however, may be partly compensated for by the small number of significant manufacturing establishments per inspector. Not far behind are New South Wales and Victoria where inspectors are almost equally thinly spread on the ground. The situation in Queensland is far worse than Table 1 suggests because industrial, factories, and shops inspectors spend a relatively small proportion of their time on occupational health and safety, with industrial award compliance being their major preoccupation.

The Northern Territory is clearly the jurisdiction best endowed with mine safety inspectors. New South Wales has by far the worst situation with regard to miners per mine safety inspector.

Mines inspectors have a much stronger presence in the workplace compared with general occupational health and safety inspectors, as Table 1 shows. There are 5,616 workers per safety inspector in Australia; for mining employees alone, there are 616 workers per mine inspector.

General Occupational Health and Safety Inspectorates

First, we discuss the regulatory strategies of the general occupational health and safety inspectorates principally found in state labour departments. Table 2 presents the numbers of convictions obtained by these inspectorates. A more detailed analysis of these statistics is provided in Braithwaite and Grabosky (1985). Data are not presented in Table 2 for the Australian Capital Territory. However, we were told that there were 'about two' prosecutions a year in the territory. This would seem to complete the picture from Table 2 of a very low level of prosecution (even if taken on a per capita basis) in the three small

Table 2
Convictions Obtained by General Occupational Health and Safety
Inspectorates, Excluding Queensland and the Australian Capital Territory

	NSW	VIC	SA	WA	TAS	NT
1973-74	—	150	—	—	—	—
1974-75	—	167	—	—	1	—
1975-76	257	154	—	26	0	—
1976-77	129	111	—	46	1	—
1977-78	151	105	39	56	1	—
1978-79	174	116	34	58	1	—
1979-80	195	127	33	57	0	2
1980-81	211	112	25	59	1	2
1981-82	174	147	18	24	1	18
1982-83	196	137	17	21	1	4
1983-84	216	—	27	—	3	3

Sources: Annual Reports; Data supplied by the inspectorates.

Compared with other areas of business regulation discussed in this book, the remaining states have relatively high levels of prosecution activity. This is particularly true of the large states of New South Wales and Victoria, and is also true of Queensland, for which data are available on numbers of prosecutions but not numbers of convictions.

In fact, the Queensland Industrial and Factories and Shops Inspectorate is among a handful of agencies of any kind in Australia which is highly prosecutorial. Between 1976 and 1984, its modest staff of 121 initiated 7,003 prosecutions, though 2,631 of these were subsequently withdrawn and 241 were unsuccessful. Of the 1,195 prosecutions in 1982-83, 684 were for failure to renew registrations of factories and shops. In 1983-84 there were two such prosecutions. Other years have seen no prosecutions at all in this area, and over 600 prosecutions for shop trading hours breaches or for the underpayment of wages to workers. In other words, this inspectorate operates by alternating prosecution blitzes between different areas among its vast array of responsibilities. There is no such thing as an average year. There are an enormous number of prosecutions each year, but often in totally different areas from the previous year.

The Division of Occupational Safety, also in the Queensland Department of Employment and Labour Relations, is also relatively prosecutorial with its responsibilities of machinery and construction safety (Braithwaite and Grabosky, 1985, 13-24). Fines are typically very low, averaging under $200 in most states in most years during the past decade (Braithwaite and Grabosky, 1985, 13-24).

For all of the agencies discussed in this chapter, law enforcement is only a part of their function. Safety education is an important involvement to a greater or lesser degree with all of them. Even with routine inspections, persuasion is regarded as a more important function than enforcement. Indeed, seven of the eight general occupational health and safety inspectorates indicated at their interview that education and persuasion were more important functions for them than law enforcement, and six of the eight thought that they devoted more resources to education and persuasion than to law enforcement.

In practice, Australian occupational health and safety regulation has relied very little on encouraging or requiring industry or individual companies to write and enforce their own codes of practice as opposed to governments writing and enforcing regulations. For nine years, South Australia has had legislative authority to require an employer to 'prepare and, as often as may be appropriate, revise a written statement setting out with reasonable particularity, the arrangements for the time being in operation to maintain the safety and health at work of his employees' (section 29a(1)(a), *Industrial Safety, Health and Welfare Amendment Act* 1976), but resources have not been deployed to ensure that such statements are written. There have not been any companies prosecuted for failing to prepare a statement.

Extensive negotiation and consultation with business and unions does take place, particularly through formal tripartite consultative committees which all of the mainland states have. However, the negotiation on these committees to date has been over what the government should put in its regulations, not over the codes of practice and corporate enforcement programmes expected of industry.

Most agencies espoused the encouragement of workers to form and demand worksite safety committees, and to elect safety representatives as a regulatory strategy (though the South Australian, Northern Territory, and Queensland occupational safety divisions did not include encouraging workers in such directions among their compliance policies). Notwithstanding the espousal of fostering grass roots union involvement by the other agencies, there has been little action to implement these ideals. Tasmania, for example, has had a legislative framework for safety committees and employee safety representatives since 1977, but at the time of our interview in late 1984, of the fifty safety representatives appointed in accordance with the act, more than forty were from government departments. The instances where safety representatives had been appointed or safety committees formed in private industry could be 'counted on the fingers of one hand'. One reason offered was that 'We have been directed politically not to get out there and wave a flag and sell it'. We may see a very different situation some years from now after the Labor states have implemented their commitment to require health and safety committees for all places of work with more than a minimum number of employees.

In practice, then, general occupational health and safety inspectorates engage in traditional government command and control regulation. The inspectorates are highly proactive, but rather rule-book oriented.

While inspection consumes most of the resources of these agencies, there are a number of other important activities. As mentioned earlier, there are safety education programmes. There is also considerable investment in all states in design review of major industrial plant prior to installation, and some activity in some states in pre-clearance of industrial chemicals. Designs for new premises are registered and approved.

In addition to approving the safety of premises and plant before it can be used, approving the competence of people before they can perform certain hazardous functions is another important part of the regulatory strategy. This is achieved through the issuance of certificates of competency as plant operators, boiler attendants, engine drivers, crane drivers, scaffolders, and the like.

Other regulatory strategies are available, but are not often used. Suspension or revocation of licence or certificates of competency has been used at some time by all general inspectorates. In every case, this action was infrequent; in most cases it was less than an annual occurrence. Adverse publicity is rarely used by general inspectorates as an alternative sanction. Written directives that certain things be done by a certain time to ensure compliance with the law (improvement notices) are used from time to time, while prohibition notices (stop notices) requiring the cessation of a particular activity which endangers health or safety, seem to be used very infrequently. Harassment, with follow-up inspections of the workplace, is the most frequently used informal sanction.

Mine Safety Inspectorates

The term 'mine safety inspectorates' is used here to include agencies responsible for enforcing health and safety in both coal and metalliferous mines and at oil and gas exploration or production projects. Except for the New South Wales Department of Industrial Relations, which refused to co-operate with our survey, these are all agencies in mines departments.

The Use of Prosecution

Low as the level of prosecution activity is on the part of some factories inspectorates, by any standard, it is even lower with mines inspectorates. In Western Australia, the state with most mine safety enforcement activity, convictions per 1,000 miners are much lower than convictions per 1,000 manufacturing workers, even though the hazards of mining employment are far greater. The average fines when convictions do occur are also lower, largely reflecting the extraordinarily low maximum penalties stipulated in mine safety statutes. In many jurisdictions, a maximum $100 fine, or even less, is all that is available for quite serious offences. Combine this with sentencing guidelines where magistrates impose 20 per cent of the maximum fine on a first offence, and one obtains a result like the following from the 1980 Annual Report of the Western Australian Department of Mines:

No prosecutions were initiated during the year, however, prosecutions commenced in 1978 following the deaths of two workmen at the Kwinana Nickel Refinery on the 8th June, 1978, were concluded.

The Magistrate's findings were handed down on the 28th May, 1980. The Registered manager was found guilty on two counts: one against Section 54 and one against regulation 8.13(1) of the Mines Regulation Act 1946-74 and Regulations. He was fined $20 on each count. The company was found guilty of an offence against regulation 8.13(1) and fined $100. The foreman responsible for the work being undertaken by the men, prior to their deaths, was found guilty on two counts: one against section 54 and the other against regulation 19.2. He was fined $20 on each offence.

The *Tasmanian Mines Inspection Act* 1968 is a classic in that it provides the same maximum penalty ($500) for negligently causing a person to be killed in a mine as it provides for using obscene language or engaging in 'unseemly or riotous conduct' in a mine (section 48).

The prosecution strategy with mine safety regulation in Australia is radically different from factories enforcement. Whereas general occupational health and safety inspectorates direct their prosecutions overwhelmingly at companies, mining inspectorates aim their prosecutions overwhelmingly at culpable individuals.

Western Australia had forty mine safety convictions between 1970 and 1982 inclusive. The only other area where there is any significant prosecution activity is metalliferous mine safety (but not coal mine safety) in Queensland (Braithwaite and Grabosky, 1985, 37-53).

With mine safety regulation, a co-operative compliance model has relatively more attraction than a law enforcement model, because of the much more frequent contact of inspectors with industry than is the case with factories regulation. Most mines of any significance in Australia can expect at least monthly government safety inspections, while other workplaces may go for many years without seeing a general occupational health and safety inspector. The consequence is that mine safety inspectors can build across time a relationship of mutual respect and accommodation with the managers with whom they are in regular contact.

Relationships of respect are also given a better chance by the fact that mine safety inspectors in Australia are generally professional peers of the managers with whom they must interact. It is unusual for a mine inspector in Australia not to have a tertiary qualification (a degree or diploma, usually in engineering), while it is equally unusual for a general occupational health and safety inspector to have one. Mine inspectors in all states are required to have a certificate of competency as a mine engineer, and at least three years experience in mine management. Generally, they have much more experience than this minimum; most states do not like to employ people who have not had at least ten years mining experience including experience as a mine manager.

For decades, mine safety laws have required mines to write their own special rules on safe transport in the mine, roof support, tipping waste, and a variety of other matters; to communicate these rules to workers through organized training; to nominate personnel with responsibility for ensuring compliance with the rules; to conduct at least weekly inspections to monitor compliance with both general regulations and company rules; to record breaches detected by these inspections and by other means in a record book maintained for the purpose at the mine; and so on. In short, mine safety regulation has long put into practice the notion that management must take the responsibility for writing, communicating, and internally enforcing codes generated by industry under the supervision of highly qualified government inspectors.

Except in Tasmania, the Northern Territory, and with off-shore oil and gas production, mine safety regulation has long involved the empowerment of elected workers as safety representatives who have the right to inspect and to stop production when this seems justified. In Queensland, in addition to local miners' safety representatives, full-time state-wide union safety inspectors with the power to stop coal production have $24,000 per year towards their salaries subsidized by the state government, and district workers' representatives for metalliferous mines have their entire salaries paid out of consolidated revenue. The Western Australian Department of Mines pays the entire salaries of five full-time union safety inspectors. Interestingly though, programmes that actively encourage the formation of workplace safety committees have never been a part of the strategy of any mines inspectorate.

The most important kind of enforcement undertaken by mine safety inspectors involves mobilizing private justice systems within mines:

We think the important thing is to take action on the spot, and you'd be aware that the strength of the unions associated with mining, and I can assure you that what we lack in, if you like, legislative strength, is more than compensated for by general acceptance of the workforce of . . . health and safety . . . I take that a little further by saying to you that misdemeanours at a mine which are registered by either the manager or the mine workers are taken care of amongst that group by standing down a person for a specific number of days, or in extreme cases, discharging that person from service . . . On the spot justice.

Q. So you encourage these informal processes?

A. Of course we do . . . It is the rule of the Queensland Colliery Employees' Union that the members of that union will not work with any person who is found to be smoking underground or to have in his possession materials for smoking . . . The tradition is, I guess . . . the tree stump, the office table justice. And maybe justice after some bartering. Management says he goes down the road for three days and his union representatives come out with a 'Jesus Christ, not that long' and they agree on two days.

Like most of the examples of tree-stump justice we were given, the following from off-shore oil regulation also concerns informal control of individual workers rather than managers.

. . . just recently we saw someone smoking in an area where they shouldn't have been smoking, and we have written to that company and advised them of it, and asked them to let us know what action they have taken against that employee.
Q. And you would rather do that than prosecute that individual?
A. Yes, the company will undoubtedly transfer him to another area, I should think. If they take no action, we just say 'Well, that personnel, that chap, isn't allowed on the rig'.
Q. And you'd have the power to do that?
A. Yes.

Mine safety inspectorates do have the resources, the expertise, and the worker–management support to contend, with a credibility that the general health and safety inspectorates do not have, that they are making informal social control succeed as an alternative to law enforcement. This does not extricate these inspectorates from the critique that their regulatory system wrongly assumes that there is always a community of interest between workers and management when it comes to health and safety.

Most of what we have said about the minor role of law enforcement in the overall regulatory strategy of general occupational health and safety inspectorates is even more true with mine safety inspectorates. All eight mine safety inspectorates saw education and persuasion as more important functions for them than law enforcement, and felt that more resources went to the former than the latter. All of them felt their goals included getting companies to do better than the minimum required by law.

Referring to his enthusiasm for self-regulation, the Northern Territory's Director of Mines echoed sentiments which were often repeated in interviews, 'Most of what we achieve, we could do without any legislation'. As with general occupational health and safety inspectorates, we must bear in mind that in addition to conducting inspections, mines departments approve plans for the expansion of mines, for roof control, contingency plans for oil spills from off-shore rigs; they issue certificates of competency for managers, deputies, electricians, and a wide array of other specialist jobs; they supervise mine rescue establishments; they undertake safety research; and they conduct safety education campaigns. Law enforcement is, therefore, only one of a variety of facets of regulatory strategy.

As with general inspectorates, harassment with follow-up inspections is the major informal sanction; directing adverse publicity against offenders is almost universally rejected; and cancellation of certificates of competency of mine managers and others, is very rare indeed.

Directives to do certain things by a certain time to ensure compliance or improve safety are usually delivered by the inspector issuing them verbally, and then writing in the record book required at each mine that the directive had been given. At the next inspection by either a government or a union inspector, the record book will be consulted, and a further entry will be made to indicate whether the directive has been complied with. No statistics are kept on the frequency of directives entered in record books, but they do seem to be a regular occurrence.

Government inspectors in all jurisdictions have the power to stop work until the area of the mine is safe, and union inspectors have the power to stop production until a government inspector arrives. All agencies claimed that stopping production was a much more severe and immediate sanction than a prosecution. As a representative of the Western Australian petroleum division said: 'We can prosecute someone. Under the direction, the maximum fine is $2,000 per day. If we shut him down it can be $100,000 a day'.

At the same time, some cynicism is justified at claims that prosecution is rejected because the same punitive function is more effectively fulfilled by shutdowns. The representative of the Western Australian petroleum division, quoted above, went on to say that there were only two shutdowns of oil rigs in 1984, and none in 1983. In mine safety regulation proper in Western Australia, the estimate of production being actually shut down in a part of, or a whole, mine (as opposed to production being slowed down by someone being pulled off a shift to fix a problem) was eight to ten times a year. In Western Australia there have been occasions when entire mines have been ordered closed for 'a day or two' while ventilation problems were rectified. The point is that, while this potent regulatory weapon is used, the frequency of its use would not seem to be greatly higher than prosecution. This is even more true in the Northern Territory where there has been only one case in recent times of a mine being shut down, albeit a celebrated one where the Ranger uranium mine was closed for four days after an exposure of uranium tailings in a pond. This was an interesting case, because it was one where shutdown was, in the eyes of the Northern Territory Department of Mines and Energy, used punitively rather than to protect workers from immediate danger:

We closed Ranger down not because there was any serious danger or an incident out there, merely an exposure of tailings in a pond which caused no danger to health or environment. However, it was symptomatic of a few laxities in the operation at that stage and also the thing was not detected by them and not reported for some time.

After indicating there had been no repetition of such laxity, the Director of Mining said that they had been given 'a message which they've since well and truly learned'.

The only other state from which we could extract information on the frequency of mine shutdowns was Queensland. In the Queensland coal industry, cases where either 'a section of a mine or a whole mine' was closed down occurred 'probably four or five times a year'. With metalliferous mines, the response was 'less than five times a year'. These shutdowns 'can go on from as little as one hour, to situations that I can recall fairly accurately, which have taken three days to correct'.

Conclusion

General occupational health and safety inspectorates are relatively prosecutorial, proactive, and rule-book oriented. However, sanctions are minimal, and are directed at companies rather than individuals.

In contrast, mine safety enforcement is directed at individuals who fulfil those management roles with safety responsibilities defined by mine safety laws. The mine safety inspectorates are equally proactive, but much more diagnostic in the way they approach safety problems. Mine safety inspectors are much better qualified; regulation tends to be more particularistic and less dominated by the rule-book, and it is pursued by negotiation within a regular ongoing relationship between professional peers: the manager and the inspector. When inspectors feel a need for punitive action, they are likely to get management or the union to mobilize private justice systems rather than prosecute. Essentially, mines inspectors act as catalysts to get managers to write their own safety rules. Mines inspectors are as much technical advisors as they are watchdogs.

The involvement of a third party besides government and business in the regulatory process — the union — is what is increasingly distinguishing occupational health and safety regulation from other areas of regulation. Safety committees and elected employee safety representatives are beginning to play an increasingly important role in regulatory strategy.

References and Recommended Reading*

*Braithwaite, John and Grabosky, Peter (1985), *Occupational Health and Safety Enforcement in Australia*, Australian Institute of Criminology, Canberra.

*Gunningham, Neil (1984), *Safeguarding the Worker: The Role of Law*, Law Book Company, Sydney.

Interim National Occupational Health and Safety Commission (1984), *Report*, Australian Government Publishing Service, Canberra.

Kirby, Michael D. (1984), 'Occupational Health and Safety — Time for Reform', Address to National Safety Council of Australia Seminar, Canberra, 27 July.

*Merritt, Adrian (1984), *Guidebook to Australian Occupational Health and Safety Laws*, CCH Australia, Sydney.

Rann, Mike (1983), *Limbs, Lungs and Lives: Occupational Health and Safety Reform*, Direct Communications, Adelaide.

5
Radiation Control

There are five main areas of radiation regulation. First, there is radiation exposure in the mining of uranium and other minerals; second, exposure in the use of uranium in nuclear reactors; third, risks in the transport of radioactive materials; fourth, exposure during commercial, medical, or scientific use; and fifth, hazards associated with disposal of used materials. In Australia, the first of these problems tends to be regulated by mines departments, the second, by the Australian Atomic Energy Commission, and the last three, by radiation control branches in state health departments. Each of these three institutional arenas of regulation will be considered in turn below.

The McClelland Royal Commission into British Atomic Testing in Australia would seem to have been presented with considerable evidence of unnecessary exposure of Australian citizens as a result of inadequately regulated use of nuclear materials. In more recent years, however, Australia has avoided the major radiation disasters which have plagued some other countries. It could be argued that in this we have been lucky since serious incidents which, fortunately, did not produce disastrous effects have occurred in all five arenas mentioned above. With mining, on 5 July 1982 about a tonne of yellowcake was accidentally discharged from the bottom of a bin at the Ranger uranium mine in the Northern Territory. Two operators were enveloped in a cloud of dust as the yellowcake escaped. Even though the workers were not wearing respiratory protection for the full period of the spill, and as a result inhaled and ingested dust, serious health consequences do not seem to have resulted (Supervising Scientist, 1983, 27-9).

With manufacturing, on 6 July 1984 about a kilogram of uranium hexafluoride escaped from the Lucas Heights headquarters of the Atomic Energy Commission when a pipe joint failed. The gas, which is used in uranium enrichment, escaped into a laboratory where four people were working, and then was ventilated out into the surrounding community. As well, in September 1985, security at Lucas Heights failed, allowing vandals to smash an underground pipe, releasing radioactive effluent into the Woronora River.

Thirdly, the risks in transport were highlighted in November 1984 when a driver was exposed in five hours to the maximum radiation dosage considered acceptable for radiation workers in one year. The driver had transported isotopes around Sydney in an improperly sealed container before delivering them to Lucas Heights, where alarm bells started ringing as soon as the truck entered the premises (*Sydney Morning Herald*, 29 November 1984).

Irresponsible usage of radiation was highlighted by a 1982 report, leaked to the press, of the Victorian government's consultative council on radiation. The report raised serious doubts about the safety of X-ray equipment being used in some Victorian hospitals, and in doctors' and dentists' surgeries, suggesting that the dose of radiation for a particular procedure may vary up to 1,000 times depending on the equipment used and the training of the operator. The Minister for Health, Mr Roper, conceded: 'What has been shown in the report is that the government's activities in the area of radiation safety have been grossly inadequate. There is a lack of effective legislation in the area and a lack of enforcement of the legislation that is there' (*Age*, 15 June 1982). Even more frightening incidents have occurred with industrial usages, as illustrated by the following remark of one government respondent:

Well we suspect that there were situations, not so much in hospitals or establishments controlled by the Department of Health, but in other circumstances there were reported incidents that were fairly horrifying. Like people having nuclear-radioactive gauges on hoppers and various places and dropping dynamite down the hold and this sort of thing to clear blockages. Which is pretty horrendous . . . That's on file, too. As a reported incident. Somebody got the hopper clogged so they dropped dynamite down.

Finally, disposal of wastes has probably been the subject of most controversy in Australia. This has ranged from allegations that forty-four gallon drums containing radioactive waste had been dumped 200 nautical miles off the Queensland coast in the 1950s, to public questioning by a former technical secretary of the Atomic Energy Commission of how the commission should deal with 1,000 used fuel rods which would remain radioactive for 100,000 years (*Canberra Times*, 6 September 1984). Perhaps the most immediate concern has been provoked by the indiscriminate dumping of lower level radioactive tailings from mineral sands mining in Queensland and northern New South Wales. Hundreds of householders who were sold the radioactive tailings in Queensland to use as fill in their backyards have been told that they must remove the health risk at their own expense, an expense that can run to many thousands of dollars when swimming pools and other structures have been built upon the radioactive fill.

Mining and Radiation

Monitoring radiation exposure during mining is a collaborative effort between mines and health departments in the states where mining occurs. In the Northern Territory, the Office of the Supervising Scientist for the Alligator Rivers Region also monitors and reports to the responsible commonwealth minister on environmental protection and health and safety at the Ranger and Narbalek uranium mines. The office generally leaves the enforcement activity to the Northern Territory Department of Mines and Energy, being content with the role of a watchdog which trusts that goodwill and the fear of exposure will exert influence:

The threat of our writing to our minister, either to advise him about a particular matter, or formally to report to him under a section of our act that would require the report to be tabled in parliament, is often sufficient for the Northern Territory or the companies or anyone for that matter to take note of what we say.

Having substantially covered the framework of mine safety regulation in the last chapter, all we need do here is to add some additional features peculiar to the regulation of radiation risks in mining. Uranium mining regulation is more like the regulation of pharmaceuticals than it is like other mining regulation. A particular project is not allowed to go ahead until investigation of the benefits of the activity are concluded, after extensive inquiry, to exceed its costs (including occupational health and safety costs). This is akin to drug regulation in which products are kept off the market until particularistic assessment concludes that benefits exceed risks, rather than the general assumption with mining that any mining activity should go ahead unless there are unusual circumstances. The Northern Territory Uranium Mining (Environment Control) Act forbids any uranium mining without an appropriate and specific authorization issued by the Minister for Mines and Energy.

When uranium mining projects are authorized anywhere in Australia the authorizations define or refer to standards, describe practices, and list the monitoring or protective measures required of each operating company as conditions for continued activity. In the Northern Territory where most activity is currently occurring, these include occupational hygiene and safety programmes which are clearly laid out in the authorizations. The companies are also required to report infringements and 'unusual events' to the Minister for Mines and Energy so that these might be fully investigated.

The mineral sands industry, which today only has a substantial presence in Western Australia, is dealt with in co-operative style. Voluntary company agreement to abide by international radiation control codes and co-operative audits of exposure levels by government and industry are the cornerstones of this regulatory domain.

In summary, regulation of radiation safety in mining operations in Australia is characterized by prior approval of projects following detailed evaluations of benefits and social costs; negotiated, contractual, or voluntaristic reliance on codes of practice which are mostly international in origin; particularism; agreements between industry and government to share responsibility for monitoring exposures and audit such monitoring (with industry doing most of the monitoring, and government most of the auditing); and total rejection of law enforcement as the regulatory model.

The Australian Atomic Energy Commission

Australia has only two operational nuclear reactors, both at the Australian Atomic Energy Commission (AAEC) establishment at Lucas Heights near Sydney. The commission is Australia's only producer of radioisotopes and radiopharmaceuticals, and has an extensive programme of nuclear research. For a staff of just over 1,000, there are forty-five full time occupational health and safety personnel. These staff have multiplied their impact by involving unions in an on-site health and safety committee and a safety review committee of outside experts.

Lucas Heights, as a commonwealth establishment, never receives visits from New South Wales state government occupational health and safety inspectors. Thus, there is no independent enforcement of compliance with occupational health and safety standards, and no chance of anyone ever being prosecuted.

In other areas, there has been a recognition of the need to separate regulator from regulatee. In 1978, the function of safeguarding against the diversion of nuclear materials to unaccountable destinations was taken away from the AAEC and handed over to the Australian Safeguards Office which, even though its officers continue to be located at Lucas Heights, answers to the Minister for Resources and Energy rather than the Chairman of the AAEC. The office is responsible for guaranteeing that Australia meets its safeguarding obligations under the Nuclear Non-Proliferation Treaty. Further independence is guaranteed in this domain by independent inspections two or three times a year by the International Atomic Energy Agency.

A degree of independent audit is also provided for with respect to monitoring exposure risks for the community and environment outside the plant. Four aspects of the waste management operations at the Lucas Heights Research Laboratories could impact on the surroundings:

First, low-level radioactive liquid wastes after treatment together with treated sewage are discharged to the regional sewer line that has its outfall on the Cronulla peninsula. Second, the ventilation of HIFAR [the reactor], and several of the research laboratories, involves discharges from stacks. These air streams can carry low-level radioactivity that is almost invariably gaseous. Third, until the mid-1960s, low-level solid radioactive waste was buried at Little Forest, an area close to the fenced section of the Lucas Heights Research Laboratories. Fourth, stormwater could carry contaminants from the site to the fresh water section of the Woronora River (AAEC, 1982).

Prior to every discharge, CSIRO officers at Lucas Heights monitor whether discharge of liquid effluent complies with an authorization under the New South Wales Radioactive Substances Act. The Metropolitan Water, Sewerage, and Drainage Board maintains its own sampling station on the effluent line near the Lucas Heights boundary fence, and the Health Commission of New South Wales carries out some monitoring for radioactivity at the various sewerage outfalls and checks the radioactivity levels of air filters on smokestacks.

The most catastrophic risk would arise from a failure of one of the reactors. This hazard is monitored by a unique semi-independent regulatory regime. Line management decisions on reactor safety are subject to audit by the Regulatory Bureau, a group of fifteen located at Mascot in separate offices from the rest of the AAEC. The director of the Regulatory Bureau does not answer to the director of the Lucas Heights Research Establishment, but rather reports directly to the chairman of the commission. On the other hand, the director of the research establishment does have effective control over the Regulatory Bureau budget; hence the description semi-independent. In a speech launching our book, *Occupational Health and Safety Enforcement in Australia*, the Minister for Resources and Energy, Senator Gareth Evans, indicated that he would 'certainly give some further thought . . . on the question of an institutional independence for the commission's Regulatory Bureau'.

The fundamental operations of the Regulatory Bureau work in the following way: operations management of the AAEC submit plans for any modifications to the reactors along with safety analyses of the projected impacts of changes to the bureau. The bureau then raises a number of questions, management comes back with answers, the bureau asks a new series of questions, until ultimately a set of satisfactory answers and amendments to plans has been made so that the bureau can submit to the commission a recommendation that the modification be endorsed. The chief executive of the AAEC explained the situation as follows:

. . . it will not endorse proposed modifications to the reactors until certain other changes are made. In other words, they'll say to me if you've put up a proposal to modify the emergency core cooling circuit in a certain way: 'Now we do not approve that until you've established the failure rate of this component at less than one in 10^5 or something. Or if you can't do that you've got to find some other way'. And they don't tell me what that other way is. In other words, it's not their responsibility to tell me how to do it, only to say whether it's acceptable or not.

The director of the Regulatory Bureau, in the following extensive quotation which outlines his regulatory philosophy, confirms that the preferred approach is one of setting performance standards rather than detailed specifications:

You can either regulate prescriptively, you can define, tell everyone just what they should do, or alternatively you can tell everyone the goal they have to achieve, giving them a degree of flexibility to meet that goal. It is, in the nuclear industry, the big difference between the approach of the Americans and the

United Kingdom. In the United States they have a completely prescriptive form of regulation. It is probably inevitable there because they have a Nuclear Regulatory Commission which is responsible for regulating a large number of operators and those operators are essentially private. In fact Americans can tell you quite horrifying stories about one utility which had never run a power station; it went straight into the reactor business . . . So the point I want to make is that in the States they have a large number of very diverse operators: diverse in competence and in responsibility. So perhaps that is forced on them, the idea of prescriptive regulations. And that means that the Nuclear Regulatory Commission is constantly churning out very, very detailed regulations on what every operator must do and they have a very extensive system of checking on that . . . they just fined someone a couple of million dollars . . . But the criticism you can make of the prescriptive form of regulation . . . is that you are really transferring responsibility away from the operator back to the regulator, because he is now coming to rely on you; if he has done it according to the book then he thinks he has done it well enough. That's a very dangerous situation . . . We always feel that the most important thing is the person who is operating the plant should have a safety concern himself. He must be worried about safety; it is not good enough that he simply feels he is meeting all the rules and regulations. In Britain they have got two main electricity generating boards. They are the only people who have reactors, so they are starting from a different base and the Nuclear Installation Inspectorate simply puts out a series of guidelines. They license reactors; they don't say for a licensed reactor it has got to meet these sorts of standards; they say, 'Look, we will want to be satisfied that in the event of this type of accident that there would be no possibility of getting exposures above these levels around the site: the goal rather than the way you achieve it'. The reason this has always been the United Kingdom philosophy is that by doing this you don't stifle the innovation of the people doing it . . . you leave the safety challenge with them . . . We have adopted a philosophy which is very much the United Kingdom one and the commission issues a thing which is called an authorization, a document of thirty or forty pages which sets down all of the goals, all of the things it wants attended to. Then the director has a responsibility to make a detailed document with arrangements on how he is going to achieve those goals. Those then come to us, and we decide whether or not they are adequate, and then we make a recommendation to the commission. If they are accepted by the commission, then . . . we eventually finish up with an approved set of regulations, a very voluminous amount of documentation.

The chief executive of the AAEC explained that the Regulatory Bureau also seems to have an extraordinarily ambiguously defined power to stop production:

The director of the Regulatory Bureau has the right to instruct me to close the reactor down. Now, I am really bound by that except if I was to feel that there was some overriding safety consideration. I mean I can't think of what that would be at this stage. There have been some arguments as to whether he should have the absolute power . . .
Q. That's not a matter of legislation?
A. Oh, no. It's a matter of internal commission policy, that's all.

Perhaps partly as a result of the performance rather than prescriptive approach to regulation, there is not an acutely adversarial relationship between the bureau and management. The director of the the Regulatory Bureau sees dangers in too 'arms-length' an approach, and advantages in being unashamedly part of the same professional club. One perceived advantage is the greater frankness with regulators who are part of the same collegial environment, and ultimately that means a greater capacity to draw out whistle blowers. It is clearly a less drastic action to blow the whistle to the Regulatory Bureau than it is to someone completely outside the nuclear scientific club. The following exchange with the director of the Regulatory Bureau illustrates the non-adversarial nature of the relationship:

Q. So how often is the commission getting a different perspective from the Regulatory Bureau than from management, so that the commission has to choose or make a compromise?
A. So far not very frequently at all, and I think the more they do the less successful we are.

The Regulatory Bureau believes that the best counterbalance against co-optation by binds to the Australian nuclear scientific club is building a stronger commitment to another club: the international 'scientific engineering safety world'. If the Regulatory Bureau and individual scientists within it are to have a name in this world, 'then you are only going to do it by showing that you have got this sort of critical nature'. So the director of the Regulatory Bureau saw his challenge as building an organizational culture, an *esprit de corps*, where his scientists feel they are judged more against the standards of scepticism and independence of the international community of safety professionals, than judged by their fidelity to the camaraderie of the Australian nuclear club.

Radiation Control Functions in State Health Departments

We discussed with the health departments in all states the role they played in occupational health generally, and radiation safety regulation specifically. The size of radiation safety groups in health departments ranged from one health physicist in Tasmania, to a staff of fifteen in New South Wales, though Victoria is about to overtake New South Wales with an expansion of staff to twenty-two.

These agencies are responsible for assuring the safe use of irradiating apparatus and radioactive substances for diagnostic purposes and treatment (i.e. radiotherapy). Industrial and research uses of ionizing radiation, including the use of unsealed radioactive substances in nuclear medicine and pathology are also monitored. Compliance with regulations concerning the safe transport and disposal of radioactive substances are other responsibilities. It is possible that the new Commonwealth Environmental Contaminants Authority will assume some of the state health department responsibilities in years to come on the question of safe disposal of wastes. Inspection of X-ray machines in medicine, dentistry, and veterinary practice is the area which consumes most resources.

The statutory framework for state radiation regulation is very similar in all the states. New South Wales has the most dated framework, while the 1984 Victorian Health (Radiation Safety) Regulations under the *Health Act* 1958 constitute one of most innovative legal frameworks for business regulation to be found in Australia. Like the Australian Atomic Energy Commission's approach, there is a strong orientation towards performance rather than specification standards. For example, instead of prescribing exactly how radioactive wastes should be disposed, Victorian regulations provide that:

A person responsible for the disposal of radioactive wastes shall release those wastes only in a manner that could not cause any person to receive more than the annual dose equivalent limits prescribed in these regulations.

The next regulation then defines an upper limit for the concentrations of radioactivity permissible at the time of discharge. A second impressive feature is the commitment not only to national uniformity but also to international uniformity. For example, Regulation 1,201 requires that transport and storage of radioactive materials be in accordance with both the Commonwealth Code of Practice for the Safe Transport of Radioactive Substances, and the International Atomic Energy Agency Regulations for the Safe Transport of Radioactive Materials, 1973. The regulation then goes on to assure Victoria the sovereignty to vary these provisions where exceptional local circumstances demand, by providing that 'Where the Code or International Regulations conflict with these Regulations then the provisions of these Regulations shall prevail'.

The heart of the regulatory regime in all states is registration of irradiating apparatus and radioactive sources, and licensing of persons qualified to use them. Licensees and employers are required to report to the health department instances of excessive exposures which come to their attention. The regulations also make it possible for organizations to be required to appoint radiation safety officers, with duties which are specified in the regulations or such other duties which may be specified as a condition of the licence. This facilitates a regulatory strategy whereby many of the monitoring and accountability responsibilities which might otherwise be borne by government inspectors are placed on the shoulders of a qualified radiation safety officer within the organization who is on hand all the time.

State regulations also impose a general duty to keep radiation exposures no higher than is absolutely necessary. For example, the regulations under section 8(1) of the New South Wales Radioactive Substances Act require that:

Every person who has in his possession or custody or uses any radioactive substance or irradiating apparatus, shall take steps to ensure that the radiation dose received by any person or any part of any person, is no greater than is absolutely necessary and that in no case does it exceed the appropriate maximum permissible dose.

Consistent with this general duty, much of the regulatory effort of radiation control in health departments is directed at educating people in ways of reducing unnecessary radiation. This may involve discouraging employers from unnecessarily requiring X-rays of employees, or teaching professionals how to achieve with two X-rays something they might previously have done with four.

There is a strong commitment to self-regulation, to getting professional associations of radiographers and others to develop and implement their own voluntary codes.

These inspectorates are, on the other hand, highly proactive. They are not heavily dependent on complaints as generators of regulatory action; their approach is to go out and randomly inspect sites where radiation is occurring. Inspectors are typically well qualified graduates in health physics, radiography, or related disciplines.

A Victorian officer could have been speaking for any of the states when he said:

The unit regards itself not as an inspectorial group or a police force but as a scientific organization, and the regulations are just to aid them to do what they are on about, and that is reduction of radiation dosage throughout the community. So if we can achieve that without using the regulations, we do it.

Self-monitoring of radiation exposures combined with government audit of the self-monitoring are crucial to the regulatory strategy in all jurisdictions. All persons who may be exposed to ionizing radiation as a result of their work must have their exposures monitored by their employer. Usually the approved method of achieving this is by the use of personal film badges issued by the Australian Radiation Laboratory, though three states issue their own. Licensees are also required voluntarily to report excessive exposures immediately.

The audit of exposure self-monitoring is generally not undertaken by health departments simply with the goal of keeping employers honest, but more as a diagnostic occupational hygiene service. To illustrate, the South Australian Health Commission spokesperson distinguished the commission's work from the overlapping work of the Department of Mines as follows:

The mines department has obligations to make sure that a mine is a safe working place, and they interpret this as including making sure that that the radiation levels are... below standards... We try to do more monitoring which is diagnostic, if you like, to try and attempt to find the causes or trends, or whatever. Mines stuff is more towards regulatory type things, like over a limit or below a limit.

This is not to deny an important element of keeping employers honest as well. When the independent monitoring of radiation exposures by health departments yields very different results from those reported by employers, they are called to account for the differences. What we have been leading to with all of the foregoing, however, is that prosecution is quite unimportant as a regulatory tool for radiation safety.

No state or territory radiation control agency has had more than one prosecution in the 1980s and most of them have had none. In addition to a strong attachment to a co-operative regulatory style, problems of proof are important in explaining this almost total absence of prosecutions.

... suppose you've got something that is relatively straightforward: the film badge comes back with a large dose on it. You have to prove (here's a very long chain of links in there) that the person was wearing that film badge, that they didn't receive any radiation dose while it wasn't being worn, that it was collected properly by the the company, that it was sent to the laboratory properly, that they analysed it properly, etc.

In addition, there is the problem common to all toxic exposures that while the average exposure over a period (a year in the case of radiation) is the criterion of importance for persuading a court of serious risk to an employee, this may not be known, and what is known — an unacceptably high exposure at one point of time — might be discounted as safe when very low exposures for the rest of the year are taken into account. So what does the South Australian Commission do when it discovers unacceptably high levels of worker radiation exposure?

... if certain high levels are reached or measured, then certain steps will be put in train to reduce them, so the first stage obviously would be re-monitoring to check ... I mean you'd look around for reasons for it. Was it a transitory breakdown in the ventilation system or was there a deep-seated long-term reason, and then, this sort of tome of causes has to be worked through, and the penalties would be directed towards ensuring that these steps to find the reason for high levels and take appropriate action are taken.

There can be no doubting that the very limited experience with prosecution in this area has been discouraging. In New South Wales there have been only two prosecutions in the last twenty-five years. One of these resulted in a fine of $500 for an offence which cost the government over $15,000 in radiation clean-up expenses. The second case has cost the health commission thousands of dollars in legal fees because the doctor concerned retained one of Australia's top QCs to appeal his sentence: a fine of several hundred dollars. At the time of interview, it had been two years since the unresolved enforcement action had been initiated.

The result is that New South Wales has an enforcement pyramid that now effectively excludes prosecution as an option for escalating regulatory response in the face of recalcitrance: 'We rely first on advice, then on a more forceful letter, then threat of licence loss'.

The ultimate step under this enforcement pyramid of actually suspending or revoking licences also occurs very infrequently in all states. Imposing special conditions on licences is another *de facto* sanction which is occasionally used. It is common for the preparation of a radiation safety manual to be required as a condition of licence; in problem cases, the commission can insist on considerable detail being recorded in such a manual with regard to listing of hazards, precautions, emergency procedures, specification of detailed lists of duties for responsible officers, constant supervision of certain areas, or appointment of specialized expertise such as a nuclear medicine specialist.

Another sanction which most jurisdictions employ is putting a notice on a machine to prevent its use until it is made safe in compliance with the regulations, or in extreme cases, the equipment or radioactive source can be seized. New South Wales is one jurisdiction which does not issue such prohibition notices. It does not have the power to do so under what is the most outdated statute in the country.

Adverse publicity is not an informal sanction which most of the states like to use. 'In such a sensitive field as radiation, it gets out of hand very quickly', we were told. In fact, regulatory efforts were directed much more at calming what were seen as alarmist media coverage of radiation hazards which surfaced from time to time. While radiation safety regulators would never dream of fostering adverse publicity for offenders, they often use the spectre of a voracious press to persuade licensees to follow their advice.

Radiation is a very emotive topic and often the warning to industry that a certain practice could result in a certain incident is very helpful. Just the expression to a user — a mine, mill, or factory — that this could get you in the newspaper, often gets prompt attention from senior management.

In summary, radiation regulation by state health departments is characterized by relying on self-regulation and professional education; imposing conditions of licence which improve prospects of low exposures; and by self-monitoring of exposures in industry combined with a government audit. Government checking of exposure levels is aimed more at a diagnostic service to licensees with problems, than at policing the integrity of their self-monitoring. Where the advice which follows problem diagnosis is ignored, regulatory response escalates to stern warning letters, to threatened revocation of licence, and to actual licence revocation, suspension, or imposition of more stringent licence conditions. Prohibition orders are also used in most states. Prosecution is almost never used.

References

Australian Atomic Energy Commission (1982), *Environmental Monitoring*, Australian Atomic Energy Commission, Sutherland, New South Wales.
Supervising Scientist for the Alligator Rivers Region (1983), *Annual Report, 1982-83*, Australian Government Publishing Service, Canberra.

6
Consumer Affairs

The Problem

Australian consumer affairs agencies received 65,388 written complaints during the year ending 30 June 1984 and at least ten times as many unwritten complaints. The major areas where consumers felt they had been unfairly treated were real estate and accommodation (17 per cent of complaints), purchase and repair of electrical goods (11 per cent), and purchase of used motor vehicles (9 per cent) (Commonwealth Minister for Home Affairs and Environment, 1984). Many of these complaints do not involve violations of law and not all of them relate to problems of enormous consequence: the New South Wales Department of Consumer Affairs has had to deal with complaints of vibrators failing to live up to their claims, while another diligent consumer counted only 400 sheets in a toilet roll advertised as containing 500.

But the victimization of the consumer is far from trivial. Consumer affairs offences can result in serious bodily injury, and can result in considerable financial cost. A perusal of the annual reports of consumer affairs departments reveals an infinite variety of 'rip-offs' which lie behind many complaints: cars sold in an unsafe condition, deception of consumers into signing exploitative credit 'agreements', misrepresentation in advertising, mail order frauds. The complaint statistics understate the problem. Most consumers cannot be bothered lodging a written complaint even when they know they are victims of significant frauds. More often they do not even know. Consumers are almost never aware when they are victims of price fixing conspiracies in breach of the Trade Practices Act, when they have bought a banned product such as a toy with an impermissible lead content, or when they have purchased a car with a tampered odometer reading (Braithwaite, 1978). Large surveys in New South Wales and the Australian Capital Territory found respectively 15 per cent and 32 per cent of petrol pumps to be giving short-measure petrol to motorists (*Sunday Telegraph*, 3 February, 1980, 7; *Canberra Times*, 13 January 1981, 1). Doubtless, many consumers were totally unaware of their victimization.

The Administrative Framework

In this chapter we will consider the work of state and territory consumer affairs bureaux and departments, as well as giving separate consideration to two more specialized commonwealth agencies: the Trade Practices Commission and the Prices Surveillance Authority. Among Australian business regulatory agencies perhaps only the Australian Taxation Office and the corporate affairs commissions face more impossible tasks than consumer affairs agencies. All jurisdictions face enormous difficulties in keeping up with the sheer number of complaints which they receive. We will see that it is these difficulties which fundamentally shape the regulatory strategies of consumer affairs agencies.

Table 1
Staffing Levels of Australian Consumer Affairs Agencies
(Including Weights and Measures Staff), 1984-85

	No. Staff	Staff per 100,000 Consumers
New South Wales Department of Consumer Affairs	481	8.4
Victorian Ministry of Consumer Affairs	170	4.2
Queensland Consumer Affairs Bureau	62	2.5
South Australian Department of Public and Consumer Affairs, Consumer Affairs Division	115	8.3
Western Australian Department of Consumer Affairs	89	6.6
Tasmanian Consumer Affairs Bureau and Weights and Measures Inspectorate, Department of Labour and Industry	37	8.4
Australian Capital Territory Consumer Affairs Bureau (Commonwealth Department of Territories)	19	7.5
Northern Territory Consumer Affairs Branch, Department of Community Development	17	12.1
Trade Practices Commission	178*	—

* At the commonwealth level, there is also the Office of Consumer Affairs in the Attorney-General's Department with a staff of twenty-five. This office is not a regulatory agency as defined in this book, as its role is limited to policy formulation. The Trade Practices Commission is the commonwealth enforcement agency.

Even though Queensland is the most decentralized state, it copes with being the jurisdiction with the greatest resource limitations (Table 1) by having only one office, located in Brisbane. This discourages country complaints, and keeps the total for the state down to a manageable 4,000 complaints a year. In country centres the bureau makes limited use of industrial, factories, and shops inspections for consumer affairs matters.

Other states create for themselves a volume of complaints impossible to meet satisfactorily with existing resources. One such is Victoria, actively seeking to regionalize with shop-front offices and a mobile unit which visited 117 towns in 1983. Apart from Queensland and the Australian Capital Territory, all states and territories have some level of regional office presence.

Regulatory Strategy

There are two quite distinct consumer protection regulatory strategies: one for weights and measures, and another for the rest of consumer affairs. Except in Tasmania, weights and measures inspectorates have now been absorbed into the 'new' consumer affairs agencies which were formed across the country between 1969 and 1974, but in all cases these older inspectorates have retained a separate identity and regulatory style. While the new agencies are primarily reactive to consumer complaints, weights and measures inspectorates are proactive, 'out on the beat' randomly checking weighing and measuring devices and trial-purchasing packages to ensure that the mass or volume claimed is correct. Weights and measures inspectors do respond to complaints, but they do not primarily rely on them as their source of information about problems. They also have more of a law enforcement orientation, in contrast to the conciliation orientation of consumer affairs officers:

I think in my experience of both consumer affairs and weights and measures, the trader understands there is a difference... A consumer affairs officer is there to negotiate in many ways, whereas the weights and measures inspector is an enforcement authority, and their reaction is: 'Do we have to do it under law. If we don't, we won't. If we do, we will'.

It should be clear by now that consumer affairs agencies have little choice but to be predominantly reactive. They cannot turn complainants away while they pursue a proactive programme of random inspections. Indeed the advent of consumer affairs agencies effected a transformation of some areas of regulation from a proactive to a reactive style.

... years ago, another agency that used to administer the Lay-by Sales Act before this department [New South Wales Department of Consumer Affairs] took it over, it was a standing joke that the way they used to enforce it was that they used to put a team of police into one of the big arcades in town and do the place over, and that was a joke, but it was true, it was how they used to enforce that act. There would be a whole lot of publicity flowing out of it.
Q. How is it different today?
Well, how it is different today is that we actually act on complaints. If there are complaints about lay-by sales and breach of the legislation, where we try to resolve the complaint, and the complaint is not resolved, we may prosecute.

Putting aside weights and measures, all state and territory consumer affairs bureaux and departments have a similar hierarchy of regulatory preferences. First, they would prefer to prevent problems by consumer education rather than deal with them after they have occurred. Failing this, their second line of defence is mediation between complainants and individual traders and negotiation of solutions to groups of complaints with industry associations. Third, a failure to resolve complaints against a trader can lead to the trader being targeted for adverse publicity. The last resort is that action is taken against the trader in the courts. This hierarchy of regulatory response is not invariate. Some states are willing to prosecute for deterrence purposes when prosecution is not a last resort, and some use prosecution before trying publicity. We will consider in turn these four elements in the hierarchy.

Education

All states produce posters or leaflets, and promote consumer education in the mass media to greater or lesser degrees. Also, school curricula are increasingly being modified to include consumer education resource kits, including audio-visual materials.

Much consumer protection legislation is also directed at requiring traders to provide educative information to consumers: care labelling for garments, ingredient labelling and date stamping for food, disclosure of interest rates computed according to a statutory formula to enable comparisons, and so on.

Queensland is the only state which could be said to devote more of its resources to consumer education than to any other area. While we have seen that these total resources are comparatively meagre, there can be no doubt that Queensland has been innovative in producing imaginative posters and leaflets, and fostering consumer education in the mass media.

Conciliation and Negotiation

Most consumer affairs resources in Australia are devoted to resolving individual complaints. Consumer affairs officers see themselves primarily as mediators rather than law enforcement officers, and see standards of 'fairness' as their guiding light more than legislative standards. Much activity is devoted to getting 'fairer' treatment of consumers in circumstances where the legal footing of the consumer is shaky. When mediation of a case runs into intransigence on the part of a trader, the consumer is often advised to take the matter for an informal but binding adjudication by the small claims tribunal or court, which exists in all jurisdictions.

If the negotiation process becomes prolonged, or is seen to be going to be unsuccessful, we don't hesitate at all. We would go off to the small claims tribunal, provided they're within the jurisdictional limits and so on, and people take that advice and go. Generally where we say to go off to the tribunal our investigators have formed a pretty clear idea that the person's got right on his side and in most cases they win.

Q. And if they're smart, they'll mention the fact that you sent them over?

They call our investigators as witnesses too, which is permissible, especially our technical officers, and this really helps the referees where they are looking at, say, a warranty matter on a motor vehicle; they take the technical advice of the engineers.

Beyond dealing with individual complaints, all the agencies look for patterns of complaints which might be solved in one fell swoop by negotiating with a company or an industry association.

If we stand back and see that the XYZ Company has a bad record in that there are so many complaints received per week, then we go and talk to that management, even bring them in here, and say, 'This is your record. Have you looked at what you're doing? Have you looked at why? Is there any way that we can help you to change your management structure or management problems or whatever it might be, to ensure that those things don't happen?' That way, we reduce the number of complaints coming in.

Sometimes such negotiation takes place against the background of an agreement, explicit or implicit, that the consumer affairs agency will not litigate even if the negotiated settlement is unsatisfactory to them.

I don't mind telling you, companies will sit around this table and say, 'Well, okay, we can see what you are on about. We don't like it but we'll negotiate and help those people only on the understanding that you're not going to take us off to court. If you want to go the legal process, well fine, let's finish the discussion. You go and do your thing'.

Such deals are often agreed to by agencies because they can produce quicker redress for complainants than can litigation. Moreover, many of the costs of a litigated settlement to business go to lawyers rather than complainants, and companies can be more generous with a voluntary settlement because the settlement is an investment in consumer and regulatory goodwill in a way that a litigated settlement can never be.

For Victoria, and to a lesser extent Western Australia, encouraging industry associations to engage in self-regulatory activities is an important part of the agency's regulatory strategy. The Victorian Department of Consumer Affairs prefers the term 'co-regulation' to self-regulation, because its goal is to get industry to work jointly with government to agree on codes of ethics and business practices, together with the means for industry associations to enforce them against their members. The Victorian commitment to this activity is so explicit that the Department of Consumer Affairs' programme objective 'indicators' for 1984-85 include assisting six business categories 'in achieving self- or co-regulation'.

All of the other jurisdictions regard business self-regulation as a desirable thing, and where it is effective, are delighted to allow self-regulation to work as an alternative to government regulation. However, they do not actively commit resources to programmes to develop self-regulation in the way the Victorians and Western Australians do. First, some of them are cynical that self-regulatory platitudes often are not translated into practice, particularly where many traders are not members of the trade associations which are supposed to be doing the enforcement. Second, there is a concern that when a serious scandal arises from the failure of a self-regulatory regime that was promoted by the agency, it will reflect badly on the agency. And third, there is concern in some quarters that encouraging trade associations can be a double edged sword, because as well as being vehicles for improving business ethics, trade associations can be vehicles for enforcing restrictive trade practices (e.g. price fixing) which are against the consumer interest.

The South Australian Commissioner for consumer affairs has been particularly outspoken in publicly criticizing sham self-regulatory regimes. It should be noted that since he issued the attack below, the situation in this industry has considerably improved.

I do not consider that there is any advantage to a consumer in dealing with an in-ground pool builder who is a member of the Master Pool & Spa Institute (SA) Inc. I am also forced to conclude that, with its present membership, there is not necessarily any significant advantage in dealing with a member of the Swimming Pool & Spa Association of SA Inc., although at least this Association does make some attempt to encourage its members to maintain appropriate standards. I do believe that if SPASA were to take a closer look at its membership, and to take heed of the comments I have made in this report, it would have the potential to offer significant benefits to the community as a responsible industry organisation. Unfortunately, however, that potential is not presently being fully realised. Although there are undoubtedly some members of both bodies who endeavour to act responsibly and fairly, there are others who are quite irresponsible and it is quite evident that there is no effective system of self-regulation in the industry (South Australian Commissioner for Consumer Affairs, 1983, 8).

South Australian and New South Wales consumer affairs agencies are moving towards an innovative co-regulatory approach via their Commercial Tribunal Acts. The New South Wales Minister for consumer affairs has explained the strategy as follows:

Where a code of practice is needed in a particular industry it is intended that machinery will be set up to bring all interested parties — industry groups, consumer and community organizations, members of the public, and people working in the industry — together to develop the code under government auspices (Paciullo, 1984).

Such codes would then be enforced through the Commercial Tribunal. The tribunal will order traders to make redress to consumers, or otherwise change their business practices when it finds codes have been violated in a particular case. Like small claims tribunals, the Commercial Tribunal will be informal and not be bound by the rules of evidence. It is envisaged that priority areas for codes will be industries where the characteristics of transactions are so unique as to fall between the cracks of broad consumer law. The New South Wales and South Australian Commercial Tribunals have also assumed responsibility for a wide variety of types of occupational licensing (e.g. licensing of motor dealers, land valuers, builders, and credit providers). Western Australia and Victoria are also looking to bring their various licensing tribunals together under one Commercial Tribunal; whether these tribunals will also aspire to the co-regulatory functions of the South Australian and New South Wales model remains to be seen.

Particularistic enforcement of fairer trading standards against a company when these standards are not covered by broad consumer law has another interesting precedent in the Victorian *Market Court Act* 1978. The Market Court was not established to handle breaches of existing legislation, but to prevent traders from 'repeatedly engaging in unfair conduct to consumers'. The idea was that the court would single out unfair traders, and deal with them individually instead of licensing or legislating for all traders in a particular industry. Only the Director of Consumer Affairs may take a trader to the Market Court, with a request that the court order the trader to desist from specified practices. The court, and the provision for negotiation of 'deeds of assurance' under the act, have not been heavily used, there being only seven deeds of assurance in effect under the act. This reflects, in part, the general unwillingness of a thinly resourced Victorian department to undertake time-consuming litigation. It also indicates the limitations of a court that can make proscriptive but not prescriptive orders. Out-and-out crooks can live with an order that they not engage in certain dubious practices of the past by shifting to another type of dubious practice in a somewhat different business.

Publicity

Directors of consumer affairs in all states except Tasmania have the power to issue public statements drawing the attention of consumers to unfair practices by a trader with the benefit of privilege against defamation. In Victoria, privilege attaches to the annual report, but only qualified privilege at common law applies to other public statements made by the director. In Tasmania, the Consumer Affairs Council has the equally effective power to produce a special report which the minister has no option but to table in parliament. Such powers are used to great effect, particularly in agencies like those in New South Wales and South Australia, which employ media professionals to maximize the impact of public warnings.

All jurisdictions except Victoria make heavy use of the annual report to name traders responsible for unscrupulous practices. This is a powerful deterrent, as the media tend to take up these reports. The following example from Western Australia is illustrative:

We usually get about two and a half full pages in the weeks after the report is tabled. It usually gets three or four minutes on the evening news, with pictures; the afternoon news would always pick something up. It can go on for days. In fact some of them go on, individual traders who don't like it, they just seem to dig deeper holes by keeping their name in the paper by complaining.

The media, however, are not always willing to take up consumer protection stories. Several agencies complained of the difficulty of getting newspapers which include a lot of motor vehicle advertising to run with a story about a motor dealer. There was even one story of a newspaper witness testifying that he was unsure that a false claim in an advertisement was placed by the advertiser or was a mistake by the newspaper. The witness admitted to a consumer affairs officer after the trial that the newspaper could not afford to lose $50,000 in advertising by testifying against a client.

A respondent from the Northern Territory Consumer Affairs Branch told the story of a land sales investigation which was handled for them by the Northern Australia office of the Trade Practices Commission. The commission put out a media release from Brisbane expressing its concern about these land sales practices in Darwin.

The North Australian rep rang me. He said, 'Now any publicity I want you to let me know'. There wasn't a word in the territory, but it made news in all the other states. Now you can draw your own conclusions.

The Victorian and Queensland directors of consumer affairs are the most reluctant to use publicity as an enforcement tool. The Victorian government named traders engaging in unfair practices until its 1982 annual report, but ceased doing so after the election of the Cain government. A limited return to the practice is planned for the 1985 annual report. It is difficult for the Victorian director to be an aggressive publicist in the consumer interest in the way his peers can in other states, because in Victoria, all press releases must be issued by the media unit of the Department of Premier and Cabinet.

Consumer protection agencies exploit 'narrowcasting' as well as broadcasting of information about the unscrupulous practices of selected traders. The most common example involves letting the finance industry know that a particular trader is a fly-by-night operator in the hope that this will exhaust his or her sources of capital for mounting new schemes of deception.

Law Enforcement

For every conviction for a consumer affairs offence in Australia, there are more than 200 written complaints that do not lead to a conviction, and conservatively over 2,000 unwritten complaints. Granted, many of these complaints do not involve an offence by the trader, but prosecution is also rarely resorted to because of the problem of keeping complaint files moving when these do relate to offences. Officers who spend time collecting evidence of sufficient quality to use in a court of law quickly fall behind on their complaint workload. They lose favour with their boss and their peers when someone else has to be assigned to take over their backlog of files. The 'speed of the line' almost inevitably forces consumer affairs agencies to be reactive rather than proactive, and settlement-oriented rather than enforcement-oriented.

In one sense, however, yielding to this inevitable pressure may be irrational for the regulatory agency which wishes to achieve its goals. It could be that the agency which allows its complaints to pile up for a time while it takes vigorous enforcement action against one offender, may deter other offenders who would otherwise have generated hundreds of complaints for the agency to deal with. Thus, a short-term log-jam in complaint resolution may be worth enduring to relieve long-term pressure on complaints. South Australia is the only state which has taken this to heart with a conscious administrative solution. Its policy on consumer affairs enforcement states:

If our legislation is properly enforced, then we 'protect' consumers by discouraging breaches of their rights before such breaches occur. Such preventive work is at least as important as the advice we provide on receiving a complaint after the damage has been done.

The South Australian Commissioner for Consumer Affairs is instituting new administrative procedures to ensure that someone stands back and looks at all offences uncovered in the complaint resolution process with a view to forming a perspective on where strategic deterrence is required. The first requirement is that *all* suspected offences detected by the personnel handling the complaints must be referred to the Investigation and Enforcement Section. The enforcement policy then states that 'All reported offences are to be the subject of "enforcement action" '. 'Enforcement action' is defined very broadly, and can involve no more than a warning letter. Nevertheless, the policy seeks to guarantee that the agency is never seen to ignore an offence. This policy contrasts sharply with the practice in Victoria, for example, where the overwhelming majority of completed investigations where breaches are detected by their enforcement section do not result in any kind of enforcement action by the Ministry of Consumer Affairs (Victoria, Director of Consumer Affairs, 1985, 15).

The South Australian consumer affairs enforcement policy (section 4.4) even allows deterrence to compromise complaint resolution in strategic cases, a 'revolutionary proposition' in Australian consumer affairs:

A request for deferral or enforcement action would not be made if it is considered that the wider consumer interest would be served by immediate enforcement action, even though this may be seen to jeopardise the outcome of a particular consumer's complaint.

The other rationale for referral to the Investigation and Enforcement Section was as follows:

The best person to decide whether or not an offence should be followed up with a view to prosecution is not necessarily the person who was investigating the matter from the point of view of getting redress for the consumer. He might, for example, be unduly emotionally involved because of the plight that this particular consumer found himself in; he might be swayed by things the trader has said in the course of negotiations; he might even be subjected to pressure by the trader who tries to do a deal — like 'If I fix up this consumer's complaint, will you promise not to prosecute me' . . . The investigation officer should be able to say, 'Look, I'm here to try and fix up this particular consumer's problem. The question as to whether any offence which you may have committed is going to be prosecuted is not my decision. I just pass the information on to somebody else'. There is a danger in doing these sort of deals. You don't get to hear about a lot of the offences if you do that because the trader who says whenever somebody complains, 'I'll fix them up, but I'll continue to do the wrong thing by those who don't complain' will find that he's able to do this sort of deal and he'll never get prosecuted.

There is the additional advantage of referral that personnel in the Investigation and Enforcement section have superior criminal investigation training, several being former police officers. Consolidation of enforcement experts in one section also permits putting all enforcement officers onto a blitz in one area. The blitz or crackdown on a particular problem 'to get a message across' to industry is a strategy much favoured by Australian consumer affairs agencies.

Not surprisingly, all of this leads to the conclusion that South Australia has emerged as the most prosecutorial of Australian consumer affairs agencies in the last two years. Table 2 summarizes consumer affairs, while Table 3 summarizes weights and measures convictions over the past fifteen years (see also Braithwaite, Vale, and Fisse, 1984).

Table 2 gives a misleading impression of the level of enforcement activity in Queensland and Tasmania. Ninety-five per cent of the convictions in these states are for the 'technical' offence of failing to comply with orders to provide information to consumer affairs officers. The fact is that in Queensland, Tasmania, the Northern Territory, and the Australian Capital Territory, prosecutions for substantive consumer affairs offences are virtually non-existent. In part, this reflects more limited consumer affairs legislation in these jurisdictions compared with the other states; in larger part, it reflects rejection of prosecution as a strategy.

Tables 2 and 3 also show that the state courts award very low fines relative to those imposed under the commonwealth Trade Practices Act. One legal officer illustrated the problem with a case of odometer fraud which, it was argued, cost the consumer $3,000 on the purchase price of an expensive used car. The dealer was fined $250. Another motor dealer in Victoria offered a consumer affairs officer a $1,000 bribe not to report an offence. The bribe was rejected and when the original offence went to court, the fine was $200.

Apart from adverse publicity and warning letters, alternative sanctions to fines are rarely used by consumer affairs agencies. In all jurisdictions, successful actions to withdraw or suspend the licenses of motor dealers, real estate agents, credit providers, and the like are even more infrequent than prosecutions. The states devote varying degrees of energy to maintaining information systems which highlight companies repeatedly coming to the attention of the agency as potential

Table 2

Convictions and Average Fines Obtained by Consumer Affairs Agencies
(Excluding Weights and Measures)

Year	Commonwealth IV*		Commonwealth V†		NSW		VIC		QLD		SA		WA		TAS		ACT		NT	
	No.	Av. Fine $	No.	Av. Fine $	No.	Av. Fine $	No.	Av. Fine $	No.	Av. Fine $	No.	Av. Fine $	No.	Av. Fine $	No.	Av. Fine $	No.	Av. Fine $	No.	Av. Fine $
1973–74	—	—	—	—	—	—	—	—	2	35	24	121	—	—	6	15	2	65	—	—
1974–75	1	5,000	4	26,875	—	—	35	51	8	66	31	109	—	—	21	18	1	100	—	—
1975–76	0	—	1	500	—	—	74	78	8	57	56	131	—	—	32	21	2	120	—	—
1976–77	0	—	16	5,345	97	162	19	148	21	82	31	155	9	—	16	64	1	200	—	—
1977–78	11	19,818	9	7,043	76	417	28	161	16	90	40	139	38	—	7	91	0	—	—	—
1978–79	2	15,500	2	13,500	64	360	16	358	30	87	#	—	63	—	24	78	0	—	—	—
1979–80	6	43,833	9	11,344	55	475	35	324	23	117	33	115	80	—	9	64	3	333	—	—
1980–81	6	53,333	10	28,940	49	808	19	541	20	192	20	78	35	—	21	61	0	—	0	—
1981–82	2	7,500	7	2,743	34	773	25	712	27	164	20	—	64	—	11	90	2	80	5	90
1982–83	3	23,333	3	17,833	54	915	24	263	29	113	103	72	82	—	23	73	2	130	2	200
1983–84	7	7,071	8	7,469	—	—	12	—	30	—	—	—	32	—	—	—	—	—	3	66

—   A dash means data not available.
*   Refers to convictions under the restrictive trade practices provisions of Part IV of the Trade Practices Act.
†   Refers to convictions under the consumer protection provisions of Part V of the Trade Practices Act.
#   SA changed over from calendar year to financial year records.

Source: Annual Reports and data provided by the agencies

Table 3
Weights and Measures Convictions and Average Fines

Year	NSW No.	NSW Av. Fine $	VIC No.	VIC Av. Fine $	QLD No.	QLD Av. Fine $	SA No.	SA Av. Fine $	WA No.	WA Av. Fine $	TAS No.	TAS Av. Fine $	ACT No.	ACT Av. Fine $	NT No.	NT Av. Fine $
1969–70	—	—	—	—	—	—	1	20	—	—	2	35	0	—	—	—
1970–71	—	—	—	—	11	56	18	24	—	—	0	—	0	—	—	—
1971–72	—	—	—	—	1	40	17	29	—	—	0	—	0	—	—	—
1972–73	—	—	—	—	7	61	7	21	—	—	0	—	2	15	—	—
1973–74	—	—	—	—	9	98	4	95	—	—	0	—	2	15	—	—
1974–75	—	—	—	—	8	62	1	20	4	63	0	—	0	—	—	—
1975–76	11	181	—	—	3	95	14	127	4	44	0	—	0	—	—	—
1976–77	25	381	—	—	6	103	15	225	2	35	0	—	0	—	—	—
1977–78	12	306	—	—	3	37	21	180	2	100	0	—	0	—	—	—
1978–79	16	401	20	147	6	73	44	214	3	17	0	—	0	—	—	—
1979–80	15	353	23	182	6	72	19	173	5	100	0	—	0	—	—	—
1980–81	6	890	21	263	9	231	18	226	11	59	0	—	0	—	—	—
1981–82	5	1,522	69	211	17	101	21	207	5	86	3	46	0	—	—	—
1982–83	—	—	39	186	22	128	43	285	1	40	14	21	0	—	—	—
1983–84	—	—	—	—	21	200	—	—	—	—	—	—	—	—	1	0

— A dash means data not available.

Source: Annual Reports and data provided by the agencies.

targets for licensing or Market Court Act actions. This situation may change with the rationalization in some states of licensing powers under one commercial tribunal. In all jurisdictions except Tasmania there also exists a power for directors or commissioners of consumer affairs to take civil action on behalf of an aggrieved customer. This power is almost never used, being saved for test cases which have the widest possible significance for consumers generally.

The South Australian Commissioner for Consumer Affairs has been an advocate of negative licensing. Instead of requiring all traders in an industry to be licensed, no barriers to entry of this sort are erected. However, the commissioner is empowered to apply for the Commercial Tribunal to withdraw the right of a particularly unscrupulous trader to operate in the industry concerned, or to impose certain conditions on continued operations. Negative licensing avoids most of the costs of administering a positive licensing system (though it also implies that the government forgo the revenue of licence fees), and abolishes the anti-competitive effects of erecting licensing barriers to enter an industry. South Australia is piloting a negative licensing scheme on rental referral agencies (companies which find suitable rental accommodation for clients).

In summary, then, with the exception of South Australia, state and territory consumer affairs agencies rarely rise above the mire of mediation to attack the underlying causes of complaints. The only way any of them show strength is through the deft use of adverse publicity. Unfortunately, the latter strategy is only useful against companies which cherish their reputation; it is a limited tool against many fly-by-night operators who move from one kind of consumer fraud to another, from state to state, from bankruptcy to bankruptcy. The problem of dealing with these people has, nevertheless, led to some tentative innovative strategies such as the Market Court, deeds of assurance which set standards of conduct above those required by the ordinary law in problem cases, and negative licensing.

Public Involvement

Most states encourage community groups which relieve them of some of the burden in dealing with complaints. These include consumer organizations, citizens advice bureaux, and specialist organizations like the Tenants' Advice Service and the Consumer Credit Legal Service in Victoria. The Australian Consumers' Association alone received 21,454 complaints in 1984. The Victorian, South Australian, and commonwealth governments also give grants to local consumer groups, which deal with many complaints.

The New South Wales Department of Consumer Affairs is seeking to expand its reach with product safety problems by working with a voluntary network of 120 product safety monitors recruited by the consumer movement.

The Trade Practices Commission

The Trade Practices Commission is partly a consumer protection, partly an anti-trust, agency. Part V of the Trade Practices Act is concerned with consumer protection matters which greatly overlap with the responsibilities of state consumer affairs agencies; it covers unfair practices such as misleading advertising and supply of goods which do not comply with mandatory standards, and implied conditions and warranties. The commission tends to refer local matters requiring mediation to state consumer affairs agencies, while the latter frequently refer matters of national significance requiring firm enforcement action to the commission. Part IV of the Trade Practices Act is concerned with restrictive trade practices: price fixing, resale price maintenance, exclusive dealing, anti-competitive mergers, and monopolization.

No business regulatory agency in Australia has been able to impose as firm an enforcement orientation as the Trade Practices Commission. To many readers, this will seem an extraordinary statement because the Trade Practices Commission has been criticized from many quarters as captured and weak (Venturini, 1980; Hopkins, 1983; Pengilley, 1984). If the commission is captured and weak, then we can only say that it follows from our study that *all* Australian regulatory agencies are so.

Admittedly, a third of the agencies in our study engage in more prosecutions per year than the Trade Practices Commission. However, no other agency takes injunction proceedings against offenders with the frequency of the commission, and apart from the Australian Taxation Office, no other agency is as frequently litigated against by companies which wish to challenge their regulatory actions. No Australian regulatory agency spends as large a proportion of its budget on litigation as the Trade Practices Commission.

It must also be conceded that the punitiveness of trade practices enforcement has a lot to do with the comparatively high maximum penalties provided for under the Trade Practices Act ($250,000 'pecuniary penalties' for offences proved to a civil standard under part IV, $50,000 criminal fines under part V), even though the federal court has never gone close to imposing a $250,000 penalty. There can be no doubt that the sanctions the commission secures from the courts are of a magnitude far in excess of those obtained by any other agency. Since it was established in 1974, the Trade Practices Commission has secured average fines (including 'pecuniary penalties', but excluding costs) of $16,630. The agency with the second highest level of fines averages $1,654, less than a tenth of the trade practices penalties. The fines and pecuniary penalties imposed as a result of commission enforcement over the past decade sum to more than four times the total fines imposed by all state and territory consumer affairs agencies. This is a result not only of the high maximum penalties provided for under the Trade Practices Act, but also of the fact that the commission has a clear written enforcement policy which favours prosecution for the biggest cases involving the largest companies.

Even though the commission often does, contrary to its policy, shy away from large unmanageable cases, there can be no comparison with the total surrender of most Australian regulatory agencies, (be they concerned with tax, corporate affairs, or food standards) to litigation in only the easy cases. The Trade Practices Commission in 1985 is up for an estimated $5-$10 million in costs concerning a restrictive trade practices case which it lost against TNT and a number of other major transport operators. Whatever one thinks of the wisdom of sinking so many resources into one case, it is evidence of the commitment to taking on large and difficult cases that no other agency can claim.

While the penalty levels seem comparatively high, they are insufficient to deter economically rational offenders in the 'high-stakes' area of regulation which is the concern of the commission. For example, in the commission's largest price fixing case against the glucose manufacturers ((1980) ATPR 40-178; (1981) ATPR 40-204, 40-238, 40-241, 40-252), each defendant corporation was fined $50,000 and required to pay legal costs of $60,000-$70,000 (a total of $630,000). Yet Grant (1984, 337) has suggested that the agreements had the potential to add $1 million per year to the defendants' income. Australian trade practices fines are in fact low compared to the seven figure penalties and occasional resort to imprisonment in North American, European and Japanese anti-trust cases.

Warren Pengilley (1984, 4), a former trade practices commissioner, suggests that 'the risk of detection and effective commission enforcement are, in many areas, slight'. He is absolutely right, but it must be said that this is even more true of other Australian regulatory agencies. The most savage critic of commission enforcement has been another former commissioner, George Venturini (1980, 428):

In the two and a half years of my experience with the Commission, despite the number of cases which were supposed to be dealt with and despite the obvious malpractices of big business in Australia, no enforcement action was ever taken under section 46 (monopolisation), section 49 (price discrimination) or section 50 (mergers). The top public service was indeed a service, but one to the ruling elite — big business and the born-to-rule government — and certainly not to the public.

Like Venturini, Pengilley (1984), and Hopkins (1983) have pointed to the concentration of commission enforcement on *per se* offences — notably consumer protection and resale price maintenance prosecutions — to the exclusion of offences requiring proof of substantial lessening of competition. This remains true today. Sixteen of the thirty restrictive trade practices cases which have produced successful court actions (to 10 May 1985) for the commission, have been for resale price maintenance. Nevertheless, the commission has now fought two monopolization and six merger cases. Only one of these eight cases produced a win in court for the commission, though some of them generated settlements which provided for a more competitive market than would have existed had there been no litigation.

The commission has therefore largely failed in 'structural' anti-trust cases which turn on showing that action is needed to prevent a market from being monopolized, but has established comparatively potent enforcement for 'conduct' cases. The latter success is no longer limited to consumer protection and resale price maintenance; to 10 May 1985, twenty cases concerning anti-competitive agreements (mainly price fixing conspiracies) had produced nine successes in court and eight exclusive dealing cases led to four commission victories.

A balanced perception of the Trade Practices Commission, we would then submit, shows the commission to be the most litigation-orientated regulatory agency in Australia; an agency capable of securing more severe sanctions from the courts than any other, and an agency with a greater willingness to take on big and difficult cases than any other. For all of this, it has proved incapable of sanctioning anything but *per se* offences. Structural anti-trust is beyond its grasp. For example, the commission is an almost irrelevant constraint on the high level of merger activity in Australia. Many would see this as a good thing, but that is a question beyond the scope of this book.

It is true that there have been a few mergers which were 'called off' after the company was advised informally that the commission would resist the merger. The commission 'considers' over 100 mergers a year. Its advice has limited authority, however, when the commission has only once prevailed in court against a merger.

An exceptional case of litigiousness though it is, the commission, like every Australian regulatory agency, puts more emphasis on administrative action than on litigation:

. . . it will always be the fact that best use of resources, both public and private, requires that most compliance work be done at an administrative level, provided the credibility of the Act is demonstrated by court proceedings when necessary (Trade Practices Commission, 1984, 3).

It is possible that the newly appointed chairman from the business community, who has signalled some shift away from litigation (e.g. Durie, 1985), will further increase the emphasis on administrative action. None of this is to say that the commission is consumed by dealing administratively with all complaints which come to it in the way that state consumer affairs agencies are. The commission refuses to deal with complaints which are not indicative of high priority matters of national concern to preserving competition or protecting consumers; it resists being ruled by the mailbag. Of 2,129 restrictive trade practices complaints during 1983-84, the commission instituted proceedings concerning seven; of 21,467 consumer protection inquiries or complaints, the commission undertook 'threshold enquiries' on only 691, of which sixteen led to court action (Trade Practices Commission, 1984, 10-11, 81-2).

The commission often turns its back on complaints in favour of pro-active administrative compliance strategies:

We had a major exercise a couple of years ago where we asked car manufac-turers, most large manufacturers of TVs, fridges, large consumer items, we asked them for their warranties, to see whether they complied with the then new manufacturers' warranties legislation. Where we thought they didn't, we told them so, and most of them changed.

Adjudication is an important element of the enforcement strategy of the commission. Sections 88 to 91 of the Trade Practices Act provide for authorization on public benefit grounds of provisions of contracts or arrangements which might affect competition, exclusive dealing, mergers, and primary or secondary boycotts. If the commission grants authorization, there is immunity from court action for the authorized anti-competitive conduct. In adjudicating whether the public benefit of a practice outweighs anti-competitive effects, the commission often negotiates an amelioration of anti-competitive practices. For example, the commission has authorized standard contracts for real estate agents only on condition that uniform commission fees be de-leted from the contracts in favour of negotiable commissions (Trade Practices Commission, 1984, 57-9). Probably the greatest achievements of the commission have been through negotiating more competitive practices against the background of the power to refuse authorization. Draft authorizations are discussed at pre-decision conferences at which parties affected by anti-competitive practices (e.g. consumer groups) are represented. From time to time, the commission adopts conditions of authorization suggested by the concerns of these third parties.

In most other respects, the Trade Practices Commission employs regulatory strategies similar to the state consumer affairs agencies: it uses adverse publicity in a rather similar fashion; it engages in limited educational activities to advise consumers and small business of their rights; and it cautiously fosters self-regulatory activity, such as voluntary recall codes for hazardous products. It does not actively encourage private actions under its act even though such actions are at least five times as frequent as commission actions. Unlike the state agencies, the commission does not become involved in licensing.

The Prices Surveillance Authority

There is an important link between the Trade Practices Commission and the Prices Surveillance Authority. The authority has responsibility for monitoring price increases in selected industries which lack, in the words of the Treasurer, the 'discipline inherent in competition'. In some ways, then, the authority is responsible for picking up the pieces from the failures, and the limited reach, of competition law. It consults with the commission to ascertain the areas of the economy where the 'discipline inherent in competition' is lacking.

The authority, with a staff of thirty-two, is a pale imitation of the Whitlam government's Prices Justification Tribunal, which had 150 personnel at its peak, and coverage of a much wider range of prices. To date the authority has only been authorized by the Treasurer to conduct public inquiries on petroleum pricing, Australia Post, Telecom, and two brands of fruit juice. Other products which are under surveillance are beer, cigarettes, float glass, concrete roofing tiles, tea, and coffee.

The two fruit juice manufacturers had their prices considered at public inquiry by the Treasurer to punish them for submitting to wage demands outside indexation guidelines by the Food Preservers Union. This is indicative of the fact that the authority is a progeny of the prices and incomes accord between the government and the Australian Council of Trade Unions (ACTU).

The only enforcement powers the authority has are against companies which refuse to co-operate in providing price and cost information. Like the Prices Justification Tribunal before it, it has never had to use such powers.

Once a public inquiry has been held, the authority produces a report making recommendations on appropriate maximum prices. Industry, however, is not bound to accept such recommendations. The only tool the authority has in holding down price increases is moral suasion. To date, the petroleum industry, Australia Post, and Telecom have shown a total willingness to yield to such suasion.

The authority has also produced a rather vague draft set of voluntary pricing guidelines in the hope that this might somehow restrain unreasonable prices.

Thus, if the Trade Practices Commission is the most litigious regulatory agency in the country, the Prices Surveillance Authority is the most toothless. In spite of this, the public hearings on Australia Post did put that monopoly under considerable public pressure for perhaps the first time in its life to provide better value for the consumer's dollar.

The Wider Domain of Consumer Affairs

Most of the agencies dicussed in this book — from the Reserve Bank to the Australian Atomic Energy Commission — have some consumer affairs aspect to their work. The generalist consumer protection agencies discussed in this chapter were all created since 1969. Some of the older specialist agencies are equally important to consumer protection. The next chapter considers one such group — food regulatory agencies — and the following three chapters discuss other key domains: drug, transport safety, and prudential regulation.

References and Recommended Reading*

Braithwaite, John (1978), 'An Exploratory Study of Used Car Fraud', in Paul R. Wilson and John Braithwaite (eds), *Two Faces of Deviance: Crimes of the Powerless and Powerful*, University of Queensland Press, St Lucia.

*Braithwaite, John, Vale, Susan and Fisse, Brent (1984), *The Role of Prosecution in Consumer Protection*, Australian Federation of Consumer Organizations, Canberra.

Commonwealth Minister for Home Affairs and Environment (1984), *News Release: Consumer Complaints*, 19 September.

Cranston, Ross (1984), *Consumers and the Law*, 2nd ed., Weidenfeld and Nicolson, London.

*Duggan, A.J. and Darvall, L. (eds) (1980), *Consumer Protection Law and Theory*, Law Book Company, Sydney.

Durie, John (1985), 'TPC to Use "Soft Approach" in Future Competition Policy Cases', *Australian Financial Review*, 1 August.

*Goldring, John (1982), *Consumers or Victims?*, George Allen and Unwin, Sydney.

Goldring, John and Maher, L.W. (1979), *Consumer Protection Law in Australia*, Butterworths, Sydney.

Grant, John (1984), 'The Economic Cost and Benefits of the Australian Trade Practices Legislation', in R. Tomasic (ed.), *Business Regulation in Australia*, CCH Australia, Sydney.

*Hopkins, Andrew (1978), *Crime, Law and Business: The Sociological Sources of Australian Monopoly Law*, Australian Institute of Criminology, Canberra.

——, (1983), 'Marxist Theory and Australian Monopoly Law', in E.L. Wheelwright and Ken Buckley (eds), *Essays in the Political Economy of Australian Capitalism, Vol. 5*, ANZ Books, Sydney.

Paciullo, George (1984), New South Wales Minister for Consumer Affairs, Speech to Australian Association of National Advertisers, 23 May.

Pengilley, Warren (1984), 'Competition Policy and Law Enforcement: Ramblings on Rhetoric and Reality', *Australian Journal of Law and Society*, 2, 1-19.

South Australian Commissioner for Consumer Affairs (1983), *Annual Report Department of Public and Consumer Affairs*, Adelaide.

Trade Practices Commission (1984), *Annual Report*, Australian Government Publishing Service, Canberra.

Venturini, George (1980), *Malpractice: The Administration of the Murphy Trade Practices Act*, Non Mollare, Sydney.

Victoria, Director of Consumer Affairs (1982), *Annual Report*, Government Printer, Melbourne.

Victoria, Ministry of Consumer Affairs (1985), *Enforcement of State Consumer Law in Victoria*, Ministry of Consumer Affairs, Melbourne.

7
Food Standards

Everyone who reads this chapter will at some stage have been a victim of
a food standards violation; at some time most of us have spent a day in
bed after purchasing a salmonella-infected chicken, or some such impure food. Equally, we all fall victim to widespread violations of quality
and quantity standards for food which do not have health implications:
the meat pie or the sausage with less than the minimum meat content,
ice cream with below standard milk-fat content, and so on. A recent New
South Wales Department of Health survey of 276 meat pies found that
73 per cent failed to meet the regulation content of 25 per cent meat,
with the meat containing not more than 33 per cent fat (*Sun-Herald*, 18
November 1984, 5).

Occasionally food poisoning causes identifiable deaths, such as the
Tibaldi salami incident in 1982, or widespread suffering, such as the
salmonella contamination at Nestle's Tongala milk powder plant which
resulted in eighty known cases of hospitalization of babies in Australia,
and unknown problems in Southeast Asian countries to which the contaminated batches were exported (*National Times*, 1-6 August 1977, 3).

Food standards offences also have important economic implications.
All Australians are familiar with the economic damage which was done
to meat exports in 1981 by traders who substituted kangaroo, horse, and
other animal meat for beef. The discovery of these practices, and the
widespread publicity which they received overseas, threatened an export
market worth $1,000 million per year. Less well known examples also
exist. In one instance, Australian producers had sold cheap Chilean
loco in abalone shells to the Japanese, which undermined the Japanese
abalone market (*Canberra Times*, 26 January 1984).

The Administrative Framework
Responsibility for food standards is highly fragmented, with state health
departments being important actors. In Queensland, New South Wales,
the Australian Capital Territory, and the Northern Territory, the central
health authority has primary responsibility for food inspection, though
local government still has an important inspection role, particularly
with the sale of prepared food.

In the other states, most of the inspectorial and enforcement activity occurs at the level of local government. State governments in Victoria, Tasmania, South Australia, and Western Australia do only a small part of the enforcement themselves, being content in most areas to monitor local government enforcement. In Victoria, this is quite formal monitoring, to the point of the state government mandating the number of food samples which must be taken by local authorities.

The most important role of the commonwealth is its attempt to co-ordinate the uniformity of food standards by providing the secretariat for the Food Standards Committee of the National Health and Medical Research Council.

The Commonwealth Department of Health has minimal involvement in enforcement, and little legislative backup for the activity it does undertake. It co-ordinates recalls nationally, and was responsible for quarantine of imports until this was transferred to the Commonwealth Department of Primary Industry in 1985. However, random sampling and testing of food at the point of import by the commonwealth is rare. Some state health departments we visited were highly critical of the failure of the commonwealth to inspect imports and to apply National Health and Medical Research Council standards to them.

I do not think that there is any evidence in Australia that anyone has used the food standards to prevent importation, but there is strong evidence that there has been negligence, I would say on the part of the commonwealth, in permitting sub-standard food. For instance, frozen fish from India. We all know what the water quality is like in India, and ice, after all, is just frozen water, so your microbiological standards are not being met. Ice does not kill organisms, it just preserves them.

The Western Australian Department of Health disputes the above statement as far as its jurisdiction is concerned: 'The Department . . . carries out monitoring programmes on a range of imported foods'. Moreover, in defence, the Commonwealth Department of Health says that it has had great difficulty in using the Quarantine Act to confiscate anything which cannot be defined as introducing disease into Australia. In addition, the Customs Service is unenthusiastic about becoming involved in food standards matters:

If we find a specific problem is causing problems over time, then we can approach them [the Customs Service] and they will make efforts to have that item included in the Customs (Prohibited Imports) Regulations. They are not that keen on it themselves. They do not see it as an appropriate use of the customs regulations. They are not seeking to build an empire out of it, put it that way.

We will see that one of the ironies of Australian food regulation is that imports are subject to the least regulation, followed by domestically produced food for domestic consumption, with the most intensive regulation being devoted to food for export. The latter is particularly true of meat, with the Export Inspection Service (EIS) of the Commonwealth Department of Primary Industry having more meat inspectors (over 2,000) than all the full-time food inspectors in the commonwealth, state, and territory health departments and local government combined. By far the most important activity of the EIS is regulation of the export meat industry. Indeed, the agency was created in the aftermath of the 1981 meat substitution scandal. In addition to their responsibilities for ensuring proper hygiene and sanitation in those abattoirs, boning rooms, and cold stores licensed to produce meat for export, EIS officers inspect every red meat carcass passing through these premises, regardless of destination.

Abattoirs and other facilities which process meat exclusively for domestic production are subject to regulation by state departments of primary industry, unless such powers are specifically delegated to the commonwealth. Agreements of this type were reached with South Australia in 1965, and New South Wales in 1983. The EIS corporate plan is to have a national inspection service incorporating all primary commodity export inspection and all domestic meat inspection by 1988.

In addition, state agriculture departments have some small inspectorial involvements with fish and poultry. State dairy industry and egg authorities, which are primarily marketing bodies, also tend to have their own inspectors and testing personnel to secure compliance with standards for these products.

Everyone sees the fragmentation of Australian food standards regulation as a problem. The meat industry has expressed a preference for a single uniform meat inspectorate (Boccabella, 1981) and the Food Industry Council of Australia, with the support of the Australian Federation of Consumer Organizations, has called for the establishment of a national food authority to oversee uniform food standards.

Even if these things happen, the fragmentation will remain considerable. Local government will continue to monitor the corner fish and chip shop's compliance with food laws by using inspectors who often also have the responsibility for inspecting buildings, and various other matters. In many cases, these inspectors will continue to be more susceptible to the pressures of fear and favour in local politics, than to the ideal of national uniformity of regulation. Poor communication will continue to pose the problems of fragmentation typified by the following statement of a Western Australian health official:

When I rang Sydney for some help, they just said blithely 'Nobody ever eats Georges River oysters when the river is in flood'. No, they export them to Western Australia.

The plan of this chapter will be to consider first the regulatory activities of health departments and local government, and then to give some separate consideration to the Commonwealth Department of Primary Industry.

Regulatory Strategy

State and local food regulation in Australia is largely in the command and control tradition of regulation, as opposed to the co-operative, partnership with industry, tradition (Reiss, 1984). Inspection of the industry is much more frequent than in other areas of regulation. Many agencies aim for quarterly inspections of food premises, and while the coverage in many parts of the country is closer to annual inspection (and fifteen months on average in the Australian Capital Territory), even this is much more frequent than inspection in domains such as occupational health and safety and environmental protection. The centralized state food inspectorates in Queensland and New South Wales are among the most prosecutorial regulatory agencies in Australia.

The enforcement orientation of the New South Wales Health Commission's chief inspector of food is indicated in the following quote:

Enforcement is really our sole function. Anything else that we're doing is ancillary. Every time we do anything else, then it's detracting from our more principal function which is enforcement. If the government wanted the whole area of food inspection to be more involved in education or conciliatory actions, then that would be recognized in terms of budget and manpower. When you look at the numbers that are involved, it should be blatantly obvious that we really don't have time for anything else other than enforcement.

There was also cynicism in this agency about self-regulation and voluntary codes, a cynicism that was quite widespread among food standards regulators:

People who are not going to breach any law anyway adopt a code. A scoundrel goes away and sees that a code is a way of getting an advantage over his competitors. That's been our experience all along with codes. The orange juice industry is known for it . . . They've got a code too.
And it seems to us that most of them get the code down, and nut away to try to pirate their competitors' customers by offering a reduced price because you've got some idiot who's going to adopt the code. Therefore his costs are going to increase, therefore I can compete with him, and therefore I've got an advantage.

Another way in which food standards regulation in New South Wales may be characterized as an extreme case of enforcement orientation is that there is a policy of fostering 'peer pressure' to keep up levels of prosecution and sampling, by displaying charts comparing the numbers of samples and prosecutions taken by different inspectors.

Other jurisdictions do not have the emphasis on law enforcement evident in New South Wales and Queensland. For them, getting compliance by 'cajoling, persuasion, and education' is more predominant. Food inspection is outcome-oriented rather than process-oriented. That is, the inspector will notice non-compliance with a food standard and will prosecute for non-compliance. Only in exceptional circumstances will he or she become involved in analysing with the proprietor just where quality control may have broken down to produce such a breach. The standards generally relate to the quality and purity of the final product, not to requirements to ensure the safety of the process of producing the product. In this aspect, food regulation differs from meat inspection conducted by the Export Inspection Service, and from pharmaceutical regulation, where, as we will see in the next chapter, much inspectorial effort is directed to monitoring the adequacy of in-process controls.

We make the manufacturer realize that he's the expert in ensuring that foods put on the market are safe, pure, wholesome, not falsely described. We're not experts in that area at all. We're experts in detecting breaches of regulations and they're two quite different things . . . Our expertise is knowing how to pick problems and how to take action against them . . . We're not in the business of advising the food industry, because they're expected to know better than we are how to rectify their problems.

Prosecutions

Table 1 indicates why we are justified in describing food standards enforcement in the New South Wales and Queensland health departments as among the most prosecutorial areas of business regulation in Australia. The other two jurisdictions with centralized food inspectorates, the Australian Capital Territory and the Northern Territory, provide a different picture. The Australian Capital Territory has a steady flow of about fourteen prosecutions a year, even though the policy of their Health Authority is one of prosecution as a 'last resort'. The Australian Capital Territory and the Northern Territory both suffer from totally antiquated and inadequate food laws. The Northern Territory Department of Health, in considerable measure, relies on bluff in regulating food standards by asking businesses to comply with National Health and Medical Research Council standards which do not have any force in territory law. There are only one or two food prosecutions a year in the Northern Territory under the laws that do exist.

The other state food inspectorates have very low levels of prosecution, as enforcement activity is primarily the responsibility of local government. In Victoria, Tasmania, South Australia, and Western Australia, state health departments are much more reactive to major state-wide problems or special circumstances, while the local government inspectors are predominantly proactive. The Victorian Health Commission secured five food convictions in the twelve months prior to our visit; the South Australian Health Commission obtained twenty-three food convictions in the ten years to 30 June 1984; the Western Australian Department of Health and Medical Services had ten food convictions in the two years to 30 June 1984; and the Tasmanian Health Department told us that there had been only one food conviction in the past four years.

While these figures for state prosecutions where food regulation is decentralized seem low, in Victoria and South Australia at least, it is clear that there is a comparatively high level of prosecution by local councils. For example, the Melbourne City Council obtained 514 food convictions in the decade 1874–84. Victorian local authorities have a

Table 1
Convictions and Average Fines in the Jurisdictions with
Centralized Food Inspectorates (excluding the Northern Territory)

	NSW		QLD		ACT	
	No.	Av. Fine $	No.	Av. Fine $	No.	Av. Fine $
1974	692	79	170†	53	7	56
1975	604	91	153	44	13	55
1976	762	91	146	53	5	32
1977	661	100	98	72	3	33
1978	525	139	130	66	18	52
1979	531	171	169	67	18	54
1980	451	200	181	78	13	102
1981	370	253	218	91	16	95
1982	400	239	157	103	10	167
1983	451	252	224	128	12	115
1984	533*	248	265	200	3‡	150

* To October 1984

† 1973-74 Financial year

‡ To April 1984

Sources: New South Wales Department of Health, Queensland Department of Health and Medical Services, and the Australian Capital Territory Health Authority

financial incentive to prosecute because the proceeds go into council revenue. In South Australia, the twenty-two councils around metropolitan Adelaide are formed into the Metropolitan County Board. We were told by the Health Commission that the board undertakes 300 food prosecutions a year. Lower levels of local government prosecutions apply in the jurisdictions with centralized state or territory government food inspection. All New South Wales local government food inspectors averaged only ninety-eight food convictions a year for the decade 1975-84.

In the centralized enforcement states of New South Wales and Queensland, from which we have the most detailed data, it is clear that for most years the majority of prosecutions are for selling adulterated meat, particularly mince or sausages with excess fat or sulphur dioxide preservative. The criticism has been made that the propensity is to go after butchers to the exclusion of larger companies.

It's easy to prosecute a small butcher, for example. It's terribly difficult to take on the supermarket retail chain with their high-powered QCs willing to take you to the highest court in the land.

Publicity
On the other hand, when a health authority does go after a large company, it can do enormous damage to the firm's reputation. Food regulators in some jurisdictions consciously use adverse publicity as a

regulatory strategy much more aggressively than do their counterparts in other areas of regulation. The Australian Capital Territory Health Authority, as a matter of routine, uses its Public Relations Section to issue a press release following a food standards conviction. The press tend to relish stories about plush hotels, such as the Lakeside, being fined for having cockroaches in the kitchen. The Western Australian Department of Health also has a standard operating procedure of having the minister's press officer notify the media of all convictions.

However, sometimes the devastating impact of such media releases can cause governments to consider the employment consequences of such tactics. The Queensland health minister's press release dominated the front page of the *Courier Mail* on 10 June 1984, pointing out that at the Suimin instant Chinese dinner factory 'even the cockroaches had salmonella', and that 'No doubt someone has eaten a crispy cockroach leg or two'. This caused complaints from the proprietor who pointed out that the scandal had forced him to lay off ninety employees. Food laws in some states (e.g. New South Wales *Pure Food Act* 1908, section 53; Tasmanian *Public Health Act* 1962, section 118) empower the government to name an offending company, to describe the details of the offence in the government *Gazette*, and to require newpapers to republish such notices with immunity from any legal action.

In Queensland, until the late 1960s, it was common for magistrates to order that placards be placed in hotels convicted for selling watered-down beer, indicating that the establishment had been convicted for that offence.

Recall, Seizure, Closure, Deregistration
Recall or seizure of below-standard food, and closure or deregistration of a food premises, have economic impacts on companies far in excess of the paltry fines typically imposed by the courts (Table 1). There have been cases in Australia of seizure of up to $200,000 worth of food. Recalls, associated with publicity, can cause longer term damage to the company. In fact, health departments sometimes deal severely with manufacturers or importers which fail to associate a recall with adequate publicity.

The idea of that manufacturer for a public recall was to put in the public notices column amongst the advertisements in the *Courier Mail* a two line recall notice saying that the food was contaminated and people who had it should take it back to their retailer and get a refund. When we saw that, the minister, on recommendation, made media statements, and went on TV calling public attention to the product.

Various mechanisms are available in different states and local councils to shut down food premises: closure orders, deregistration, and licensing; even negative licensing, as in the the following provision from the New South Wales *Pure Food Act,* section 39A(1):

Where any person carrying on a business of selling food has been convicted of an offence against this Act or the regulations, the court, on that conviction, or that court or any other court of petty sessions at any later time, may, on the application of an officer of the Department specifically authorised by the Minister for the purpose, make an order prohibiting that person from engaging in the sale of food, or in the sale of food of such class or description as may be specified in the order, for such period as the court may determine and specify in the order.

It is difficult to know with any certainty in such a fragmented regulatory system just how often food premises are shut down, but it seems to happen only a few times a year, even in the larger states.

The Export Inspection Service of the Department of Primary Industry

We have already noted that the Export Inspection Service of the Commonwealth Department of Primary Industry is primarily concerned with inspection of red meat for export and for domestic consumption in New South Wales, South Australia, and the Australian Capital Territory. The need to check every single carcass at the abattoirs concerned creates the most intensive form of inspection in any area of Australian business regulation. As many as sixty commonwealth meat inspectors can be permanently located at one abattoir. Even with other exports, such as fish and grains, inspection of processing sites tends to occur weekly, and never less frequently than monthly. Some fish processing establishments have full-time inspectors during their peak season.

The chicken meat industry, in contrast, is subject to almost no inspection by the commonwealth and most state governments, for there is very little export of chicken meat. However, chicken processors sometimes request inspections for exports to the Singapore and Malaysian markets.

Unlike any of the other regulatory agencies we visited, the regulatory regime of the Export Inspection Service is subject to the strict scrutiny of foreign governments. Since 1979, the government of Iran has had an officer posted in Australia to observe that meat slaughtered for export to that country is killed according to religious requirements. The United States Department of Agriculture also has officers permanently stationed in Australia to ensure that meat, shellfish, and certain fresh fruits destined for the American market are subject to inspection to their standards.

The US does not extend its legislative and legal controls to Australia. No foreign country can, but they can always go to another supermarket.

To this end, American officials actually conduct occasional inspections on meat processing premises in Australia.

A lot of people are outraged on nationalistic grounds. They say, 'What right have these people got just to barge into our premises?' Well, no right other that the fact that we want to export meat to the United States, and we have to conform to their requirements.

Most violations of the Meat Inspection Act and the Export Control (General) Regulations are dealt with informally by the inspector or the senior veterinary officer at a particular plant. Such informal action can escalate from condemning a single carcass to condemning a whole day's production (if, for example, it was found that processing rooms were not running at prescribed temperatures), stopping a slaughter chain, shutting down a whole section of a plant, shutting down the whole plant, withdrawing the export registration of an establishment which authorises the preparation of meat for export, or withdrawing an export licence from a person or company. The decision to take the latter more drastic action is made in Canberra. While export licensing is a function of the Australian Meat and Livestock Corporation, a marketing organization dominated by industry nominees, in practice it is difficult for this body to ignore appeals by the EIS to withdraw a licence.

Licensing actions and deregistration can take many forms. Abattoirs found violating the requirements for export to Muslim markets have had their 'Halal status' withdrawn for a period to cut them out of these markets until they conform to appropriate standards. Similarly, processors found violating the American Department of Agriculture requirements for the United States market have had their licences to export to the United States withdrawn. The Woodward Royal Commission (1982), following the meat substitution scandal, found certain individuals to be culpable in this racket. Certain processors now have licences conditional upon these individuals being excluded from meat preparation areas. Twelve individuals have now been blackballed from the industry in this way.

These informal sanctions are very powerful indeed in the impact they can have on companies. This explains the minimal resort to prosecution by the EIS as a regulatory tool.

Because of the nature of the system — prosecution involves judges, prosecutors, policy people, and A.G.s — it involves time, whereas the administrative remedies are so simple: just so quick and clean and devastating . . .
If we stop production on a plant for a day, you are probably looking at a $20,000-$30,000 penalty. If we condemn a shipment or a container of product because it is not sealed properly, outside the regulations, then the consequences probably amount to some thousands of dollars.

Given the importance of informal sanctions such as condemnation of product and stopping production, it is surprising that the EIS does not keep any statistics on the frequency with which such sanctions are used. The Commonwealth Department of Primary Industry was criticized by the Woodward Royal Commission for inadequate flow of information from the field to the head office (Woodward, 1982, 3). Despite this, and the subsequent recommendation of consultants (Price Waterhouse Associates, 1982, 11), the service struggles on without a standard enforcement manual, or a statistical system for monitoring the implementation of enforcement strategy. On the other hand, a small program review section was established in 1984 to conduct audits of inspection activities. One goal of the section is to encourage uniformity within and between regions.

It is striking that the EIS, as the largest business inspectorate in Australia, rarely prosecutes. Prior to the Woodward Royal Commission, prosecution was not used at all as a regulatory strategy. Now it is used exclusively for frauds which potentially threaten Australia's meat exports, such as meat substitution or non-approved manufacture and misuse of official stamps. It is not used for 'operational' offences which threaten the hygiene of meat. From the establishment of the service in 1982 to the end of May 1985, there were ten convictions for frauds of various kinds with an average fine of $4,080. The latter figure is inflated by one case, prosecuted by the Trade Practices Commission, which resulted in a fine of $30,000.

Investigations of such frauds are initiated by the compliance section of the service, who then refer them to the Australian Federal Police for detailed investigation and ultimate prosecution.

The EIS also uses adverse publicity as a sanction less than most Australian business regulatory agencies. This stems from the fact that the perceived first priority of the agency is to protect the reputation of Australian export industries:

Q. Would you ever use the PR people in the department when you shut down a plant, just to let the rest of the industry know that you mean business?
A. No. We'd use them the other way, to try and stop the criticism.

A second deterrent has been fear of defamation actions. In 1984, one of Australia's largest meat exporters threatened to sue the Commonwealth Department of Primary Industry over a press release referring to the discovery of rams' legs in a quantity of goat meat destined for Southeast Asia (Austin, 1984).

The system of devoting enormous resources to checking in-process controls on the quality of exports, while comparatively minor resources are devoted to protecting domestic consumers, arouses occasional antagonism from health department officials. One state health department officer, after recounting some instances of his state department of primary industry losing interest in impure food problems after it was found that exports were not involved, issued the following blast:

They [state and federal departments of primary industry] are only concerned about protecting exports and they never show any interest in protecting Australian citizens.

While food inspection generally is among the most prosecutorial of business regulatory activities in Australia, the largest inspectorate, the EIS, is an exception in its rare resort either to prosecution or to adverse publicity as sanctions. However, the service regularly uses the informal administrative sanctions available to it by virtue of the capacity of their multitude of inspectors to condemn products and to stop production.

The threat of deregistration or licensing action against meat exporters is also very real; the severity of such action gives the EIS enormous regulatory clout.

Conclusion

Food regulation is characterized by the highest frequency of inspectorial scrutiny of any area of business regulation in Australia. The toughest scrutiny is reserved for food, particularly meat, for export. Industries dominated by domestic sales, a notable example being the chicken meat industry, are, in most states, free of the direct government inspection of quality control on the production line that is observed with exports. These products are, nevertheless, subject to state health department inspections of the quality of food at the point of sale.

Imports are subject to the least control, there being very little random inspection of food at the port of entry, nor any inspection of manufacturing premises whence the food came.

References and Recommended Reading*

Austin, N. (1984), 'Meat Industry in Crisis Over Writ', *Weekend Australian*, 4-5 August, 1.

Boccabella, L. (1981), 'New Meat Protest in Asia', *Age*, 31 August, 1.

Price Waterhouse Associates (1982), *Review of Effectiveness of the Revised System for the Documentary and Physical Control of Export Meat*, Australian Government Publishing Service, Canberra.

Reiss, Albert J. Jr. (1984), 'Selecting Strategies of Social Control over Organizational Life', in Keith Hawkins and John M. Thomas (eds), *Enforcing Regulation*, Kluwer-Nijhoff, Boston, 23-35.

*Woodward, A. (1982), *Report of the Royal Commission into Australian Meat Industry*, Australian Government Publishing Service, Canberra.

8
Drug and Medical
Device Regulation

The horror of the thalidomide disaster, in which many Australian babies died or were born with missing limbs and other deformities, ushered in a comprehensive approach to drug regulation for Australia in the 1960s.

Medical devices, which range from basic equipment, such as syringes, to high-technology devices, such as heart pacemakers, have also been a source of major disasters. In 1983 at least five people died when imported heart valves crumbled in the chests of patients (Australian Federation of Consumer Organizations, 1984, 15). Thousands of Australian women have used the Dalkon Shield intra-uterine device which has caused death, sterility, and forced many women into massive surgery, including hysterectomy.

Drug regulation, though not medical device regulation, is distinguished from other areas of Australian business regulation by its comprehensiveness. Government monitoring intrudes at the level of developing the product (requiring that drug testing protocols are adequate), approving products for marketing, assessing quality control during manufacturing, checking the quality of the final product, regulating prices, and monitoring advertising and other promotion.

While the regulatory coverage is so comprehensive, the resources deployed to undertake all of these tasks are slight compared with the thousands of public servants involved in food regulation discussed in the previous chapter.

We will consider drug regulation first, and then devote some separate treatment to medical device regulation at the end of the chapter. In both areas, we will see that most of the important regulatory activities are the responsibility of the Commonwealth Department of Health, although state health departments complement this work in many areas.

Regulation of Drug Development
This is not an important area of regulation in Australia, because little drug testing goes on here. Most of the data on the safety and efficacy of drugs for which approval is sought for marketing, are collected in other countries, notably the United States and Europe. There have been major frauds where scientists have generated false data to misrepresent the safety and effectiveness of drugs (Braithwaite, 1984, chapter 3). In the United States, this has led to the Food and Drug Administration devoting considerable resources to auditing human and animal trials on new drugs. Violations of good laboratory practices regulations in that country are criminal offences.

Australia is now moving towards adopting a voluntary code of good laboratory practices to improve the accountability of data collection on new drugs. The Commonwealth Department of Health does not have any staff devoted to auditing the honesty of research on new drugs that does occur in Australia, though contract laboratories which conduct basic testing for sterility, pyrogens, etc., have been subjected to inspections by the National Biological Standards Laboratory (NBSL), a former division of the Commonwealth Department of Health, which in late 1985 was incorporated into the Therapeutics Division. Protocols for trials on human subjects are, however, subject to study-by-study approval by the health department. The National Health and Medical Research Council also has voluntary codes on informed consent and protection of privacy for patients involved in clinical trials of new drugs.

Approval of Drugs for Marketing
Drugs, motor vehicles, aircraft, ships and most electrical appliances are the only types of products which cannot be sold in Australia until their design passes government approval. On the basis of analysis of thousands of pages of information in new drug applications undertaken by the Therapeutics Division of the Commonwealth Department of Health, the Australian Drug Evaluation Committee (ADEC) recommends to the health minister whether new products should be allowed on the market. This committee is dominated by eminent medical practitioners and pharmacologists from outside the health department. Its work is divided among seven specialist sub-committees which make recommendations to the full committee.

While the states are happy to leave new drug approval decisions to the commonwealth, the commonwealth does not have the power to prohibit drugs which are manufactured and sold within one state from ingredients sourced within that state. This is in the hands of the states through their legislation covering therapeutic goods. The commonwealth exerts control through forbidding imports of drugs or ingredients under the Customs (Prohibited Imports) Regulations. Since most Australian pharmaceuticals are either imported or made from imported ingredients, this method of control has a much broader reach than it would at first seem.

The Customs (Prohibited Imports) Regulations also underpin restrictions the commonwealth places on promotional claims which pharmaceutical companies can make about their products. No pharmaceutical company has ever been prosecuted for importing a banned product, or for illegally importing a product without the approval of the health department. Instead, cancellation of the privilege to import drugs under an 'honour system' is the sanction used. That is, pharmaceutical importers can be put to considerable additional costs by requiring them to seek individual approval for importation of every batch of any pharmaceutical that enters the country. Cancellation of importing licences of pharmaceutical companies has occurred 'about five or six times in the last three years'. In every case, these licences have been restored once the health department became convinced that the company had mended its ways.

Regulation of Prices

Of the approximately 8,000 drugs on the Australian market, 560 (available in 1,200 different forms, and as 2,000 different brands) are subsidized by the commonwealth under the Pharmaceutical Benefits Scheme (PBS). Drugs under this scheme account for over 90 per cent of consumption, thereby giving the commonwealth effective control over most drug prices. Patients pay nothing, $2, but generally $5 for PBS prescriptions, while the commonwealth pays the pharmacist the rest of the bill.

Other than for unique products, the Commonwealth Department of Health will not give a PBS listing to a product for which the company is asking too high a price. Pharmaceutical companies do not have any choice but to negotiate with the health department over a PBS price, because doctors are reluctant to put their patients to the expense of buying drugs which are not subsidized by the scheme. The parties negotiate on the basis of prices of suitably equivalent alternatives, of prices charged in other markets, and of cost information supplied by the companies.

Therefore, PBS listing becomes an important regulatory tool. The health department can decide to discourage consumption of a drug which has a higher risk-benefit ratio than its competitors, which has been the subject of complaint from the National Biological Standards Laboratory for sloppy quality control, or which is expensive compared with alternative therapies, by refusing PBS listing, or by delisting the drug. About thirty products a year are removed from the PBS list, but most of these are products which have been superseded or which have fallen into disuse, resulting in the company withdrawing them from the market. Because of the disastrous financial consequences of delisting, the mere threat of it can quickly pull a company into line.

Regulation of Drug Quality

Drug quality regulation, which is primarily the responsibility of the National Biological Standards Laboratory, is more like the regulation of the purity of red meat than regulation of the quality of other food. That is, considerable emphasis is placed on detecting problems at their source by inspecting the effectiveness of in-process controls, and the adequacy of manufacturing procedures, rather than relying solely on NBSL's random testing of final products. In the terms of Chapter 16, it is diagnostic rather than rulebook inspection.

Pharmaceutical manufacturing processes are inspected for compliance with a voluntary code of Good Manufacturing Practices (GMP) which was originally based on a mandatory GMP code existing in the United States. Voluntary compliance characterizes the whole approach to drug quality regulation in Australia. There has not been a commonwealth prosecution concerning drug quality under the Therapeutic Goods Act since the 1960s.

Only three commonwealth inspectors are assigned to monitoring compliance with the GMP code throughout the country, though three more are soon to be employed: a far cry from the sixty commonwealth meat inspectors which can be permanently based at one large export abattoir. Because it is the states which have licencing powers over pharmaceutical plants, the commonwealth inspector is always accompanied by a state inspector. Except in New South Wales, where experienced inspectors are employed, the state inspectors have limited experience with GMP requirements, and all states rely heavily on the commonwealth inspectors.

The NBSL also tests the quality of the final product. Twelve per cent of the antibiotics fail these tests. However, such is the backlog that in the majority of cases, by the time the company is notified that a batch has failed, some or all of the batch has been sold.

The most damaging thing the NBSL can do to a company is insist on a recall of products. Single recalls have cost Australian pharmaceutical manufacturers up to a quarter of a million dollars. In 1983, there were sixty-three recalls of therapeutic goods: drugs and medical devices. All of these recalls are undertaken voluntarily or as a result of fear of product liability suits, or fear of reprisals from the Commonwealth Department of Health (e.g. PBS delisting). The health department, at the time of writing, does not have any power to order a pharmaceutical company to recall a product. However, Trade Practices Act amendments introduced into the parliament in late 1985 will make this power available.

This has been perhaps the most extreme example to be found in Australia of a secretive, negotiated approach to business regulation. The Australian consumer movement has been critical of the secretiveness with which drug recalls are handled (Australian Federation of Consumer Organizations, 1984), so that outlets like *Choice* magazine have been able to include in its regular listings of recalled products only that tiny minority of drug recalls which are made public. Even some senior state health department officials were aggressively critical during our interviews of what they saw as a 'deal between manufacturers and the commonwealth' to keep the lid on drug recalls:

There is a tacit agreement not to prosecute at the other end of the line, nor to give them any adverse publicity. So when a product fails, and is out there in the marketplace, you never see it in the newspapers, although it's happening all the time. We would have two or three recalls a week of a drug or therapeutic device. Some of them could be of grave significance, but never ever reach the press.
Q. Sorry. I don't understand what the nature of the agreement is?
A. There is a tacit agreement that a recall will be put in place without it ever being public. But we are alerted to the problem.
Q. What is the industry giving for that?
A. What they are giving in return is co-operating with voluntary GMP compliance.

Since the first draft of this chapter was sent to the Commonwealth Department of Health, and following representations by the consumer movement, the department has agreed to make information on therapeutic goods recalls available to consumer groups on a regular basis in future.

Monitoring Advertising and Promotion
Under the Broadcasting and Television Act, the health department has the power to regulate the advertising of therapeutic goods on the airwaves. This is used effectively to ban the advertising of prescription drugs on radio and television. In theory, print media regulation of drug advertising is a state responsibility, but, in practice, the states rarely use their legislative powers. They see it essentially as an area where the commonwealth has the expertise, even if it does not have the power.

Nor does the commonwealth have adequate legislative authority to control the major area of pharmaceutical advertising: medical journals. The power to ban imports under the Customs (Prohibited Imports) Regulations is used to require companies to seek the approval of the department for all promotional material used during the first three years of sale. On occasion, the department has required companies to write to all doctors retracting claims or adding warnings when the approved promotional material was ignored. After the first three years, reliance is placed on industry self-regulation (see Najman *et al*, 1979). The Australian Pharmaceutical Manufacturers Association has a code of conduct which includes promotional claims. However, no company has ever been fined, removed from membership, or otherwise sanctioned for breaching the code.

Controlling the Overprescribing of Drugs
The Commonwealth Department of Health devotes significant resources to countering the effect of drug company promotional material

that encourages the over-prescription of drugs. First, a vehicle for achieving this is the regular educational publication in favour of rational prescribing: the *Australian Prescriber*. This is delivered free of charge to medical practitioners.

Second, the department sends counsellors to discuss prescribing behaviour with doctors whom PBS statistics reveal to have unusually heavy prescribing patterns. Doctors who intransigently continue to prescribe products for conditions which are contra-indicated or beyond approved indications can be called before a committee of inquiry. This is a committee of peers from the medical profession. The committee can recommend ministerial reprimand, reprimand with gazettal, suspension or revocation of authority to write PBS prescriptions, and obtain refunds of prescriptions inappropriately written. Reprimand with gazettal has the advantage that state medical boards routinely check the *Gazette*, with a view to monitoring the need to take deregistration action against doctors.

Unfortunately, doctors sometimes conspire with pharmacists to defraud the Pharmaceutical Benefits Scheme. For example, some doctors pay their personal pharmacy account with PBS scripts to the considerable profit of both doctor and chemist. Pharmacists also frequently perpetrate this kind of fraud without the aid of doctors. Steroid prescriptions for racehorses can be paid for by the PBS, the quantity of medication on a script can be changed (so that the pharmacist claims the cost of filling a prescription for 100 tablets when the actual number was thirty), and claims can be made on unused repeat scripts (see Hickie, 1981).

The Commonwealth Department of Health has programmes for random audits of repeats in pharmacies. There are six to eight prosecutions a year of pharmacists and doctors for prescription offences, and on average fifteen committees of inquiry a year into the prescribing practices of particular doctors. One of these committees of inquiry in 1983-84 resulted in a recommendation that a pharmacist's approval to supply pharmaceutical benefits be suspended for four months. Sometimes such enforcement action is followed by deregistration proceedings by a state pharmacy board or a state medical board against a pharmacist or doctor.

Medical Device Regulation

Medical devices provide a stark contrast to the comprehensiveness of drug regulation. There is no regulation of medical device testing and development, no requirement for design approval prior to marketing, no regulation of prices, no regulation of advertising and promotion, and minimal regulation of the quality of devices. The latter is the responsibility of two beleaguered officers at the Australian Dental Standards Laboratory, a branch of NBSL.

Following an attack on medical device regulation by the Australian Federation of Consumer Organizations (1984) in the aftermath of the heart valve deaths mentioned in the introduction to this chapter, the health minister promised to spend $1.3 million in the area. It is not yet clear what the nature of the new regulatory strategy will be. However, a register of devices available in Australia will be established and there will be at last some evaluation of high risk items prior to marketing approval. Recruitment of fourteen new medical device regulatory staff in the NBSL is under way.

Conclusion

Drug regulation is unique in the comprehensiveness of the regulatory regime; commonwealth regulation impinges at all stages from product testing to the promotion and quality control of the final product. Most aspects of this regulation are very thinly resourced, however. There are, in fact, more than a thousand Commonwealth Department of Health officers concerned with drug regulation, but over 70 per cent of these work at the routine business of processing PBS claims.

Notwithstanding the inadequate resources, Australia has a reputation for being one of the countries which is reasonably tough in granting marketing approval for drugs, and in holding pharmaceutical prices down. In contrast, regulation of quality control and promotion of drugs, and all areas of medical device regulation, are more *laissez faire* than in other OECD countries.

References and Recommended Reading*

Australian Federation of Consumer Organizations (1984), *Deadly Neglect: Regulating the Manufacture of Therapeutic Goods*, Australian Federation of Consumer Organizations, Canberra.

Braithwaite, John (1984), *Corporate Crime in the Pharmaceutical Industry*, Routledge and Kegan Paul, London.

*Darvall, L.W. (1980), 'Prescription Drug Advertising: Legal and Voluntary Controls', in A.J. Duggan and L.W. Darvall (eds), *Consumer Protection Law and Theory*, Law Book Company, Sydney.

Hickie, David (1981), 'Favourite Fiddles of the Crooked Chemist', *National Times*, 11-17 January, 304.

Najman, Jackob M., Siskind, Victor, and Bain, Christopher (1979), 'Prescription Drug Advertising: Medical Journal Practices under Different Types of Control', *Medical Journal of Australia*, 1, 420-4.

9
Transport Safety

The Problem

Road accidents kill about 3,500 Australians and cost the community an estimated $1,000 million, or 2 per cent of gross national product every year (Commonwealth Department of Transport, 1984, 1). Therefore, an important area of business regulation becomes the safe design of motor vehicles. Although there is no way of knowing, probably a minority of accidents are partly or wholly attributable to vehicle faults. The greater importance of safe vehicle design is in accepting the inevitability of crashes from whatever cause, but requiring vehicle designs which minimize the injury to occupants when such crashes occur. Large scale problems with the design and quality control of motor vehicles do occur regularly. For example, the Australian Capital Territory Motor Registry reported that 207 of 1,089 Holden Commodores presented for inspection, in the eighteen months to August 1984, had been rejected for registration because of floor pan cracks (*Canberra Times*, 5 October 1984, 1).

Accidents also occur with sea and air transport. The remarkably high frequency with which ships sink was described by Charles Perrow: 'There were 71,129 ships in service worldwide in 1979, and 400 of these were lost' (1984, 184). Although air transport is relatively safe, between 1973 and 1984 the world's major airlines had 1.8 fatal accidents per million landings, and for Australia, the rate was 0.06 (*Canberra Times*, 25 January 1985, 7). Regulatory authorities, nevertheless, remain concerned at the spectre of massive accidents, such as the 1979 Air New Zealand crash in Antarctica in which 257 perished. While Australia's airlines have an exemplary safety record, sixty-one people died in general aviation accidents in 1983 (Johnston, 1985).

This chapter is concerned with road, sea, and air safety regulation in Australia. There is no rail safety regulatory agency; the state and national rail authorities are trusted to regulate themselves.

Motor Vehicle Safety

We are not concerned here with road safety policy generally, but only that aspect of it which involves regulating business. That means, primarily, the regulation of vehicle design. The Office of Road Safety in the Commonwealth Department of Transport does all of the regulatory legwork on vehicle design, but the decision making responsibility rests with a joint commonwealth/state body, the Australian Motor Vehicle Certification Board (AMVCB).

The investment in this area of regulation is modest compared with other OECD countries. Twenty-six public servants in the federal Office of Road Safety have the responsibility for assuring the safe design of approximately the same variety of car makes and models as is the responsibility of over a thousand officers in the National Highway Traffic and Safety Administration in the United States. As a review prepared for the Commonwealth Department of Transport concluded: 'The annual cost of AMVCB operations is around $1.1 million. It is not unusual for the Courts to award road crash victims up to $2 million in compensation, in cases of serious injury such as quadriplegia. In other words, the certification system has only to reduce the road crash injury toll by one quadriplegic per year to have paid the cost of its operations' (Vehicle Regulatory Review Team, 1982, 27).

Demonstration of compliance with Australian Design Rules for motor vehicle safety (ADRs) for a particular vehicle category is required for registration of a motor vehicle in all states. The states, not the commowealth, have the legislative power to put vehicles which do not comply off the road.

Type Approval

Australia has a 'type approval' system of regulation. This means that a prototype of a new vehicle model is certified, at least three months before it comes on the market, by AMVCB, as complying with all applicable ADRs. AMVCB then issues a compliance plate approval. The manufacturer is authorized to affix a compliance plate to each vehicle it manufactures of that particular type for a specified period. The presence of a compliance plate on a vehicle is taken as proof by state motor vehicle registration authorities that a vehicle complies with ADRs.

The Office of Road Safety satisfies itself that it can advise the AMVCB to approve a new model by receiving test reports from the manufacturer which demonstrate compliance with ADRs. In other words, the manufacturer is essentially trusted to conduct its own tests to show that vehicles comply with the law. Most OECD countries have this kind of 'type approval' system.

The United States is a major exception with its 'self-certification' system. Under this approach, the government limits itself to rulemaking and enforcement. Manufacturers certify themselves, on the basis of their own testing, that they comply with the design rules. Once the new model is on the market, the government then tests randomly selected production vehicles to assess compliance. Non-compliance can mean mandatory recalls and/or penalties.

Unlike the American system, the Australian approach is very much like the strategy we saw in the last chapter with the approval of drugs: a new type of product is not allowed on the market until its design is approved. Where motor vehicle regulation has differed from drug regulation to date, however, is that once a type approval has been granted, there has been no monitoring of quality control, or independent government testing of final products to ensure that they comply. This is a concern because it could well be that many production line vehicles attain lower standards than prototypes which may be constructed of 'gold-plated parts'.

In modern mass production techniques it is inevitable that occasionally the spread of tolerances for individual components will lead to a particular vehicle failing to perform as intended. It is also inevitable that there will be occasional failures of production processes . . . (Vehicle Regulatory Review Team, 1982, 119).

In recent years, Australia has been the only OECD country with a type approval system which has not devoted a considerable proportion of its vehicle safety regulatory resources to inspections and checks on manufacturers' facilities and quality assurance systems, and to the inspection and testing of production vehicles (Vehicle Regulatory Review Team, 1982, 126-7). The consequence has been a worrying level of non-compliance of production vehicles with ADRs.

The Review Team has also been given details of a number of cases in which it appeared that vehicles granted Compliance Plate Approval may not in fact have complied with all applicable ADRs. Examples of seat belts which fail to operate correctly, steering columns which intrude further into the cabin in a crash than would be expected if they complied . . . doors which do not stay latched, and windscreens with inadequate light transmittance, are only some of the cases mentioned. In the Team's view there is adequate information available in Australia to suggest that the AMVCB is not succeeding in ensuring that all vehicles presented for registration do in fact comply with applicable ADRs (Vehicle Regulatory Review Team, 1982, 131).

While the minister for transport is not willing to invest in a facility for independent destructive testing of cars after they have come off the production line, he has agreed to the recommendation of his vehicle regulatory review team, that there be visits to manufacturers' premises to audit quality control systems. Such audits of manufacturing operations are expected to occur on average every eighteen months from 1985.

It has also been agreed by the minister for transport that in future the emphasis on checking test results will be increasingly on audit inspection of test facilities as well as the traditional examination of test reports. One is entitled to be cynical that there will be a substantial increase in inspectorial presence during manufacturer tests without an injection of many extra staff into the Office of Road Safety. This is because the office has been totally overwhelmed by the basic task of simply reading the reports it gets from the companies.

For twenty-seven months between 1980 and 1982, '38,995 submissions were received . . . of those, 4,965, or 12.7 per cent, were examined. The examination rate of safety submissions was only 9.3 per cent, but that for environmental submissions was 27.0 per cent' (Vehicle Regulatory Review Team, 1982, 79-80). However, the review team report points out that the situation is not quite as bad as it seems, because if one excludes 'carry-over submissions', 30 per cent of submissions were examined. 'Carry-over submissions' are those in which a manufacturer simply calls up a previous submission, claiming that there has been no change to affect compliance during the previous twelve months.

The Office of Road Safety has freed some resources for audits of testing sites by reducing the amount of written information which must be submitted on how companies conduct their tests, thus reducing the paperwork burden on the agency.

It is to be hoped that substantial monitoring of actual tests can be achieved because, as one senior officer said, 'I think it possible, in fact probable, that some manufacturers cheat'. Overseas experience, such as the fining of Ford $US7 million for an emissions testing fraud, would seem to confirm this concern (Fisse and Braithwaite, 1983, 55-62). Audits of test facilities are now also expected to occur on average once every eighteen months from 1985.

In short, in 1985 it remains fair to say that not only is there no testing of production line cars (as opposed to prototypes), but the testing of the latter is done by the manufacturer itself rather than by an independent authority. Also, not only is there a dearth of on-site government audit of these tests, but the government does not even find the resources to read most test reports which are posted to it, and is now solving this problem by asking the companies to send them only summary reports.

On the positive side, monitoring of manufacturing plants to ensure that prototype compliance is translated into production vehicle compliance is beginning to occur. By the end of 1985 it is also planned that one production line vehicle of each new model will be visually inspected for compliance with ADRs. However, the car will be selected by the manufacturer, and one must remember that destructive testing is required to assure compliance with many of the most important ADRs.

Imports and Components

Imports pose a particular problem with assuring production line quality control to make type approval credible. In 1985, the Office of Road Safety completed agreements with overseas safety authorities to perform the same audit and surveillance function being implemented in Australia. This was prompted by severe problems of import non-compliance:

The Review Team was told that considerable numbers of motor vehicles for which compliance has not been demonstrated (beyond those contemplated in ATAC's approval of private imports) are being imported into Australia. These vehicles get registered. Most of these vehicles are luxury cars, many second-hand from countries with lower motor vehicle requirements than Australia.

Many of these vehicles are known not to comply with ADRs (Vehicle Regulatory Review Team, 1982, iv).

Another difficult regulatory problem is sub-standard components which, when installed, bring the vehicle into non-compliance with ADRs. Australia, unlike other OECD countries, does not have a component approval scheme under which all components intended for fitting to motor vehicles which could affect any ADR would have to be certified. There are not even mandatory standards for vital safety-related components such as new tyres. With the introduction of 'world car' programmes, where the same basic vehicle is being sold in a number of countries, including Australia, the financial incentives for producers of cheap imitation parts are growing:

. . . a growing number of counterfeiters, parts manufacturers who duplicate easy-to-sell fast moving parts, offering them as genuine replacements, and importers of overseas second-hand parts, pose a safety hazard to Australian motorists.

Late in the Review, the Team's attention was drawn to a flourishing trade in second-hand and sub-standard parts for Japanese cars being imported from Japan and Taiwan. Many of the parts and components being imported clearly do not comply with Australian standards. The Team was given evidence of doors which do not comply with ADR 29, and engines which do not comply with ADR 27, A, B, or C being offered for sale to the trade. The prices at which these items are being offered would allow repairers to make large profits. The Team was told that some insurance companies have encouraged the use of cheap imported components for smash repairs (Vehicle Regulatory Review Team, 1982, 70, 227).

State Regulations

An overly simplistic picture of Australian vehicle safety regulation has been painted to this point. While the ADRs are the centrepiece of state vehicle registration requirements, they are not the whole story. All states and territories have their own additional regulations. These generally pre-date the ADRs. While the ADRs are mostly complex technical standards, which frequently require expensive testing to ascertain compliance, the state regulations tend to be verifiable by visual inspection, or simple non-destructive testing. They vary enormously. To take a simple example, the states have quite different regulations concerning the permissible length and width of buses. The Australian Transport Advisory Council develops draft regulations, but one survey of the four eastern states found that 40 per cent of the draft regulations had not been implemented by any of the states (Vehicle Regulatory Review Team, 1982, 101). Attempts are continuing at securing agreement on incorporating the state regulations into uniform ADRs.

The Legal Status of Australian Vehicle Design Regulation

Clearly, the solution to this problem is to enact uniform national regulations, but the Office of Road Safety and the AMVCB do not have any legislation which gives them a legal identity. This means that there is no ability to enforce decisions against manufacturers. The only sanction available to the board is to withdraw compliance approval and to rely on state registrars to refuse to register vehicles of the manufacturer from whom compliance approval has been withdrawn. This drastic action has never been taken. Moreover, it would be inappropriate, in circumstances where a testing fraud was proven some years after a model was sold, to punish innocent owners by withdrawing their registration. What the AMVCB has done, on occasions when it has been dissatisfied with the quality of testing by a company, is grant provisional compliance plate approval for twelve months, during which tests must be redone.

Another consequence of the AMVCB's lack of legal status is that it cannot prosecute those who misuse compliance plates, such as scrap metal merchants and others who manufacture unapproved plates. Also compliance plate fraud is at the heart of the problem of imports which do not comply with ADRs, yet there do not seem to have been any state government prosecutions for compliance plate fraud. The absence of any legal status for the board also means that compliance plates cannot even be legally protected as a trade mark.

Further, the board lacks the power to order recalls of vehicles discovered as a result of investigation of consumer complaints to be unsafe. Recall is entrusted to a voluntary code of the Federal Chamber of Automotive Industries.

All of these problems led the Yeend Report (1977), and the review team of 1982 to justify the need for commonwealth legislation with the following reasons:

- to enable AMVCB to act directly against manufacturers (e.g. by enforcing recalls) rather than indirectly against owners through state law;
- to enable AMVCB to prosecute anyone found fraudulently misusing compliance plates;
- to authorise collection of fees [for issuance of compliance plates];
- to enable ADRs to be legally cited in commonwealth law;
- to protect members of AMVCB and ATAC against legal proceedings;
- to enable AMVCB to prevent sale of components or accessories which would, if fitted to a vehicle, degrade its performance below ADR standards;
- to enable AMVCB to prevent import of vehicles which do not comply with ADRs (Vehicle Regulatory Review Team, 1982, 178-9).

These recommendations have not been acted upon. It is the failure to take this action, and the acceptance of federal responsibility for motor vehicle safety without federal legislative authority or adequate resources to give effect to the responsibility, which has created the non-uniform, gap-ridden system of regulation described above. Some ADRs are considerably higher than standards in other countries, but the chaotic regulatory system which 'enforces' these rules provides implausible guarantees of compliance on any basis other than the corporate social responsibility of manufacturers.

Marine Safety

An individualized design approval approach to ship safety has existed for 100 years. Ship surveys are the responsibility of the ship safety branch of the Commonwealth Department of Transport; however, vessels which do not travel overseas or interstate are the responsibility of state marine authorities. The latter survey commercial vessels and recreational vessels above a specified size.

Australian ship certification systems rely on approval of design at the drawing stage, surveillance during construction, and visual and nondestructive testing of the final product. On occasion, ships which are constructed overseas for the Australian market are inspected during construction in the country concerned. While design approval is ship-by-ship, standards are quite detailed, so that discretion for the surveyor is restricted. Ships in service are resurveyed annually.

The strongest deterrent against ships operating without a current survey certificate is that if the ships are lost or damaged, they lose their insurance coverage. For Australian ships, refusal of permission to go to sea after failing to pass survey is also a financially damaging sanction. A foreign ship found in an unseaworthy state is required to be brought to a seaworthy condition before proceeding on its voyage. Also, prosecutions can follow when ships are considered sub-standard due to negligence. The commonwealth secured thirty-seven convictions under the Navigation Act for sub-standard ships at an average fine of $1,870 in the six years to 30 June 1984. All defendants were the masters of foreign vessels.

Random inspections at ports, and inspections prompted by complaints from seamen and waterside workers, complement annual surveys. Thus, the system for ship design approval is in every way more rigorous than the type approval of motor vehicles. It is also a much better resourced regulatory regime at the federal level. There are 100 regional surveyors and head office personnel devoted to ship safety in the Commonwealth Department of Transport. In addition, there are state government officers devoted to ship surveying. Even Western Australia, with a relatively small shipping industry, has nine officers devoted full-time to ship surveying in its Department of Marine and Harbours.

Beyond design safety, there is regulation of the safety of navigational practices at sea. Enforcement in this area again is primarily directed at the master. A serious navigational offence can be made the subject of a Court of Marine Inquiry under either state or commonwealth legislation, depending on whether the offence occurred in state or commonwealth waters. Such an inquiry can lead to the master or mates losing their livelihood through loss of certificates of competency. Seamen in turn can be fined by the master for offences under the Navigation Act. The master has extraordinary powers of a magistrate while at sea and can deduct the fine imposed from the seaman's wages (section 115 Navigation Act). There is provision for appeal against the fine when the ship returns to port. The master also has effective law-making powers at sea, it being an offence punishable by imprisonment for a seaman wilfully to disobey a lawful command (section 100).

Most of the state marine authorities have dozens of marine inspectors who launch hundreds of prosecutions for navigational offences every year, but only a handful of these prosecutions (e.g. eighteen out of 868 in Western Australia during 1983) are directed at commercial operators. Mainly it is speeding offences in recreational boating that predominate.

Air Safety Regulation

Air safety regulation is primarily a responsibility of the Commonwealth Department of Aviation. It is better resourced than the other two areas, with some 550 persons engaged in the flight safety standards function of the department, with a large number of the remaining 11,000 officers, such as air traffic controllers and accident investigators, also having central safety functions.

Airworthiness certification of civil aircraft is a type approval similar in principle to motor vehicle certification. However, it is a more rigorous type approval which builds in firmer guarantees that production models will meet the specifications in the air navigation orders.

An aircraft type proposed for use in Australia firstly has its full specifications, drawings, and design calculations scrutinized for compliance with Australian standards. A team of between four and eight experts then visits the manufacturer's factory for a period of two to six weeks. The design methodology, quality control procedures, and methods for demonstrating compliance with standards are evaluated during this period. Compliance must then be demonstrated by tests which must be witnessed by the source country's authorities. Critical tests may also be witnessed by officers of the Commonwealth Department of Aviation. Copies of these test reports are then sent to Australia.

During the construction of each aircraft, all quality checks and steps in the production process are signed off by an officer employed by the manufacturer but responsible to the national airworthiness authority. Source national authorities also directly supervise approved flight testing programmes. Source country authorities and, occasionally, Commonwealth Department of Aviation pilots fly confirmatory tests. Once an aircraft is accepted, periodic airworthiness checks are a continuing requirement. There are also random checks and audits of the maintenance work which has been carried out by licensed aircraft maintenance engineers. Operators are given notice of most inspections, a feature of the regulatory regime which has been much criticized by the Australian Federation of Air Pilots and some board of accident inquiry reports. Unlike the situation with motor vehicle regulation, the Air Navigation Regulations require approval for aircraft components for use as replacements (regulation 41).

As with ship safety regulation, grounding non-complying aircraft is an important weapon (Smith, 1984). There has been at least one recent case where the entire fleet of a general (non-passenger) aviation company has been grounded for non-compliance with maintenance requirements.

Another powerful sanction which is used, though rarely, is the withdrawal or variation of licences for general aviation companies. Flying schools, for example, can be rated as private schools, commercial schools, or integrated commercial schools; operators who fail to meet the requirements of a higher rating can have their licence varied to a lesser rating.

Suspension and cancellation of individual licences are much more common measures. Each year about 100 pilot licences are suspended for varying reasons, mainly for short periods pending operational investigations. While the majority of these are for private licences, suspensions of commercial licences also occur. Aircraft mechanics, engineers, air traffic controllers, and similar licensed personnel are also subject to suspension. In licensing matters, safety concern is given priority over concern for justice in that suspected offenders are effectively assumed guilty until proven innocent. The general practice is to suspend licences pending a full investigation of the behaviour or competence of a licence holder.

Given the potency of these alternative routes to obtaining compliance, it is perhaps not surprising that prosecution is comparatively infrequent, at least in corporate regulation. While there were about a hundred prosecutions of private pilots in four and a quarter years to 31 March 1984, there were only thirteen convictions of aviation companies or individuals acting on behalf of companies. The average fine was $278, obviously a pittance compared with the economic consequences of grounding aircraft or suspending a licence, though in one case in 1982 a sentence of eight and a half months imprisonment was imposed following a serious accident.

Aviation safety prosecutions are unusual in Australian business regulation because a comparatively high thirty-seven per cent of cases are unsuccessful. The complex causes of aviation accidents or near-misses is perhaps one explanation for this.

An interesting feature of aviation regulation is that much enforcement is particularistic rather that universalistic. Companies are required to comply with operations and maintenance systems and manuals which they themselves prepare with the approval of the Commonwealth Department of Aviation (Air Navigation Regulation 43(4)), and there have been cases of prosecution for failure to comply with a company operations manual as opposed to an industry-wide standard specified in the air navigation legislation.

A unique feature of aviation regulation is a concerted attempt bureaucratically to separate the accident and incident investigation function from the enforcement function; investigations are the responsibility of the Bureau of Air Safety Investigation.

The reason for the split is that we are concerned in the bureau that if it seemed that our information from investigations is used for punitive measures, we'll have a drying up of the source of the information, and we won't get the real details of what happened in the accident so that the function of prevention can be fulfilled in the future.

Thus, the policy of the bureau is against handing over, to the enforcement divisions of the department, information such as witness reports from pilots, which might incriminate the pilot. A similar rationale exists for a system of immunity whereby if a pilot reports an occurrence that the department would not have otherwise become aware of, then the pilot is immune from any punitive action.

Conclusion

It is paradoxical indeed that while road travel causes by far the greatest loss of life, followed by sea travel, followed by air travel, the commonwealth government devotes most resources to air safety, followed by ship safety, followed by motor vehicle safety. It might be contended that state governments spend enormous amounts on motor vehicle safety through their vehicle registration functions (and traffic police), but this would confuse the issue because it remains the case that the safe design of motor vehicles is primarily a commonwealth function, while the state motor vehicle registries are primarily tax collection agencies. In any case, to the extent that motor vehicle registration amounts to safety regulation, it is not business regulation in the terms of this book, but regulation directed at individual owners of vehicles.

All these areas of transport safety regulation share with drug regulation the primary regulatory commitment of approving the safety of the design of particular products (cars, ships, planes) *before* they are allowed to be used.

Safety approval of ships, and more particularly of aircraft, are subject to greater follow-through than the crude type approval of motor vehicles. Motor vehicle regulation lacks assurances that prototype compliance will be matched by production vehicle compliance which will last throughout the life of the machine.

In all three areas, there is also considerable investment in ensuring that approved vehicles are used safely. With motor vehicles, this is not a matter of business regulation, but primarily police enforcement against private motorists. With sea and air navigational safety, corporate enforcement is achieved principally by licensing and other actions to prevent use of craft, and secondarily, by prosecution.

References

Commonwealth Department of Transport (1984), *Australian Design Rules for Motor Vehicles*, Office of Road Safety, Canberra.

Fisse, Brent and Braithwaite, John (1983), *The Impact of Publicity on Corporate Offenders*, State University of New York Press, Albany.

Johnston, Elizabeth (1985), 'Flying "Cowboys" Spark Call for More Regulation', *The Australian*, 17 July.

Perrow, Charles (1984), *Normal Accidents: Living with High-Risk Technologies*, Basic Books, New York.

Smith, Dick (1984), *Two Years In the Aviation Hall of Doom*, ACORP, Sydney.

Vehicle Regulatory Review Team (1982), *A Review of the Australian Vehicle Regulatory System*, Commonwealth Department of Transport and Construction, Canberra.

Yeend, F.E. (1977), *Report to the Australian Transport Advisory Council*, Commonwealth Department of Transport, Canberra.

10

Prudential Regulation

Introduction

Few people living in Australia today remember the failure of the New South Wales Savings Bank more than fifty years ago. Bank failures were not uncommon during the colonial era, with catastrophic consequences for many, particularly small depositors. More recent times have seen citizens stranded by the collapse of insurance companies. While there is a current debate on the degree to which financial institutions should be regulated, few would disagree that some level of regulation is necessary not only to protect small depositors, but in furtherance of economic policy generally.

The critique of prudential regulation has been that it has purchased stability for the financial system at the price of restricting competition which might result in more innovative financial services for customers and greater allocative efficiency. The regulatory regime, it is argued, has effectively erected barriers to entry for new competitors. This critique has less force today in the wake of major deregulatory activities by the present federal government, most notably, the opening of the banking sector to foreign competition.

The challenge of minimising risk to the depositor, or to the insured, while promoting general economic well being is the task confronting prudential regulators in Australia today. The main agencies of Australian prudential regulation are three commonwealth bodies: the Reserve Bank, the Office of the Insurance Commissioner, and the Office of the Life Insurance Commissioner.

Our research into these three agencies followed the usual format: see above, pages 5 and 6.

At the Office of the Insurance Commissioner, we spoke to two officers, including a senior legal officer, designated by the commissioner for this purpose, and followed our usual procedures. We now indicate for the record that the commissioner does not endorse all the views expressed at the interview by the designated officers and quoted in the remainder of this chapter. In response to a draft with which we supplied him, the commissioner by letter dated 18 June 1985 stated: 'I categorically disown each of the quoted passages (i.e. those found on page 129, 134, 135 and 136) They are not my views nor do they reflect my administration of the Insurance Act'. However, we are ourselves satisfied that the interview in conjunction with other source material is sufficiently cogent to be drawn upon in our analysis of prudential regulation as a whole.

Regulatory Functions

The Reserve Bank employs 3,700 people, and is responsible for a variety of tasks pursuant to the *Reserve Bank Act* 1959, the *Banking Act* 1959, and the *Financial Corporations Act* 1974. These include acting as the nation's central bank, printing and managing the banknote issue, holding and managing Australia's international reserves, serving as banker and financial agent for governments, and regulating the money supply. In addition, the Reserve Bank determines appropriate standards of financial practice management for banks in Australia, other than state banks which are the responsibility of state governments. It is this business regulatory function which is our concern here. Whilst the bank enjoys a degree of independence, it is ultimately responsible to the common-wealth through the Federal Treasurer (Campbell *et al.*, 1981, 16-31).

Banks are influenced in what they do by the volume of their holdings of cash and other very liquid assets. The Reserve Bank may directly influence the liquidity of most trading banks through the mechanism of statutory reserve deposits. Trading banks subject to the Banking Act are required to maintain a statutory reserve deposit account with the Reserve Bank based on a proportion of their Australian deposits. The volume of statutory reserve deposits varies with the levels of deposits and with the statutory reserve deposit ratio.

Monetary policy is implemented primarily through the Reserve Bank's operations in the money and securities markets with the aim of influencing the availability and cost of funds and thus, over time, the demand for money and credit. Direct controls on interest rates are confined to housing loans for owner-occupation.

By agreement with the Reserve Bank, trading banks subject to the *Banking Act* 1959 have undertaken to hold, at all times, a proportion of their total liabilities in Australian currency (other than shareholders' funds) within Australia in the form of 'prime assets', i.e. prescribed high quality, liquifiable assets. If a bank were to be in danger of breaching the prime assets ratio requirement, it would have to correct the situation promptly under supervision of the Reserve Bank. The Reserve Bank aims to ensure that there are sufficient funds available in the market to meet the banking system's need for liquid assets. Individual banks should normally be able to handle their liquidity requirements without recourse to the Reserve Bank; any assistance provided by the Reserve Bank would be at its discretion.

In addition, the Reserve Bank monitors banking operations by requiring the regular supply of statistical information, and by reviewing reports of periodic audits of each bank by the Commonwealth Auditor-General. The monitoring process includes an ongoing assessment of each banking group, including subsidiary finance companies and associated merchant banks. Among the factors considered are earnings, capital adequacy, distribution of risk, and maturity structure of liabilities and assets.

Compared with those of the Reserve Bank, the goals and functions of the Office of the Insurance Commissioner are narrow in focus. The major responsibility of that office is the financial supervision of the 180 general (non-life) insurance companies carrying on business in Australia. The Office's objective is the protection of the security of policy holders against insurer insolvency.

The Office relies, in the main, upon the timely submission of quarterly and audited annual financial and other returns by authorized companies. Each company must, at all times, satisfy certain minimum paid-up capital and solvency requirements and satisfy requirements in respect of their reinsurance arrangements.

Where an authorized insurer has contravened, or failed to comply with applicable provisions of the Insurance Act, or is about to become unable to meet its liabilities, the Federal Treasurer may appoint an inspector to investigate its affairs. An inspector so appointed has wide ranging powers of inquiry into the affairs of an insurer, and may make recommendations which can lead to the Treasurer issuing formal directions relating to the conduct of a company's affairs. A company can be directed to cease issuing or renewing policies. If a company's liabilities exceed its assets, it can be placed in liquidation.

Unlike the Life Insurance Act, the Insurance Act does not embrace wider matters of consumer protection such as advertising or contractual arrangements between policy holders and insurers. These issues have been left to the Trade Practices Act and state legislation. Secrecy provisions of the Insurance Act require the permission of the Federal Treasurer before other agencies can be notified of any malpractice detected. However, legislation currently being implemented, the *Insurance Contracts Act* 1984 and the *Insurance (Agents and Brokers) Act* 1984, address certain of these issues. The Offices of the Insurance Commissioner and the Life Insurance Commissioner will administer the Agents and Brokers Act in its application to their respective categories of business. The Insurance Contracts Act establishes new principles of law governing contractual relationships between insurer and insured. Both of these acts identify offences and prescribe penalties.

Having asked what the Office of the Insurance Commissioner's responsibility was with regard to deceptive advertising, we were told by one of his officers: 'Nothing to do with us'. In this regard we will see that the

Office of the Insurance Commissioner has a narrower statutory mandate than does that of the Life Insurance Commissioner. We then inquired how the office might respond to information suggesting that the director of a general insurance company was shifting the company's assets to Switzerland.

We would get very disturbed, but our chief concern is solvency. Now there is nothing to stop a person from transferring assets of a company to Switzerland. It's a perfectly legitimate business decision to transfer funds to Switzerland, but we would only be concerned if this threatened their solvency.

An authorized insurer is required to maintain, in Australia, sufficient assets to satisfy the solvency requirements of the Act. Where it appears that investment decisions may lead to the inability of a company to be able to meet its liabilities in Australia (or generally) then an inspector may be appointed and appropriate directions issued.

The Office of the Commissioner's regulatory role is based to some extent on the principles of *laissez faire* and *caveat emptor*. To be sure, the Office from time to time requires amendments to be made to reinsurance arrangements, disputes the adequacy of outstanding claims provisions, and refuses to approve assets for the purposes of the solvency requirements of the act. But when asked, in light of a recent case of asset stripping involving an insurance company, whether the public interest would be better served by an expanded regulatory role, one of the staff of the Office said:

With respect to the general health of the insurance industry, the thing that sorts that out is very much Adam Smith's invisible hand. Competition does that. People learn very quickly who to stay clear of. They learn it from friends and neighbours and brokers and vicars.
Now if somebody is going to go 'kaput', or if somebody is good, people will learn ... Competition has sorted out the insurance industry. It's as simple as that.

In fact, the Office faces a constant risk of companies going 'kaput'. As the Commonwealth Treasury said in its submission to the Campbell inquiry, 'a relatively high proportion of general insurance companies are maintaining financial standards close to the minimum standards of the Act' (Commonwealth Treasury, 1981, 215). It warned of 'the responsibility of a major catastrophe leading to companies incurring significant losses' (Commonwealth Treasury, 1981, 215). Since 1978, general insurance companies in Australia have failed at the rate of about one per year.

The Office of the Life Insurance Commissioner was created in 1945, following the collapse of a number of insurance companies in preceding decades. Aside from the winding up of two life companies which were insolvent when the Life Insurance Act commenced, Australia has not seen a life insurance company collapse since the agency was created. All life offices today could be described as stable.

Life companies are required to establish and maintain statutory life insurance funds to secure policy liabilities, and to lodge audited accounts, balance sheets, and statements of business in prescribed forms. No person may act as an auditor until approved by the commissioner. No life insurance policy may be issued unless the premium rates for its class have been certified as adequate by an actuary. Every company is required regularly to cause an actuary to make an investigation into its financial condition, including a valuation of its policy liabilities for which a minimum valuation basis is prescribed. An abstract of the report of the actuary must be lodged with the commissioner.

The Act provides for an active supervision of the affairs of registered companies. The Life Insurance Commissioner may demand any information from a company in relation to its business, authorize an inspection of a company upon sufficient cause, issue directions subject to review, petition the Federal Court of Australia for judicial management or liquidation, and be heard by the court in any application for transfer or amalgamation of life insurance business. The commissioner may also direct the amendment or withdrawal of any form of proposal, policy, or canvassing matter if misleading or not in compliance with the act.

The whole basis of internal control by the actuarial profession minimizes the possibility that an Australian life insurance company would now become insolvent. In the unlikely event that solvency may be in doubt, suasion and ultimately direction would be used to strengthen prudential guarantees. The purpose of this oversight is to prevent avoidable collapses, to minimize losses, and effect smooth exit from the industry in the case of failure. That is, the regulatory regime accepts that failure can be desirable in weeding out inefficient operators, but where failure occurs, maximum protection must be afforded to the weak.

Among others, the indicators of company performance which are routinely monitored by the Life Insurance Commissioner and his staff are trends in the volume of new business written, the forfeiture rate of policies, interest rates earned on funds, and business overheads.

The regulatory approach of the Office of the Life Insurance Commissioner is less interventionist than in other countries. In the United States, investments, policy conditions, and premium rates are subject to direct regulation, while under the Policy Holders Protection Act in Britain, policy holder guarantee arrangements ensure that policy holders do not suffer major losses when a life office fails.

Other financial institutions (building societies, credit unions, finance companies) are subject largely to state government regulation, in part, through credit acts administered by consumer affairs agencies, whose regulatory strategies are discussed in Chapter 6.

Barriers of Entry to Banking and Insurance Industries

Licensing is a key to the regulation of banks. Licences can be issued subject to conditions. In addition to initial capital requirements, directors and management are expected to have appropriate qualities, qualifications, and experience before licences are issued. Proposed operational management plans are scrutinized to provide for satisfactory protection of depositors. Strict limits on individual shareholdings are maintained in order to avoid the dominance or control of a bank by one or a few shareholders.

Unlike the banking industry, there are no formidable barriers to establishing a general insurance company, beyond having to meet certain statutory criteria. These include minimum paid up capital and solvency requirements, satisfactory arrangements for reinsurance, and the Office's satisfaction that the company will be able to meet its liabilities. Beyond this, the policy is one of an open door. Every application has been routinely approved, as long as it has complied with certain objective financial standards. Even some of the statutory criteria are widely subject to exemption. For example, when one company recently fell into difficulties, leaving $7 million in unpaid insurance claims, it was found to be one of 124 companies exempted from a provision requiring a registered office in Australia (Totaro, 1985).

Where an authorized insurance company is acquired by a new owner, the conditions of authorization continue to apply to the company. Such permissive standards may not continue, however, in the aftermath of the Bishopsgate affair. In this case, a viable insurance company was acquired by an individual with no previous background in the insurance industry, and against whom criminal charges were pending at the time. The company quickly collapsed, the person in question disappeared in the wake of allegations that he had embezzled $19 million from the company, and the Office of the Insurance Commissioner began to consider amendments to the act which would require higher standards for those seeking to establish or to acquire an insurance company (Munton, 1985).

Applicants for registration under the Life Insurance Act must demonstrate the adequacy of their management and financial resources. Other than basic solvency requirements, the Life Insurance Commissioner has discouraged acquisition of life companies by persons suspected of unsavoury designs on company assets:

To a certain extent it's done by friendly persuasion. It's not spelt out in the act ... [One] individual was very keen to take over a life insurance company, and the owner was very keen to sell it to him. It was only the persistent questions that we asked during the negotiations for sale that dissuaded the prospective purchaser from acquiring the company.
There was one individual in the finance field who acquired a company with considerable assets that he could use for legitimate purposes, as far as he was concerned, but they weren't investments in the best interests of the policy holders. Now he wasn't aware of this impropriety, and when he found that the commissioner was going to ask a number of difficult questions, and perhaps use the annual report to comment adversely on company performance regarding the use of the assets, he backed off and he sold out again.

Regulatory Strategies

The approach to regulation taken by each of the three agencies is that of informal consultation and suasion. The Governor of the Reserve Bank saw his bank's role as that of a monitor:

The Reserve Bank's approach to supervision is predicated on the view that the prime responsibility for the prudent management of a bank's business lies with the bank itself. Our approach is directed toward satisfying ourselves that individual banks are following management practices which limit risk to prudent levels, and that those prudential standards are being observed and kept under review as circumstances change (Johnston, 1984, 152).

Despite the existence of severe penal clauses in the Banking Act, officials of the Reserve Bank have never contemplated the use of criminal sanctions. Indeed, any formal legal action is regarded as unnecessary and inappropriate, in light of the close, co-operative relationship between the bank and the banking industry.

Rather, the Reserve Bank's regulatory style has been characterized by one commentator as 'vice regal influence by suasion' (Livingstone, 1984, 22). The traditional deference of bankers to informal requests by the Reserve Bank was also noted in our interview.

We just ask banks to do certain things and they've done them. It's characteristic that we do so by asking banks to do something without a piece of direct legislation.

In reality, Reserve Bank suasion cannot be ignored by the banks because it is backed up with formidable latent powers. Under the Banking Act, the Reserve Bank can actually assume control and carry on the business of a bank (section 14(2); section 65). It can recommend to the Treasurer that a bank's licence be suspended. Moreover, the penalties that courts can impose for offences are draconian compared with other regulatory statutes. Forfeiture of gold can be ordered (section 49). Penalties of imprisonment are available (section 49); and a bank which is short on its statutory reserve deposit account is liable to a penalty of 8 per cent per annum of the value of the shortfall (section 26(1)); that is, if a bank had $10 million less than it was required to hold in its statutory reserve deposit account over a year, this could cost it $800,000. Such potent sanctions have never been applied, nor are they ever likely to be, but it may be that the Reserve Bank can walk so softly because it carries so many big sticks.

One advantage of a policy of never using formidable powers is that the industry comes to view suasion as granting them a privilege they ought not to abuse. Consequently, they often yield to Reserve Bank suasion in areas where the guidance is not in fact backed up by legislation. For example, the bank, in the past, has successfully called for restraint in lending for speculative non-residential real estate and for imports (Martin *et al.*, 1984, 124).

Early in our interview, it became apparent that the very idea of serious misconduct in the banking industry was almost beyond comprehension. Having asked what the consequences of a bank's wilful non-compliance with Reserve Bank requirements might be, we were told:

The scenario which you envisage has never existed . . . It is inconceivable given the basis of authorization.
Not only has it not occurred, but I think it would be absolutely inconceivable with the sorts of bodies that would be authorized by the Governor-General to have licences.

The relationship of the Reserve Bank to the institutions which it regulates was likened to a marriage. It was quite apparent that the metaphor implied not the tempestuous aftermath of an impulsive union, but rather a relationship based upon years of mutual trust and understanding.

I think that by dint of the gateway to getting into the industry and then the nature of the relationships between those in the industry, the question of pursuing misconduct to the point of action would be very unlikely.

When we probed about the likely consequence of persistent non-compliance by a bank we were told:

. . . In a situation where one of the institutions which falls under our responsibility under the Banking Act fails to do so, I'd regard it as the breakdown of a marrriage, and it's time for a divorce. It's not a matter of pursuing to the courts . . . they just can't fail. If they fail, it's time to put asunder, and I suppose that's the ultimate regulatory deterrent.

In fact there never has been such a putting asunder; no bank has ever had a licence suspended or withdrawn.

Some evidence of the approach taken by the Reserve Bank came to light in the events surrounding the collapse of the Bank of Adelaide in 1979. A subsidiary of the Bank of Adelaide, the Finance Corporation of Australia, encountered difficulties as a result of certain real estate investments which, at best, proved to be unwise. During March and April of 1979, the Reserve Bank monitored the situation on a daily basis, with particular concern for the substantial assistance which the bank was giving to its subsidiary. Later in the year, when the bank itself began to founder, the Governor of the Reserve Bank quietly advised the chairman of the Bank of Adelaide that he had two days in which to arrange a merger with another bank, or else the Reserve Bank would seize control as it is authorized to do under the Banking Act. In the event, a merger was arranged with the ANZ Banking Group Ltd, thus avoiding the necessity for a dramatic, and public, intervention.

During the 1983-84 financial year, the Australian Bank, a small bank which had been recently licensed, encountered considerable difficulties when $3.5 million in bad debts to one customer had to be written off. This enhanced the bank's vulnerability, given its fairly modest capital base of $30 million. An external audit of the bank's loans department was ordered, and its capital base was significantly expanded through new share issues to large commercial entities such as Lend Lease and MLC. However, the full extent of the Reserve Bank's role in encouraging these remedial measures is shrouded in secrecy.

In recent years, a number of questionable practices of Australian banks have come to light. The Commonwealth Special Prosecutor, in discussing the use of banking services in furtherance of tax evasion schemes, criticized the banking industry for permitting the use of multiple bank accounts for round-robin transactions (Redlich, 1984, 117). Returning by car to Canberra after our interview at the Reserve Bank, we heard a radio news bulletin that the ANZ Banking Group Ltd and a former branch manager were ordered to pay about $6 million in damages to a Swiss bank. It was found that a letter of introduction sent to the Swiss bank on behalf of a Sydney customer was deceitful, and was a negligent mis-statement of the customer's integrity (*Canberra Times*, 12 May 1984, 1).

The Reserve Bank, however, does not regard misconduct by bank employees as its responsibility. Reserve bank involvement is limited to those affairs which affect a bank's viability, the stability of the banking system, or monetary policy in general.

The Office of the Insurance Commissioner also relies substantially upon the voluntary compliance of those companies which he regulates. Describing the approach taken in inspecting a company's accounts, a representative of the Office told us:

We don't do it looking to a possible prosecution, because that's not our aim. In fact it is the furthest thing removed from us. We don't see ourselves as a prosecuting agency at all.

The prosecutorial role of the Office of the Insurance Commissioner has been limited exclusively to sanctioning companies delinquent in submitting regular reports, and even this has dropped off in recent years. In 1980-81, there were convictions for sixty-two offences by thirteen firms; 1981-82, thirty-two offences by six firms; and 1983-84, nine offences by two firms.

Like the Reserve Bank, the Office also regulates by means of obtaining voluntary compliance with informal guidelines which lack the force of law. Personal contact is regarded as important, and examiners from the Office are assigned to oversee particular companies for a period of years.

There is a very thorough consultative mechanism between the companies and us. Most of the company directors and company managers know Mr Tickle (the commissioner) and I. Most of the examiners are on first-name terms with someone in each company.

The Office of the Insurance Commissioner endeavours to cultivate goodwill in the industry from:

... contacts individually developed, from phone calls, from finding things out, remembering names, ringing people up on a first name basis, making sure always that if someone does ring up we do give them the right answers as soon as possible, and we expect that in return. I am regarded as a virtual reference on insurance law. People ring me up, companies ring me up, big solicitors (who have got any sense) operating for insurance companies will ring me up . . . they use me a lot.

The Life Insurance Commissioner also relies largely on the power of persuasion and informal exchange with the industry. Where matters are not covered by the Life Insurance Act, circulars are prepared in association with the industry containing guidelines. These have included, for example, guidelines dealing with promotional statements and benefit illustrations to be used by the companies in their marketing literature.

One area of regulation contained in section 50 of the Life Insurance Act places a maximum on the amount of surplus which can be transferred to shareholders or to another life insurance statutory fund. It has been necessary on occasion for the Life Insurance Commissioner to reject accounts and valuation abstracts of companies where this restriction has not been observed.

We do quite a bit of arguing with companies on their treatment of their resources between the different types of policy holders. To a certain extent it's done by friendly persuasion. It's not spelt out in the act.
If a company contravenes the conditions of the act by transferring too much surplus to shareholders, we reject the accounts . . . we do a fair amount of correspondence with companies . . . we usually manage to reach agreement.
You talk to the company and see what they can do about it. Tell them we are getting worried and, as a last resort, we would have to go to an investigation . . . they don't want to go to court any more than you do, and they will generally come to the party, unless you have got a real crook.

Despite the availability of criminal sanctions under the act, the commissioner has never had cause or seen fit to prosecute any company; penal provisions have remained unchanged since 1945. Nor has the commissioner ever sought to deregister a life office except, of course, as a result of companies merging operations. The negotiated regulation style occurs against the background of the commissioner's considerable power to order the amendment or withdrawal of any policy if it contains misleading material, or is not in compliance with the act. When asked if he should adopt a detached, arm's length relationship to the industry, the Life Insurance Commissioner replied:

We don't want to keep them at arm's length; we want to talk to them. We want to ring them up and say 'I don't like this. I don't like that. I'd rather you do it this way'.
Personally, I think it is a damned good thing if we take a business point of view. Because we're looking for the future of the industry itself, and I regard the purpose here as being to further the industry, not to hinder it. I think too many government regulators regard themselves as hindering and stopping things as much as they can. That is not my point of view.

The essence of the Life Insurance Commissioner's regulatory strategy is rejection of direct intervention in favour of monitoring the work of approved actuaries and auditors paid by each life office.

Publicity

Whilst publicity plays but a minor role in prudential regulation, there is some variation in its use by the three agencies. The Reserve Bank itself keeps a low media profile, so much so that a financial journalist has commented:

To write about the Reserve Bank is akin to seeking an entree to ASIO. Almost everybody is off the record, or only on it with the sparse information already available in Bank publications (Preston, 1980, 29).

The Bank, moreover, quite explicitly rejects the use of adverse publicity as a regulatory tool, regarding such a strategy as incompatible with the goal of maintaining public confidence in the financial system.

The Office of the Insurance Commissioner tends to avoid the active use of publicity, but allows nature to take its course. An incident involving misconduct on the part of an insurance company 'certainly becomes known around the industry, and it will get published in the *Financial Review*'.

In the course of our interview at the Office of the Insurance Commissioner, we asked about the use of annual reports to name delinquent companies:

Q. Would you name companies for failure to lodge?
A. No.
Q. For failing to adequately assure prudential standards?
A. Christ, no! We could not do it. The act prevents it, section 126. [Firms in] the insurance industry know each other quite well. The big companies know each other. The *Financial Review* has expertise in that area.
The information would not come from us. Indeed, if somebody contacted us I would say 'Secrecy provision. I am not allowed to speak'.

Indeed, section 126 of the act provides for a fine of $1,000 or imprisonment for three months for disclosing any information about a person except to the Commonwealth Treasurer, or with the Treasurer's approval.

When official action is taken against an insurance company by direction of the Commonwealth Treasurer, however, press coverage almost inevitably follows. Not long after our interview, the Treasurer issued directions under section 62 of the Insurance Act which prevented Crest Insurance Co. from issuing and renewing policies. As predicted, the following morning's *Australian Financial Review* covered the incident (Buduls, 1984). It was the second time the minister had so acted in four months.

Beyond this, matters of concern to the office of the Insurance Commissioner are covered in addresses to industry groups, and in annual reports, without naming specific miscreants.

The Life Insurance Commissioner employs publicity as a regulatory tool, but to a limited extent. On rare occasions adverse comment on a particular firm's operations may be threatened as noted above. The annual report has called attention to inappropriate practices, without naming specific offending firms. For example, a recent annual report stated:

The last two Reports drew attention to problems which have emerged in recent years in ensuring equity in treatment of policy holders. These problems have increased rather than receded, and now constitute the greatest area of concern for the Commissioner (Life Insurance Commissioner, 1984, 22).

It has been more common for the Life Insurance Commissioner quietly to issue circulars to all life offices drawing attention to unacceptable practices, such as misleading advertising, and issuing guidelines to prevent such practices.

The Future of Prudential Regulation

The future of prudential regulation in Australia seems destined to involve significant changes. With licences being offered to sixteen new banks, the Reserve Bank may be expected to adopt a more formal regulatory posture. As the Governor of the Reserve Bank conceded:

So far, the Reserve Bank has carried out its supervisory function on an informal basis. In the light of the probable expansion of the Banking system, it is possible that a more formal and legally explicit basis might need to be developed (Johnston, 1984, 152).

Developments in the insurance industry appear likely to influence the regulatory process as well. As noted above, the Bishopsgate collapse inspired moves toward a closer scrutiny of entry to the industry and acquisition of companies. Diversification of insurance activities, particularly the involvement of life insurance companies in the general insurance field, would appear to make the distinction between life and general insurance industries somewhat less meaningful, and to invite a rationalization of insurance regulation.

Most significant, however, are the profound changes currently occurring in the Australian financial system. Rapid deregulation does not herald a *laissez faire* financial future, but rather a refined and flexible regulatory structure which will oversee newly emergent financial institutions in addition to the traditional.

The desirability of increased scrutiny of merchant banks, for example, was strongly highlighted by Special Prosecutor Redlich:

By virtue of their privileged positions within the Australian and international money market and their relative lack of regulation, merchant banks provide a ready means for criminals and evaders to launder moneys. Two merchant banks have already been investigated by this office and numerous irregularities have been uncovered which are the subject of ongoing investigations. These irregularities include laundering of moneys through false bank accounts, suspect dealings in the commodities future market, promotion of tax avoidance schemes, poor accounting practices and breaches of Reserve Bank (Foreign Exchange) Regulations (Redlich, 1984, 119).

Foreign exchange regulations have since been relaxed, but the Special Prosecutor was critical of the Reserve Bank's failure to act under those parts of the *Financial Corporations Act* 1974 which have thus far been proclaimed.

The future of prudential regulation is thus likely to see a paradox. Responsible agencies are likely to operate with greater formality (Weston, 1984, 222), but within a regulatory framework which is less rigid than that of the past. Also, informal strategies will continue to operate: new banks which have yet to develop a 'track record in the marketplace may be expected to hold . . . proportionately more capital and/or liquidity than a well established bank with a diversified deposit base and loan portfolio' (Brady, 1984, 10).

References and Recommended Reading*

Brady, N.J. (1984), 'Licensing and Supervision of Banks: The Role of Central Banks', Paper presented to LAWASIA Conference on International Banking in the Asian Region, Sydney, 21 May.

Buduls, A. (1984), 'Keating Acts Against Sydney Company: Crest Ordered to Cease Operations', *Australian Financial Review*, 8 June.

Campbell, J.K. *et al.* (1981), *Australian Financial System: Final Report of the Committee of Inquiry*, Australian Government Publishing Service, Canberra.

Commonwealth Treasury (1981), *The Australian Financial System: Treasury Submissions to the Committee of Inquiry into the Australian Financial System*, Treasury Economic Paper No. 9, Australian Government Publishing Service, Canberra.

*Johnston, R. (1984), 'The Reserve Bank: Its Place in the Galaxy', *Canberra Bulletin of Public Administration*, 11, 3, 149-54.

Life Insurance Commissioner (1984), *Annual Report 1983*, Australian Government Publishing Service, Canberra.

Livingstone, D. (1984), 'Changing Times in the Australian Financial World', *The Chartered Accountant in Australia*, June, 22-24.

Martin, V., Beetham, R., Cleary, D., and Hancock, K. (1984), *Australian Financial System: Report of the Review Group*, Australian Government Publishing Service, Canberra.

Munton, Joellen (1985), 'Law Lingers over an Embezzler's Loophole', *Australian Financial Review*, 31 July.

Preston, Y. (1980), 'The Good Wife of Martin Place Wants to be Pure — But Not Yet', *Australian Financial Review*, 2 May, 29-31.

Redlich, R. (1984), *Annual Report of the Special Prosecutor 1983-84*, Australian Government Publishing Service, Canberra.

Totaro, Paola (1985), '$7 Million in Unpaid Insurance Claims', *Sydney Morning Herald*, 29 June.

*Weston, R. (1984), 'The Regulation of Trading Banks', in R. Tomasic, *Business Regulation in Australia*, CCH Australia, Sydney, 217-38.

11
Anti-Discrimination Policy

Introduction

Perhaps the darkest chapter in Australia's history would be devoted to discrimination. The genocide of the Aboriginal population in the nineteenth century was followed by the enactment of numerous statutes and ordinances restricting their freedom of movement, disrupting families, and otherwise branding them with a mark of inferiority (Rowley, 1970; Tatz, 1984). Aboriginal Australians were not even entitled to vote in commonwealth elections until 1962 and, until it was repealed in 1967, section 127 of the Australian Constitution required the exclusion of Aboriginal people from census enumerations. Consequently, for most of the twentieth century, Australian governments, businesses, and individual citizens alike were free to discriminate against Aboriginal people in matters of employment, public accommodation, and the provision of goods and services. The grim legacy of this second class citizenship may be seen in vital statistics: the life expectancy of Aboriginal people is twenty years less than that of non-Aboriginal Australians (Fraser, 1984, 43); the Aboriginal infant mortality rate is nearly three times higher (Commonwealth Department of Health, 1984, 244); the rate of unemployment is five times higher than that of the general population (Fraser and Fraser, 1984); and the rate of imprisonment is up to fourteen times higher (Walker and Biles, 1985, 22; Commonwealth Department of Aboriginal Affairs, 1984, 137).

The history of racial discrimination in Australia was by no means limited to its Aboriginal population. Indeed, Australia was better known throughout the world not for its ill-treatment of Aboriginals, but for the White Australia Policy: the systematic exclusion of non-white immigrants dating from federation until the 1960s.

Institutionalized racism in Australia became increasingly untenable, however, in the aftermath of the war against Hitler, and in a post-colonial era when the populations of most of the world's nations were predominantly non-white. For Australia to be accorded any moral standing in the new international arena, profound changes were in order.

The first Australian anti-discrimination law was the South Australian *Prohibition of Discrimination Act* 1966, which made racial discrimination a criminal offence. Almost another decade was to pass, however, before further legislative developments occurred.

The 1970s saw an emerging sensitivity to other forms of discrimination in Australia: discrimination against women, and most recently, discrimination against the disabled. Although South Australia was the first jurisdiction in the common law world to allow women the vote (in 1894), women throughout Australia were denied equal employment opportunities, equal pay for equal work, and faced much greater barriers than men in obtaining credit, accommodation, and access to public services. Married women were prohibited from permanent employment in the commonwealth public service until 1966 (Scutt, 1983, 225-8). The rate of female unemployment in Australia today is significantly higher than the male rate (Australian Bureau of Statistics, 1984, 136).

Over and above the affront to emerging standards of gender justice, the economic dependence of Australian women imposes significant costs on a society which fails to utilize fully many of its most talented people. A great proportion of government funds allocated to welfare services and to income maintenance programmes are necessitated by this imbalance, whether for the young single unemployed woman, the supporting mother, or for the aged pensioner.

The constitutional basis for commonwealth involvement in the anti-discrimination field derives from the corporations power, and ratification of a number of international instruments. These include, *inter alia*, the International Convention on the Elimination of All Forms of Racial Discrimination (1975), the International Covenant on Civil and Political Rights (1980), and the International Convention on the Elimination of All Forms of Discrimination Against Women. States are free to legislate concurrently as long as their legislation is consistent with federal law.

Common Patterns of Anti-Discrimination Policy

The most noticeable characteristic of anti-discrimination programmes in the various jurisdictions of Australia is their patchwork nature. To begin with, neither Queensland, Tasmania, Western Australia, nor the Northern Territory had anti-discrimination legislation or agencies in place at the time of our interviews, although Western Australia has since enacted legislation.

The legislative framework and administrative structure of anti-discrimination policy in the commonwealth and the states of New South Wales, Victoria, and South Australia vary somewhat, as is indicated by Table 1, but their basic operating principles are quite similar (Mills and Ronalds, 1984). The regulatory posture of Australian anti-discrimination agencies is almost entirely reactive. That is, the agencies in question

Table 1
Commonwealth and State Anti-Discrimination Agencies

Jurisdiction	Agencies	Statutes
Commonwealth	Human Rights Commission (Commissioner for Community Relations) (Sex Discrimination Commissioner)	*Racial Discrimination Act* 1975 *Human Rights Commission Act* 1981 *Sex Discrimination Act* 1984
New South Wales	Anti-Discrimination Board (Equal Opportunity Tribunal)	*Anti Discrimination Act* 1977
Victoria	Commissioner for Equal Opportunity (Equal Opportunity Board)	*Equal Opportunity Act* 1984
South Australia	Commissioner for Equal Opportunity (Sex Discrimination Board) (Handicapped Persons Discrimination Tribunal)	*Racial Discrimination Act* 1976 *Sex Discrimination Act* 1975 *Handicapped Persons Equal Opportunity Act* 1981

respond to complaints lodged with them, rather than patrol and actively seek out examples of discriminatory practice.

There are provisions in both commonwealth and state law, however, for matters to be investigated without prior complaint. In Victoria, for example, section 41 of the *Equal Opportunity Act* 1984 specifically provides for the Equal Opportunity Board to refer matters for investigation that have not been the subject of complaint. This had led to major investigations and policy change in Victoria, for example, regarding recruitment policies in banks and enrolment policies in schools of obstetrical nursing. In the period July 1983-June 1984, there were fourteen matters referred by the Equal Opportunity Board under these provisions.

Each agency has little or no recourse to criminal sanctions. None of the state agencies we visited had ever brought a prosecution, although the Commonwealth Human Rights Commission has on rare occasions referred apparent offences under the Racial Discrimination Act to prosecuting authorities. These have involved such procedural matters as failure to attend a compulsory conference, and intimidation of complainants. In no case, to date, has a matter proceeded to prosecution. Agency executives in any event regard the criminal process as inappropriate to their mission. Rather, the agencies employ a two-fold strategy, combining the conciliation of individual complaints with various programmes of public information.

The focus of those few penal clauses which do appear in anti-discrimination legislation is striking. Before its repeal by the *Equal Opportunity Act* 1984, one statute, the South Australian *Racial Discrimination Act* 1976, made discriminatory practice in employment or the provision of public accommodation a criminal offence. In each of the three state jurisdictions, it is an offence to publish an advertisement which breaches the act.

All other discriminatory practices, however, are defined as 'unlawful', and thereby are subject to civil, but not criminal remedies. Criminal liability does attach, however, to various acts such as intimidation of complainants, and refusal to co-operate with agencies in the investigation and conciliation process.

Nevertheless, the remedies that are at the disposal of tribunals are significant. For example, the Victorian Equal Opportunity Board, in the *Wardley* v. *Ansett* case which was referred to it in 1978, awarded Deborah Wardley $14,000 damages plus $40 per day until she was taken into the Ansett pilot training programme, a requirement that was also included in the order. Settlements in New South Wales have ranged from $1,000 to $35,000.

Variations in Anti-Discrimination Strategy

The two strategies which most markedly differentiate the anti-discrimination agencies under review are the use of publicity, and the inclination to refer matters to judicial or quasi-judicial bodies for determination. The two are inextricably linked, as far as the state agencies are concerned; there exists no specialist tribunal to which the Commonwealth Human Rights Commission might refer matters not amenable to conciliation.

Conciliation is essentially a private process. Indeed, the terms of an agreement reached through conciliation may explicitly preclude disclosure of a matter. Only when attempts at conciliation break down, and a matter is referred to a tribunal or a court, does it enter the public domain, and thus become accessible to the media. Whilst the four agencies under review endeavour to conciliate each of the complaints which they entertain, those in New South Wales and Victoria appear less reluctant to refer matters for judicial determination.

The South Australian Commissioner for Equal Opportunity informed us that she has a particular philosophical preference for conciliated settlements over formal adjudication. She maintained that conciliation results in more effective remedies, and carries a greater potential for attitude change.

Also significant, however, is the risk that the tribunal may decide against the complainant. Subsequent media attention accorded such cases could discourage members of the public from complaining in future, and could reinforce prejudicial attitudes within the community.

The commitment of the Human Rights Commission to conciliation is similarly grounded in philosophy as well as strategy. The commission contends that their ultimate *raison d'etre* is attitude change, which is better achieved by positive means than negative sanctions. It is the shared view amongst commission staff that parties feel more committed to an outcome which has been reached freely, by mutual agreement, rather than one which has been resolved through formal adjudication.

Strategic considerations also enter the commission's overwhelming preference for conciliation over adjudication. In contrast to the situation in the three states, there is no specialized commonwealth tribunal to hear cases arising from unsuccessful attempts at conciliation. The Sex Discrimination Commissioner may refer complaints to the commission itself for inquiry, however. In addition, the commission may issue a complainant a certificate which will confer standing to seek a remedy in a civil court, but commission involvement ends there.

This is regarded as particularly inappropriate in the case of complainants from deprived circumstances. As an officer put it:

You're asking the disadvantaged and inarticulate, those who are intimidated by court appearances and court processes, to take their own remedy.

Officials of the Human Rights Commission are extremely cautious in their use of publicity, because of their concern over possible backlash and eventual polarization. 'Publicity only confirms people in their attitudes', we were told.

If you publicize matters of discrimination, and you are seen to be attacking people, say police or power figures in towns . . . you will divide the community down the middle on racial lines, and people who mightn't have a firm view soon develop one. So you polarize communities.

Moreover, the legislation prohibits officers from disclosing particulars of complaints, the conciliation process, and its outcome. The Human Rights Commission does, however, use positive publicity, particularly in country areas. It is more their style to:

. . . go in quietly, unannounced into towns, working quietly, and then, at the end of it all, publicizing our visit, the kinds of issues we dealt with, the kinds of discrimination, the forms of it encountered, the outcome, in an anonymous way, and then talk about how we obtained co-operation of the parties, and how better understanding has been developed, and how procedures have been implemented . . .

Whilst officials of the Human Rights Commission are aware that anti-discrimination bodies in New South Wales and Victoria take a different approach to publicity, they still adhere to the principle that attitude change is best achieved through positive inducement:

Is the publicity you get from court outcomes a good kind of publicity for changing attitudes, or not? We decided quite clearly that it wasn't. We'll talk to our counterparts in Victoria and New South Wales at the Office of the Commissioner for Equal Opportunity and the Anti-Discrimination Board, and they'll say 'What you need is a good case'. They'll talk about the Wardley case as being a landmark case in Victoria. They'll talk about other cases in New South Wales as being good cases because [they] focused the public attention. You can argue both ways on that, and in the early days when we were forming the *modus operandi* under this act, it was to the contrary.

The Human Rights Commission explicitly avoids the use of threat:

You can't conciliate if people are threatened, because that makes them anxious and angry; in other words, they're not open to themselves, and to the impact that they might have had on others.

The approach taken by the New South Wales Anti-Discrimination Board stands in stark contrast to the low-key style of the Human Rights Commission. Because it is empowered to refer matters to the Equal Opportunity Tribunal for public adjudication, the Board uses the implicit threat of public visibility to encourage conciliation.

The board has used publicity as both a conciliatory tool and a regulatory tool. The media relishes the individual conflict in discrimination cases of the small person against a large organization.

In order to be successful in conciliation, you need to be able to speak at ease with the captains of industry. You need to be able to speak their language. You need to be able to offer them assistance in self-regulation, but at the same time you need a stick out there that says, 'Listen, if you don't comply voluntarily, then compliance will be forced on you in a public determination of the complaint'.

Our high media profile has been critical in bringing about the resolution of complaints. Large companies calculate the negative publicity of being named as an alleged discriminator, particularly companies which sell to women consumers. Such companies have indicated that they have a 'settle at any cost philosophy'.

Recently we had a complaint against a large multinational company . . . because of the nature and image of the company it would have held the company up, if it went public, in a way that would have ridiculed them. The cartoonists wouldn't have been able to resist it, and it would have been a 'page oner' as we call it . . . Then they did a calculation, that if this was referred from here — where it was private and confidential — to the tribunal, the sheer reference of that would force it into the press, and on to page one, they believed, but worse still, into the cartoon sections of the paper. So they calculated that one single action would cost them a million dollars in publicity. Being a multinational, it would be picked up by the wire services . . . So they were prepared to settle.

It was observed that government agencies which are the subject of complaints are much less sensitive to adverse publicity than is private enterprise:

Government departments seem almost immune to bad publicity. Some seem to take a perverse delight in it. Further, some argue that the only way a policy, a practice, or a situation can be changed is for the department to be ordered by the tribunal to make the change.

If the 'X' matter — the sexual harassment case last year that went to the tribunal against (a senior public servant) — if that had been filed against the managing director of a major public company, they would have settled in conciliation months before they went to the tribunal.

Moreover, the high visibility of contested cases involving public sector respondents has a salutary effect on the willingness of businesses to co-operate:

I can't describe how much more responsive companies are to sexual harassment cases because of the 'X' matter.

Nevertheless, reactive, complaint-based conciliation has its shortcomings as a regulatory strategy. Perhaps most significant of these is the problem of access to justice on the part of disadvantaged individuals. Not all complainants are themselves disadvantaged, nor are they drawn necessarily from disadvantaged groups. A significant proportion of complainants under sex discrimination acts, for example, are male. A representative of one of the agencies we visited remarked:

We look after the poor, the oppressed and the articulate middle class, and not necessarily in that order.

Individual complaint-centred remedies, moreover, fail to address the problem of biases which are essentially structural in nature. An aggrieved complainant may be one of hundreds or even thousands of similarly situated victims of discrimination. The inefficiency of tackling widespread discrimination on a case by case basis is patently apparent.

Whilst the Commonwealth Sex Discrimination Act and the New South Wales Anti-Discrimination Act contain provisions for representative complaints, these preclude the award of damages to the affected class. This detracts significantly from the utility of this group-remedy.

One of the more distinctive characteristics of South Australian anti-discrimination policy is the readiness of the Commissioner for Equal Opportunity to use positive publicity, explicitly congratulating companies in instances where they have engaged in exemplary conduct.

Because it was an issue that we wanted to discuss, and because we'd had a complaint against them in the past and they'd taken steps to rectify the situation, and we were really pleased with the present standard they've got on that issue, we use their names and release to the press what a great job they've done, and that more organizations should do that.

More than one Commissioner, labouring under weak legislation, has invoked the 'Bluff Act' from time to time in order to facilitate conciliation.

Saying that we are going to the tribunal sometimes has an element of bluff because often we have not got the evidence that would be likely to succeed . .
The other thing that we do is to take up complaints that could be exempted under the legislation . . .
Organizations where there are fewer than six employees, for instance, are not covered, but where we had complaints of sexual harassment in those small organizations we have taken them up, sent the employer a letter which does not specifically say that the act covers the situation, and yes, I admit that, in effect, this could imply that we are suggesting we have jurisdiction . . . And we've managed financial settlements on that as well. Where indeed we really don't have any power in that area.

The Victorian commissioner has had considerable success in working with, and through, trade associations. The Australian Hotels Association assisted in obtaining members' compliance with the Equal Opportunity Act. The Victorian Employers' Federation and the Victorian Chamber of Manufactures provide each of their members with copies of the commissioner's information bulletins.

The Tension between Advocacy and Impartiality in Anti-Discrimination Agencies

Australian anti-discrimination agencies play two roles, roles which are often incompatible. On the one hand, they are charged with advancing a cause: that of removing discriminatory barriers in Australian society. It is their task to impress upon the Australian public that discriminatory practice is wrong, and to act as advocates for the victims of discrimination. On the other hand, the primary strategy which they employ to achieve the goal of a non-discriminatory society, that of conciliating complaints, requires a certain degree of detachment and impartiality. The four agencies we visited vary somewhat in the manner in which they manage this tension between contradictory roles.

The Victorian Commissioner for Equal Opportunity places great importance on maintaining an image of impartiality.

The job of the conciliator is just as much to prevent somebody being hounded if they are conforming to the Equal Opportunity Act as it is to get them to conform to the Equal Opportunity Act if they are not . . .
The way we set the scene is extremely important. We go out to see a respondent in the first instance. We write a letter saying there has been a complaint, giving a brief outline of what it is and saying that we feel the best way to sort the matter out is to come and discuss it . . .
We explain to both sides that what we are trying to do is first of all understand exactly the situation from the complainant's point of view, then to understand exactly what it is from the respondent's point of view, and only after that to put those two things together and try to resolve the problem. We are very aware and concerned about our responsibilities equally to the respondent and the complainant, and I believe that this comes through in the trust we usually enjoy from both.

The New South Wales Anti-Discrimination Board, however, gives a somewhat different emphasis to compensating for the differences in skills and resources which complainant and respondent would bring to a conciliation setting:

Sometimes, if the evidence warrants, it is a role of supporting what the complainant clearly deserves under the law, or of advocating on behalf of a respondent if the view is that the complainant makes excessive claims. As Counsellor I have taken the view that sometimes I must take an active rather than a passive role in protecting the rights of, in particular, the complainant. It is my belief that complainants, particularly those who are the victims of sexual and racial harassment, may and have become depressed and demoralised by the discriminatory action they have suffered. With weakened self-confidence they find it difficult to negotiate directly with the respondent and it is only with active support of the Counsellor that a settlement can be effected which protects their rights and ensures a resolution which conforms to the legislation. The Counsellor has a duty under the law to 'endeavour to resolve the complaint by conciliation'. How this is to be accomplished the law leaves to the discretion of the Counsellor (Niland, 1981, 7-8).

An officer of the Human Rights Commission used the term 'controlled bias' to refer to the conciliation process. The commission does assist the complainant to develop his or her case and ensures that the respondent is provided with all relevant information. Commission conciliators do not press complainants to seek a particular level of settlement.

The South Australian Commissioner for Equal Opportunity is required by law, once a complaint has been entertained, to assist the complainant in the preparation of his or her case. Whilst some respondents might be entitled to regard this with scepticism, the commissioner opined:

We have a general feeling in the community, particularly in the private sector . . . that we're not there to aggressively use the legislation, but we are there and have an expectation that those organizations will comply with the legislation. There's been a consistently high level of co-operation from respondents, and again an expressed satisfaction at the outcome when the matters are conciliated.

The Human Rights Commission and the New South Wales Anti-Discrimination Board both engage in specific community relations programmes. The commission has undertaken what it terms 'whole town projects', where a team will visit a town, and encourage the formation of human rights committees. Team members will address a meeting of concerned citizens and advise:

Look. Get together as an identifiable group in the community. Stand by the Aboriginal people. Be identified with them. Be a focus point for them to come to you. Be a reminder in your community that racial discrimination will not be tolerated. If you're up to it, confront discrimination.

The goal of the team is to develop the capacity of local communities to respond to problems of racial prejudice and discrimination. The 'ten towns project' of the New South Wales Anti-Discrimination Board was launched after the fatal shooting of an Aboriginal man in Moree in 1982. Teams were sent to each of ten New South Wales country towns to meet with community leaders to identify particular sources of friction within the community, and to encourage local organizations and interested citizens to assume some responsibility to reduce conflict in the locality.

In keeping with the characteristic styles of education and conciliation in response to complaints of discriminatory practices, the state anti-discrimination bodies take a consultative approach to the problem of discriminatory advertisements. The Victorian Commissioner for Equal Opportunity was at the outset reluctant to use those criminal sanctions available to her.

Magistrates, when we started, gave no indication that they thought the Equal Opportunity Act was a sensible provision. I thought that if we prosecuted, and the person was fined fifty cents or something equally trivial, it would be very detrimental to my credibility.

As an alternative to the criminal process, the commissioner sought to enlist the support of the press in preventing offending conduct.

We got very good compliance from the newspapers early in the piece. As soon as the Equal Opportunity Act came into operation I went and interviewed the managers of the classified ads section of the *Herald*, the *Australian*, and the *Age*. On two different occasions, in the case of the *Age*, I addressed all the women — and I say women because they were all women — who were at the telephones taking classified ads about what they could and couldn't accept in compliance with the Equal Opportunity Act. I had an ongoing dialogue with them and, in fact, I saw them as being probably the most important enforcers of the act at one stage. They were really the frontline troops. Indeed I went and had what I would describe as a rallying session with them, and told them that I saw them as our frontline troops, and what a great job they were doing.

At the time they were receiving a lot of abuse over the telephone, so I felt it was extremely important that to begin with they understood the philosophy of the act, and what it was achieving. Then after they had been monitoring the ads for about three months, I thought it was time to go and see them again, and tell them about the change that has occurred, and the success of what I thought they had been doing, and generally getting them to feel that it was all worthwhile. They loved the sense of achievement, they really did.

The co-existence of commonwealth and state laws in New South Wales, Victoria, and South Australia has been accompanied by both legal and administrative difficulties. A complaint in late 1980 of racial discrimination under the New South Wales Anti-Discrimination Act inspired a challenge to the constitutionality of the act on the ground that it was inconsistent in part, if not in spirit, with the Commonwealth Racial Discrimination Act, and thereby invalid under section 109 of the Australian Constitution. The High Court of Australia upheld the claim in *Viskauskas* v. *Niland* (1983) 47 ALR 32. The commonwealth government, not wishing to displace state anti-discrimination laws which appeared to be functioning satisfactorily, and which were consistent with Australia's international obligations, amended the federal act to permit the continued co-existence of commonwealth and state statutes. Nevertheless, the retrospective application of these amendments was subsequently ruled invalid in *Metwally* v. *University of Wollongong* (1985) 60 ALR 68. At the time of writing, the validity of both commonwealth and state anti-discrimination laws remained under legal challenge.

However, such concurrent jurisdiction continued to pose organizational as well as legal difficulties, including a certain rivalry between the Human Rights Commission and relevant state bodies, the duplication of limited personnel resources, and the difficulties encountered by prospective complainants in selecting the most advantageous jurisdiction in which to lodge a complaint. The solution chosen was to negotiate co-operative arrangements between the commonwealth and each of the state anti-discrimination agencies to permit the state bodies to act as agents of the Human Rights Commission and to deal with complaints under both state and federal law. Commonwealth funding was provided for these additional responsibilities.

Whilst the complainant retains the right to choose whether to proceed under commonwealth or state law, advice to the prospective complainant will, in most instances, be provided by officers of the state body. This is likely to continue the existing regional variation in anti-discrimination policy and practice.

Anti-discrimination agencies operate under conditions of severe resource constraint. Conciliation is a labour intensive process, and Victorian and South Australian agencies endeavour to achieve conciliation through face to face meetings rather than through correspondence. They thus have fewer resources to devote to public information and community relations functions.

Activities of the Human Rights Commission have been noticeably constrained by staffing limitations. As a representative of the commission told us:

The hallmark of the operation of the Racial Discrimination Act has been lack of resources . . . Our operations have been restricted largely to Queensland, New South Wales and, to a lesser extent, Victoria. We have virtually ignored Western Australia, South Australia, and the Northern Territory, except for the most serious of matters that, because of national publicity, could not be ignored.

Since there is no state anti-discrimination machinery in place in Queensland, the opening of a Human Rights Commission Brisbane office, albeit with a skeletal staff, was heralded as an important event. The resignation of the director of the office after four months reflected her feelings of futility when endeavouring to cope assisted by a staff of only three trainees.

Given the willingness of the commonwealth government to share concurrent responsibility with those states wishing to be active in the anti-discrimination domain, it seems likely that the Human Rights Commission will continue to concentrate its efforts in the information and promotion areas, and will become less involved in the conciliation of complaints, except perhaps in the Australian Capital Territory, and those jurisdictions without anti-discrimination legislation.

From Individualistic to Structural Initiatives

Anti-discrimination agencies face a dilemma over the allocation of resources to structural as opposed to individual remedies. Agencies devote considerable attention and resources to assisting individual complainants. Indeed, it would be very difficult to turn one's back on a disadvantaged and victimized individual. Structural remedies may prove to be more cost effective, however. To a certain extent, the Human Rights Commission appears to have recognized this, as reflected in the considerable resources which it devotes to the Information and Promotion Branch, its largest area. In addition to approaches involving public information, a number of other structurally orientated initiatives have been developed in recent years.

One relatively unusual regulatory device which exists in the anti-discrimination domain is the use of monetary incentives to industries which further regulatory policy. The commonwealth government has recently introduced a scheme of special cash rebates for employers taking on additional female apprentices in specified trades. Employers may receive up to $4,000 tax exempt for each additional female apprentice recruited.

Another initiative to be introduced in conjunction with the emerging deregulation of the banking industry involves provision for equal employment opportunity as a condition attached to the granting of new banking licences.

Commonwealth anti-discrimination programmes have recently seen the development of significant initiatives in self-regulation. Whilst previous programmes were based upon the conciliation of individual complaints and upon community education, it was recognized that these initiatives were unlikely to have any significant large scale impact on employment opportunities for women for many years. Some of the largest employers in the private and public sectors were thus invited to join a voluntary pilot programme to improve employment opportunities for women in their workforces.

Within broad guidelines proposed by the Office of the Status of Women in the Department of the Prime Minister and Cabinet, thirty-one participants in the programme were invited to develop their own strategies for 'affirmative action' consistent with the conditions and environment of their respective industries. A senior executive within each participating firm was given responsibility for developing the company's affirmative action strategy.

The programme included the setting of numerical goals, and provided for self evaluation at the end of the pilot phase. Recommendations which emerged from the pooled experience of participating firms contributed to the design and the diffusion of improved programmes, and to legislation requiring the adoption of affirmative action plans for all organisations with over 100 employees.

Developments in the law may also have significant structural implications. Women and members of racial minorities may be disadvantaged not only by explicit discriminatory practices, but also by height, weight, educational, or other requirements which may be irrelevant for the purpose at hand. Actions claiming 'indirect discrimination', the exclusion of persons by means of unreasonable and unnecessary requirements or qualifications, appear likely to increase over the next decade. These may involve class actions to obtain injunctive relief for members of a disadvantaged group, in addition to individual complainants.

The Uncertain Future of Anti-Discrimination Policy

The Human Rights Commission is unique amongst all of the regulatory agencies under review in that its legislation contains a 'sunset clause'. Section 36 of the *Human Rights Commission Act* 1981 provides that the act will cease to be in force after five years.

The future contours of Australian anti-discrimination policy remain unclear. Late in 1985, the commonwealth government heralded the introduction of an affirmative action programme for women's employment, backed by legislation. This appeared likely to involve a form of enforced self-regulation, where employers would be required to lodge plans with a specified authority, subject to adverse publicity in the event of non-compliance. Proposals to enact an Australian Bill of Rights continue to meet with considerable controversy. Reluctance to offend the sensibilities of the states militates against a bill with substantial powers. Persistent challenges to the validity of commonwealth and state anti-discrimination laws suggest that Australian governments have accorded low priority to reform in these areas. Whilst a renewal of the Human Rights Commission seems assured, the nature of the powers it will be given and role it will play in its reincarnated state are uncertain. They seem destined to be determined by the federal politics of the day.

Other countries such as the United States impose criminal penalties for many discriminatory practices. Under the United States federal system, the Bill of Rights is superior to state law. By contrast, it seems apparent that Australian governments will continue on the path of seeking to reduce discrimination through consensus and co-operation. Even such strategies as making government grants and contracts conditional upon the achievement of recruitment quotas and timetables, have so far been unpalatable to most Australian governments.

References and Recommended Reading*

Australian Bureau of Statistics (1984), *Yearbook Australia 1984*, Australian Bureau of Statistics, Canberra.

Commonwealth Department of Aboriginal Affairs (1984), *Aboriginal Social Indicators, 1984*, Australian Government Publishing Service, Canberra.

Commonwealth Department of Health (1984), *Annual Report for the Year 1983-84*, Australian Government Publishing Service, Canberra.

Fraser, B. and Fraser, S. (1984), 'Must These Children Keep Dying?', *Australian Society*, 3, 6, 27-8.

Fraser, S. (1984), 'Aborigines: Australia's Third World', *Populi*, 11, 3, 31-56.

*Mills, H. and Ronalds, C. (1984), *Anti Discrimination Laws in Australia*, Metal Trades Industry Association, Sydney.

Niland, C. (1981), 'Investigation and Conciliation', Paper presented to a Seminar on Anti-Discrimination Law and Practice, University of New South Wales, 19-20 June.

Rowley, C. (1970), *The Destruction of Aboriginal Society*, Australian National University Press, Canberra.

*Scutt, J. (1983), 'Legislation for the Right to be Equal: Women, the Law and Social Policy', in C. Baldock and B. Cass (eds), *Women, Social Welfare, and the State*, George Allen and Unwin, Sydney, 223-45.

*Tatz, C. (1984), 'Aborigines and Civil Law' in P. Hanks and B. Keon-Cohen (eds), *Aborigines and the Law*, George Allen and Unwin, Sydney, 103-36.

Walker, J. and Biles, D. (1985), *Australian Prisoners 1984*, Australian Institute of Criminology, Canberra.

12
Fraud against the Government: Medical Benefits, Tax and Customs

Introduction

The growing salience of the commonwealth government in Australian life is bemoaned by some, and deftly exploited by others. At $2,000 million per year, the price of universal health care is not trifling. One conservative estimate suggests that an additional $100 million is added to the bill each year as a result of fraud and over-servicing by Australian medical practitioners (*Medical Practice*, 1983). Most Australian doctors have formed companies, for purposes of tax minimization, if not for the efficient administration of their practices; some pathology practices employ hundreds of people.

The majority of taxpayers comply, if at times begrudgingly, with the requirements of the Commonwealth Commissioner of Taxation. But many do not. The burdens consequently borne by honest taxpayers have been enormous. According to the Commissioner of Taxation, at 30 June 1984, 54,886 objections had been lodged by 33,551 taxpayers against disallowance of their claims arising from participation in tax avoidance schemes including company and trust stripping cases. The tax and other amounts disputed totalled $1,523 million (Commonwealth Commissioner of Taxation, 1984, 16). It should be noted that this awesome figure which the Commissioner is seeking to recover does not include losses from tax evasion: the understatement of income, or failure to state income altogether. The government's Draft White Paper (1985, 36-7) on tax reform estimated a loss of at least $3 billion in revenue from tax evasion and an even greater loss from avoidance.

Evasion of duties by commercial importers through deliberately understating the value of imported goods constitutes a further drain on the revenue. And again, the stakes are high. In one simple case, in 1984, conniving importers evaded an estimated $7 million in duties by smuggling T-shirts, not bothering to declare them at all.

Multinational enterprises are able to exploit the tax (and tariff) systems of various nations by transfer pricing – selling goods to a subsidiary at a low price in low tax countries, while selling the same goods at higher prices to high tax countries (e.g. Crough, 1981).

But the cost of fraud against the government is more than financial. The prestige and authority which the medical profession enjoys in Australia today is threatened by decay from within. The inequity of the taxation system has been significantly amplified. Widespread beliefs that 'tax is optional for the rich' have undermined the confidence of ordinary citizens in the legitimacy of the legal order and the social justice of Australian society.

Three agencies having responsibility for the prevention and control of fraud against the government by companies or by individuals in corporate clothing, are the Commonwealth Department of Health, Health Services Financing Division (prior to May 1985), the Australian Taxation Office (ATO), and the Customs Service of the Commonwealth Department of Industry, Commerce, and Technology.

The distinctive characteristics of all three regulatory regimes are first, their reliance upon the systematic monitoring of documents as the primary method of detecting misconduct, and second, their frequent use, when compared with other regulatory agencies, of prosecution and/or massive civil penalties in response.

The ATO and the Customs Service are primarily concerned with efficiency in collection of revenue: $34,000 million and $9,000 million per year, respectively. The Health Services Financing Division, on the other hand, is concerned with efficiency in the provision of funds for health care, approximately $2,000 million per year. The actual processing of Medicare applications, and dispensation of payments, are the responsibility of the Commonwealth Health Insurance Commission, an independent statutory authority.

Two of the agencies, the Commonwealth Department of Health and the ATO, along with the Commonwealth Department of Primary Industry (see Chapter 7), stand out among all of the regulatory bodies visited in the course of our research, for the unprecedented extent to which they were subject to unrelenting criticism and scrutiny during the period 1981-84. This attention arose, of course, as a result of revelations of widespread abuse of the commonwealth medical benefits programme, colloquially termed 'medifraud', and the massive growth of 'bottom of the harbour' tax avoidance schemes (Joint Committee on Public Accounts, 1982; Costigan, 1982a).

Inspired by a number of revealing newspaper accounts in 1981, growing suspicion of widespread medical benefits fraud was confirmed early in 1982 when even the Australian Medical Association (AMA) estimated that over 800 of its members were engaged in gross abuse of the medical benefits programme at a cost of $100 million per year (Joint Committee on Public Accounts, 1982, 3).

Late in 1981, two Victorian corporate affairs investigators revealed that complex tax avoidance schemes, based on company asset stripping, had proliferated during the 1970s (McCabe and La Franchi, 1982). This was resoundingly confirmed by an interim report of the Costigan

Royal Commission which discovered, incidentally, in the course of its inquiry into alleged corruption of the Federated Ship Painters and Dockers Union, the existence of widespread tax evasion (Costigan, 1982a).

The medifraud and bottom of the harbour scandals focused persistent media attention on the will of the commonwealth government to address each of these problems, and on the implementation of government policy by the responsible agencies.

In the case of medical benefits fraud, it provoked a major reorganization of the Commonwealth Department of Health, and a doubling of resources devoted to the control of fraud and over-servicing. By the 1984-85 financial year, 206 officers were assigned to the task, at a cost of $8.1 million per year. In addition, a dozen officers of the Director of Public Prosecutions, and about twenty Australian Federal Police officers were assigned to work full time on medical benefits fraud.

In the case of the Australian Taxation Office, it gave rise to increases in human resources, and to legislative changes including the first revision of the penal provisions of the Income Tax Assessment Act in nearly fifty years. The office, and the public prosecutors working with it, wiped most of the well known tax avoidance schemes of the 1970s off the map through adopting, for the first time in its history, an aggressive, if selective, attitude towards promoters of tax avoidance.

Medical Fraud and Over-Servicing

The Commonwealth Department of Health is concerned with two distinct forms of medical benefits abuse: fraud and over-servicing. Fraud is an unambiguous concept; section 129 of the *Health Insurance Act* 1973 prohibits the making of false or misleading statements on documents used to obtain medical benefits.

One doctor, for example, after having his lawn mown, had his gardener sign an assignment form for an after hours consultation. The doctor received $24. Other doctors have forged the signatures of patients whom they had not visited, or have billed the commonwealth for a consultation longer than the one actually held. Medical benefits fraud is punishable by disqualification from participation in the medical benefits programme, and by a fine or imprisonment.

Over-servicing is a more complex matter, and refers to services not reasonably required for the adequate medical care of a patient. A common type of case involves repeated home visits to elderly patients, without legitimate medical justification.

The determination of over-servicing involves a sensitive professional judgement, however, and over-servicing may not be intentional. It is, moreover, of considerable importance that a regulatory regime not have a chilling effect on the provision of adequate medical care; doctors must not be discouraged from providing a medical service when it is warranted. Persistent over-servicing may result in an order to refund payments made for services deemed to be excessive.

Tax Avoidance and Evasion

The ATO is responsible for the implementation, and not the formulation of tax policy. Its primary responsibility is the efficient collection of revenue. The inordinate complexity of tax laws, the proliferation of 'loopholes', and the resulting inequities of the tax system have been the work of successive governments. Indeed, on four separate occasions in 1978, the Commissioner of Taxation called the attention of the Federal Treasurer to the proliferation of tax avoidance schemes in the aftermath of High Court decisions facilitating avoidance (*Slutzkin* v. *Federal Commissioner of Taxation* (1977) 12 ALR 321). It was not, however, until December of 1980 that the *Crimes (Taxation Offences) Act* 1980 closed the loopholes permitting trust and straw company stripping, and it was not until June 1981 that the new part IV A of the *Income Tax Assessment Act* 1936 was passed. This now permits certain forms of recovery of tax avoided by income splitting through the use of family companies and trusts.

The two basic forms of misconduct which the ATO encounters in the course of its revenue collection role are tax evasion and tax avoidance. Tax evasion, an explicit breach of the law, encompasses such conduct as failure to submit an income tax return, or deliberately understating one's income. The *Income Tax Assessment Act* 1936 specifies such conduct as punishable by penalty equal to double the amount of under payment.

Tax avoidance, on the other hand, involves minimizing one's tax burden by breaching the spirit, if not the letter, of the law. Technically, the law may not require the payment of tax in a set of circumstances, although the policy of the law would say that that tax should be paid (Parsons, 1984, 57). In the 1970s, for example, ambiguities in the law permitted the buying and selling of companies to create deductions, not for any legitimate commercial purpose.

Gains from tax avoidance activity, if disallowed, are subject to civil recovery with penalty surcharge. The commissioner makes an assessment; the taxpayer can then lodge an appeal to the commissioner which, if rejected, can be taken to a Taxation Board of Review, and ultimately to the courts. The widespread use of substantial civil penalties is perhaps the most characteristic regulatory tool of the ATO.

Customs Offences

Commercial importers are required to declare their goods under the Customs Act on or before arrival. Required documentation, including invoices and bills of lading, are lodged at that time. The most common forms of fraud against customs authorities are valuation fraud, where the full value of the goods in question is not declared, and tariff classification abuse, where imported goods are incorrectly classified.

Detecting Fraud Against the Government

Agencies responsible for the prevention and control of fraud against the government rely heavily on the monitoring of documents. The regulatory regimes which most readily lend themselves to this type of surveillance are medical benefits and taxation. The task is greatly facilitated by the technology of electronic information storage and retrieval.

In the medical benefits area, a Fraud and Over-servicing Detection System (FODS) was established in the Surveillance and Investigation Division of the Commonwealth Department of Health. Information from each medical practitioner's benefit claims forms and accounts (receipt and patient claim forms) was stored in a data base and subject to systematic analysis. It was thus possible, routinely and automatically, to determine if a given practitioner has billed for more than twenty-four hours of consulting time in a given day, for example, and to identify those practitioners whose billing patterns appeared anomalous, given their specialty and the geographic area in which they practice. Aberrant practices were identified for further, more intensive, investigation. The health department employs similar methods to detect fraud by pharmacists in conjunction with the pharmaceutical benefits scheme.

The argument has been made that most of the cases singled out for prosecution thus far have been general practitioners, and that a great deal of abuse by specialists has gone unpunished (Rupert Public Interest Movement, 1984, 11). This occurred in part because the FODS system, in its early stage of development, more readily singled out deviant billing practices from a large peer group of comparable doctors.

The billing practices of a general practitioner were more meaningful in contrast with the average of a more numerous peer group. FODS was also criticised as costly, as well as for having been a 'very blunt instrument' by an external consultant's report (Field, 1984).

The Taxation Office is also able to identify tax avoidance practices by monitoring trends in individual returns.

We've always monitored tax avoidance . . . Avoidance, generally speaking, depends on the taxpayer manufacturing a deduction in some way or another. When a taxpayer who has been returning a taxable income of $100,000 every year for the last eight years suddenly returns a taxable income of nil, and that taxable income of nil is the result of a claim of a deduction for purchase and sale of shares in some sort of Curran scheme, it's totally obvious to us . . .

While such more blatant examples are undoubtedly detectable, when the Auditor-General reports that assessors average between 2.4 and 11.4 minutes on each income tax return, depending on the type of return, one wonders about the capacity to detect more subtle avoidance (Australian Audit Office, 1984, 16). Even more difficult is the detection of tax evasion, where income (other than wage or salary income) is understated or unstated. The sheer volume of the task confronting the ATO is daunting. Their objective is, by 1992, to increase post assessment audits from 0.4 to 2 per cent of all tax returns lodged each year by non-salary and wage earners. It has been suggested that the burdens of the ATO could be reduced substantially through better use of computer technology in processing tax returns (Australian Audit Office, 1984a, iii).

Whilst in years past, customs control was based on physical inspection, today it is primarily based on the monitoring of documentation.

The emphasis is on companies keeping appropriate records that we can then check in a documentary sense. Otherwise commerce would just grind to a halt.

The department has established a data base which permits random selection of invoices for physical compliance checks.

In addition to that, of course, if we have reason to believe that in the commercial area certain suppliers' documents may be suspect, or that examination in respect of certain goods may be suspect, we are able to feed into our computer systems flags for the officer checking the documentation to pay particular attention to these aspects. That in turn may lead to more detailed checking and perhaps physical documentation.

The department, moreover, is seeking to enlist the support of customs agents in introducing online entry of invoice data.

The department runs a computer entry processing system. If certain agents and importers choose to avail themselves of that system, they can hook into the Customs computer, and they can create the necessary documents in their own office. They can lodge entries prior to the vessel's arriving or the aircraft arriving, and all customs documentary checks are done prior to the goods arriving. But it is better for them and better for us as it gives us more chance to look at the documents. Impediments to delivery can be resolved in many cases prior to the arrival of the carrying vessel.

The detection of valuation fraud remains a problem for the Customs Service. An importer may present invoices suggesting that the consignment is valued at a certain price, and that the specified amount has been remitted overseas. There may, however, have been a second payment by some other means. Lack of access to banking records was cited as an impediment to assembling sufficient evidence to sustain prosecutions.

Each agency also discovers offences as the result of third party complaints. Approximately 50 per cent of medifraud cases coming to light have arisen from information provided by patients and associates of the offending doctor. One unlucky doctor, who may have been a competent medical practitioner, but who was obviously unskilled in the art of deception, was 'dobbed in' for fraudulent billing jointly by his wife and his jilted receptionist.

The Commissioner of Taxation has also relied on tip-offs from members of the public. No rewards are payable by the Taxation Office for information leading to recovery of unpaid taxes as is the case in the United States.

On the other hand, the Customs Service receives public complaints, often motivated by financial self interest. Fraudulent valuation of imported goods gives a competitive advantage over locally produced products or imported products on which full duty has been paid. Local manufacturers and honest importers thus have no qualms about calling fraudulent activity to the attention of customs authorities.

Enforcement Strategies

A significant characteristic of the three agencies is their enforcement orientation. Unlike most of the other regulatory bodies we studied, each of the three has a written enforcement policy.

An example of written enforcement guidelines for commercial breaches appears in the *Australian Customs Service Manual*:

(2) Prosecution proceedings should be taken in the following circumstances:
   (a) cases involving deliberate evasion or attempted evasion of the revenue or circumvention, or attempted circumvention of Customs and Excise controls;
   (b) gross negligence;
   (c) serious instances of negligence or carelessness involving short payment of revenue in excess of $1,000;
   (d) repeated transgressions of a minor nature where the company concerned has made no effort to comply with Customs requirements despite counsellings and/or warnings;
   (e) recidivists.
(3) Consideration is to be given to joining company management along with the corporate body where the elements of the offence can be directed to individuals.

The Commonwealth Department of Health claimed to have adopted an aggressively prosecutorial stance in the aftermath of the attention it received in the early 1980s.

The department received severe criticism by the Public Accounts Committee. They implied an attitude of leniency and being soft on doctors. That is not on anymore, and it has nothing to do with the change of government.

The primary purpose of prosecution, according to the department, was not the recovery of moneys, but to punish offenders and to deter misconduct.

The Commonwealth Department of Health Surveillance and Investigation Division was one of only two of the ninety-six enforcement agencies we visited which had set a target number of prosecutions. Their goal was 100 successful prosecutions each year, leading to eighty disqualifications from the medical benefits programme. This emphasis on a 'darg' led to the criticism that the health department was more interested in quantity rather than quality, and was therefore pursuing the easy, simple fraud cases at the expense of the larger frauds (Rupert Public Interest Movement 1984, 7). It was suggested in our interview that because of the length of time involved in investigating an offender and in bringing him or her to trial, the recently heralded crackdown on medifraud would not be reflected in prosecution statistics for at least two years. Data from the previous four years confirm that the department has a long way to go to achieve its annual target of 100 convictions (Table 1).

In contrast to its strict law enforcement approach to the question of medifraud, the strategy adopted in the face of over-servicing was one of counselling. The department employed its own medical doctors as counsellors, who called upon those medical practioners whose billing patterns suggested that they may have been over-servicing.

Table 1
Commonwealth Department of Health:
**Prosecutions of Providers for Medical
Fraud Offences 1980-84**

Period	Convictions	Charges Proven but no Convictions*	Unsuccessful	Total
1980-81	12	3	1	16
1981-82	10	9	1	20
1982-83	5	8	7	20
1983-84	6	6	6	18

* Amendments to the Health Insurance Act, which came into effect on 1 November 1982, provide for disqualification from the medical benefits programme when two charges are proven.

Source: Commonwealth Department of Health

The first call was more of a courtesy visit. The counsellor inquired if the doctor had encountered any difficulties with the medical benefits scheme, and asked if she or he could be of any assistance.

Those who we believe are over-servicing will naturally attract priority visiting, with greater frequency. Their practice patterns are of course monitored following these visits to see if they cut it out or not.

On a subsequent visit the counsellor may have requested an explanation for aberrant billing practices. Should an appropriate response not be forthcoming, a case may have been referred to a Medical Services Committee of Inquiry (MSCI). This panel of five medical practitioners includes four doctors appointed by the Commonwealth Minister for Health in consultation with the AMA. The system of committees is not without problems, however. It was estimated in 1984 that the New South Wales Committee had a thirteen year backlog of cases (Field, 1984, vi). The responsibility for administering the secretariat tasks for MSCIs, and referring matters to them, was transferred to the Health Insurance Commission in May 1985.

Should the committee find that over-servicing has in fact occurred, it can recommend to the minister that the doctor in question be counselled, reprimanded, or that the doctor's name be gazetted (and thereby made public in the commonwealth government *Gazette*), and that he or she be required to re-pay the benefit payments for the services determined to be excessive. Only $44,000 in repayments determinations resulted from the MSCIs during the twelve months to 30 June 1984. Recent consideration has been given to replacing the committees with permanent independent tribunals, subject to normal administrative appeals procedures.

As noted above, the Australian Taxation Office sees its primary responsibility as one of efficient revenue collection. To this end, the determining factor in its decision to invoke the legal process (civil or criminal) has tended to be that of cost-effectiveness. In response to criticism by the Auditor-General that more resources could have been applied to handling sales tax avoidance, the Commissioner of Taxation replied: 'The fact is that at the time the limited number of officers available with the necessary experience and skill were devoted to work of a higher priority' (Commonwealth Commissioner of Taxation, 1984, 29).

The task confronting the ATO is an impossible one. In his 1984 annual report, for example, the commissioner considered the problem of trust stripping schemes: schemes designed so that income of a family trust was purportedly distributed through a chain of trusts to persons or entities associated with a promoter, so that they pay no tax on the income. The commissioner reported the identification of 5,000 target trusts which had participated in one or more trust stripping schemes (Commonwealth Commissioner of Taxation, 1984, 19). Pre-tax strips of company profits were considered on the next page of the annual report; there, 6,059 companies had been targeted. Against the background of such figures, a referral of only eight cases to the special prosecutor, Mr Gyles, during 1983-84 for further investigation and prosecution under the *Crimes (Taxation Offences) Act* 1980 hardly provides an historic lesson in deterrence for rational tax offenders (Commonwealth Commissioner of Taxation, 1984, 19). By April 1985, a further twelve cases had been referred to the Director of Public Prosecutions (DPP).

On the other hand, the real sting in the taxation commissioner's tail does not come from referring cases to the DPP for criminal enforcement. By 31 August 1984, $370 million had been recovered through civil remedies from the pre-tax strips of company profits mentioned above, and recovery of $200 million in unpaid tax was predicted for the following twelve months (Commonwealth Commissioner of Taxation, 1984, 21). This by far exceeds any reasonable expectations of financial penalties which might be imposed through the criminal process.

The principal regulatory strategy employed by the ATO is the administrative imposition of additional tax. Consider a further illustration. Prosecutions for breaches of the Sales Tax Assessment Acts and the Sales Tax Procedure Act netted total fines during 1982-83 of $313,-886 (Commonwealth Commissioner of Taxation, 1984, 84). In contrast, additional tax charged for failure to furnish sales tax returns, for furnishing false returns, or for understating the sale value of goods during 1982-83 was $75 million (Commonwealth Commissioner of Taxation, 1984, 83). The same annual report also noted assessments on 148 taxpayers involved in 'paper' sales tax schemes for $108 million tax and $100 million additional tax. Clearly, it is the threat of administrative imposition of additional tax which is the most potent threat to the dishonest taxpayer. In addition to the greater financial stakes involved, this route to enforcement is also more powerful because of the less onerous burdens of proof on the state compared with the criminal process.

None of this is to say that the Taxation Office is a non-prosecutorial agency. In fact, it is by far the most prosecutorial business regulatory agency in Australia. While the numbers of prosecution cases are much lower than the cases where penalty taxes are administratively imposed, they are still at a staggering level. In 1982-83 there were 102,345 prosecutions. Perhaps a majority of these were of individuals rather than companies, which are the concern of our study. However, within this number there are whole categories of prosecutions which are almost entirely the province of corporate offenders.

The most important category of this kind is prosecutions for breaches of the Sales Tax Assessment Act and the Sales Tax Procedure Act, of which there were 4,396 in 1982-83. No other business regulatory agency in Australia has anywhere near the number of prosecutions in this category alone.

The criticism of the ATO cannot be that it fails to prosecute, because it does so on a monumental scale. Even so, the Auditor-General has said that 'if more staff were engaged in areas devoted to enforcement activities, the effectiveness of the ATO's operations would be enhanced' (Australian Audit Office, 1984a, iii). But a louder criticism has been that the ATO prosecutes the minor cases while eschewing substantial investigative effort on major tax criminals with the excuse that these are matters for the DPP and the Australian Federal Police. Granted, by early 1985 the ATO had twenty-seven people on secondment to the DPP on various task forces.

The minor nature of most ATO prosecutions is evidenced by the average fine for the 102,345 cases in 1982-83 of $76. To be fair to the ATO, the maximum penalty for the great bulk of these cases — failure to lodge returns — was, until recently, a mere $200. The ATO contends that its lodgement enforcement policy is geared toward the tax avoiders and high income taxpayers. Moreover, in response to an earlier draft of this chapter, the ATO advised us that eighty people were engaged in assessing high profile bottom of the harbour promoters, not to mention 215 officers employed in the various Recoupment Tax Sections of the office, who have a large role in assessing bottom of the harbour matters. These do not seem to us to be very large numbers for an agency with over 15,000 officers, nor do they change the fact that prosecutions continue to be for minor offences, and that the recent exception to this pattern — major criminal cases against bottom of the harbour offenders — was in some measure prodded by extraordinary external pressure generated by the Costigan Royal Commission.

Special Prosecutors Gyles and Redlich have both been especially critical of the paralysis of the Taxation Office when confronted with major offenders. The following quotations from Mr Redlich's 1984 annual report illustrate:

The shortage of investigative officers with accounting expertise has seen some important matters left for months, and in some cases years, before investigation is commenced . . .
Until now the major criminal has had no need to fear the investigative resources or techniques of the Taxation Office. They seemed well aware of the fact that the Taxation Office did not have the means, and often lacked an appreciation of its own expertise to move quickly in taxing the proceeds of crime . . .
The Taxation Office must, as I have reported previously, reorder its priorities and tackle more complicated taxpayers affairs, otherwise the increase in resources will be of only marginal significance (Redlich, 1984, 103).
The apocalypse of the 'bottom of the harbour' was not, save for its magnitude, an exceptional example of a bureaucratic inefficiency. Rather it was indicative of a degree of malaise within regulatory bodies (Redlich, 1984, vii).

The Australian public might indeed ask that if the largest business regulatory agency in Australia, one with over 15,000 employees, has to pass responsibility onto others for dealing with its most difficult cases of non-compliance, whether by its own choice or that of its political masters, then what hope is there for any agency to deal with our worst white collar criminals? Recent penalty increases under the Income Tax Assessment Act may increase the incentive to pursue criminal as well as civil remedies with major cases: companies can now be fined $50,000 plus three times their unpaid tax for falsifying records. At the nub of the problem is the commissioner's total preoccupation with cost-effective revenue maximisation:

The Taxation Office too often elected not to unravel the corporate structure which a criminal employed to hide his assets because Tax officers could spend that time dealing with straightforward returns of other taxpayers and thereby recover the same or greater revenue (Redlich, 1984, 131).

This was short-sighted cost-effectiveness indeed. It created a climate in Australia where ruthless offenders knew that so long as they maintained their affairs in a sufficiently complicated manner as to render taxation investigation 'cost-ineffective', they would be left alone while the authorities chased the easy dollars of less dishonest citizens. This has not only encouraged tax fraud, it has discouraged more honest citizens from being totally open with a tax system which they have increasingly perceived as rotten.

Whether or not to pursue investigations which cost more than they recoup from offenders is a general dilemma business regulators must confront. The Commonwealth Department of Health, for example, has not recovered from dishonest doctors the $8 million a year spent on medical benefits enforcement. Certainly they cannot claim, as does the Taxation Office, that new audit staff recoup an average of ten times their salary.

Of the three agencies concerned with the prevention and control of fraud, the health department placed greatest emphasis on the deterrent value of prosecution, at least at the time of our interview in late 1984.

I suspect that the activity we take on the fraud side, as we escalate our numbers of prosecutions and as we escalate our numbers of disqualifications, will have a beneficial spin off effect in terms of over-servicing as well. Doctors are just going to say, 'This system, it bites'.
Doctors at 'X', where Doctor 'Y' lives, must be thinking twice about the service they give to patients. They know Doctor 'Y' has got to re-pay $120,000.

From time to time, medifraud prosecutions also have a general educative function:

Occasionally, to demonstrate to the community at large, to the medical profession, and to the judiciary that fraud is a problem and it does exist, we will lay 150-200 charges against each of a number of doctors.

It should be noted that the deterrent value of medifraud prosecutions lies not so much in the criminal penalties which might be imposed in the event of conviction, but in the threat of automatic disqualification from the medical benefits programme should two charges of fraud be proven in court. There had only been four such disqualifications to May 1985, however.

The Customs Service relies more heavily than the other two agencies upon informal administrative responses to corporate misconduct, such as withdrawal of privileges which make life easier for importers:

Provision exists for an importer to move goods between bond stores or to move them to his own premises with permission of the Customs Service. Such privileges may not always be granted. People must maintain the correct records of the way their cargo is moving, how it's accounted for. If they don't match up, permission to remove their goods can be cancelled.

Customs authorities, of course, are empowered to inspect all cargo, and can make life very difficult for an importer should they require that a forty foot container be opened on the waterfront.

Informal administrative arrangements of the Taxation Office include late lodgement programmes made available to tax agents to assist them in the management of their workload. If tax agents do not strictly comply, their arrangement is cancelled, and their clients face late lodgement penalties.

The Customs Service also makes considerable use of prosecutions as an enforcement tool. However, Figure 1 shows that there has been a considerable drop in these cases. In fact, the number of convictions each year during the 1980s has been at only a quarter of the level in the mid-1960s. This drop is partly due to the re-allocation of resources to investigate corporate breaches after clearance at the barrier. The prosecutions are of two main types: the larger group involves customs offences by individual passengers detected at the barrier, the second, excise and revenue offences. The second group are the predominantly corporate offences.

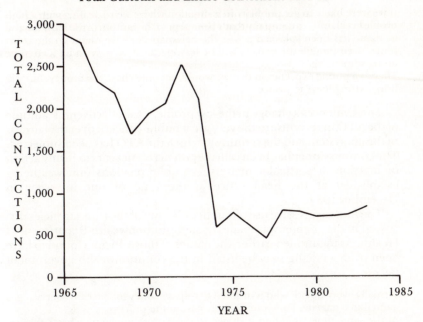

Figure 1
Australian Customs Service
Total Customs and Excise Convictions 1965-85

Publicity

The three agencies concerned with preventing and controlling fraud against the government vary markedly in their use of publicity as a regulatory tool. Customs officials tend not to call media attention to their actions. On the other hand, the threat of a dumping notice, which would ultimately reach the attention of the world trading community, has prompted exporters to alter their prices.

The exporter will commonly want to avoid adverse publicity inherent in the publication of a dumping notice, and he will say, 'Well, don't do that. I'll undertake to raise my export price to the normal value level'.

The Taxation Office has occasionally used publicity as a regulatory tool, but not aggressively so. This may be explained in part by the traditional low profile of the office, and for its very great concern to protect the privacy of an individual taxpayer's affairs.

Nevertheless, the names of offending taxpayers were published in the Commissioner for Taxation's annual report, along with amounts of assessed tax and penalties. This annual list of tax evaders received good press coverage in most states. In late 1985, however, the Taxation Office announced that it had abandoned the policy of systematically naming defaulters.

Occasionally the office will prosecute in order to attract media atten
tion for purposes of public reassurance as much as regulation.

If we were likely to get publicity in a situation where we're dealing with a high
profile tax claim — a company that's been sent to the bottom of the harbour and
its name has been splashed across the newspapers — we might go the court
route, even though the penalty will be less, because we have to be seen to be
doing something.
There's a public expectation that we would not only chase the money, but will
bring wrongdoers to justice.

This evidences a change in the low profile, 'cost-effectiveness' attitude
of the ATO in response to the very great public concern over the fairness
of the tax system and the scrutiny to which the ATO has been subjected.
The commissioner has been called upon in recent years to justify action
or inaction in particular matters. A public relations unit was being
established at the head office at the time of our interview in
December 1984.

The most aggressive use of publicity by any of the three agencies discussed in the chapter was made by the Commonwealth Department of
Health. As mentioned earlier, the names of those doctors found to have
been over-servicing may be listed in the commonwealth government
Gazette:

Virtually every doctor who is ordered to re-pay money for excessive servicing is
named in a gazette. Everyone. That is part of the process.
At the same time, attention is drawn to the gazette notice by a press release.
In addition, their names have been published in the department's annual
report.

Disqualification from the medical benefits programme attracts more
attention, for a number of reasons.

With fraud, the minister will normally issue a press release, and we will
make sure that the press release comes to the attention of the media...
When we disqualify a doctor, there is fairly extensive publicity about
that fact. The primary stated purpose is to ensure that patients are not
caught out by going to a doctor who is disqualified and then they go
along to get a refund and they can't get one... I suppose it is true to say
that the secondary unstated purpose is in fact deterrence.

We put ads in the paper. We put them in the *Australian* and the *Sydney
Morning Herald*. We put them in the local paper, like the *Campbelltown
Star*. We also require the doctor to display in the surgery a sign saying he
is disqualified. We tell him where he has got to place it.

We give him a form and we also require him, before he gives a service
to any patient, to hand that form to that patient. The form reads 'I am a
disqualified practitioner. If you come to me and I give you a medical service you won't get benefits for it'.

Self-Regulation

The three departments differ in the extent to which they are able to foster self-regulation in furtherance of their aims. The organized medical profession has a vested interest in maintaining a public image of propriety and rectitude, and as such, one would expect it to be most actively involved in the suppression of medical benefits abuses. The Medical Services Committee of Inquiry system relies very heavily upon professional review mechanisms. On the other hand, the profession tends to be defensive and generally reluctant to discipline members who have engaged in misconduct.

The Commonwealth Department of Health not only endeavours to consult the medical profession about steps to be taken to control abuses, it actively involves the profession in the regulatory process. Nominees of the profession sit on Medical Services Committees of Inquiry, as noted earlier. In addition, the department provides professional organizations, the AMA, and the various medical colleges, with systematic information regarding over-servicing trends and practices.

We might, for example, advise them that ENT specialists in North Adelaide are abusing item no. XYZ in terms of over-servicing.

It is expected that the professional organizations will then exercise peer pressure to discourage abuses.

The majority of the commercial community importing goods employ the services of customs agents. Licensed by the Collector of Customs under the Customs Act, customs agents are intimately familiar with invoice and documentation procedures. A National Customs Agents Licensing and Advisory Committee, consisting of representatives of the Customs Agents Federation of Australia and the Customs Agents Institute of Australia assist the department in controlling entry to the profession by conducting preliminary background investigations and interviews of prospective agents. Whilst ultimate power of apppointment and suspension resides with the minister, the department at the time of our interview was considering providing some decision making powers to the National Customs Agents Licensing and Advisory Committee.

Because of the diversity of its clientele, self-regulation is less of an option for the Taxation Office than it is for the Department of Health or the Customs Service. The office takes great pains to disseminate rulings to taxpayers.

We're about explaining the laws to them. We try to explain as much as we can in order to avoid inadvertent non-compliance.

The Australian Taxation Office is introducing an alternative approach to processing business tax returns, which would involve abandoning the traditional methods of assessment by its own officers in favour of a system of self-assessment by business taxpayers. An internal review of assessment procedures suggested that it might be more cost-effective to accept business returns at face value, but to use resources otherwise devoted to assessment to subject a greater number of companies to investigation (McCathie, 1985, 3). Whether the increased threat of investigation will constitute a credible deterrent to evasion of tax remains to be seen.

Substantial decentralization of operations characterized the regulatory regimes of the health department and the ATO, although a more centralized management system was introduced at the health department in the aftermath of criticisms by the Public Accounts Committee when department officers in Victoria disclosed to a number of doctors that they were being investigated. The Joint Committee of Public Accounts drew attention to wide variations from state to state in the number of successful prosecutions and in the amount of funds involved in those cases prosecuted (1982, 87).

Prior to 1979, the operations of the ATO were considerably decentralized. There was no co-ordinating body for investigations and audits. Generally speaking it was left to the local knowledge of the Deputy Commissioner in each state to concentrate on particular projects and areas for investigation. The Auditor-General has called attention to substantial interstate differences in patterns of investigation and prosecution with regard to the collection of sales tax. A new directorate in the head office has been formed with a view toward establishing a uniform national prosecution policy.

Conclusion

Compared with other areas of business regulation in Australia, customs, tax, and medifraud (in the latter case, at least until mid-1985) are relatively prosecutorial regimes. This is so even though customs prosecutions have declined dramatically since the 1960s, and tax and medifraud enforcement has been under public attack for 'catching the minnows while ignoring the sharks'.

It has also been shown that use of adverse publicity and appealing to relevant licensing bodies to suspend licences of customs and tax agents, and to deregister doctors are also used from time to time as alternative enforcement tools. More important than any of the above, however, are the ways these agencies can effect control through administrative actions: withdrawal by the Customs Service of privileges to move goods to warehouses without physical inspection, or for weekly settlement rather than settlement for each transaction; penalty tax assessments by the Taxation Office; and recoupment of medical benefits payments and disqualification from participation in the medical benefits programme.

Finally, negotiation is central to the strategies of all three agencies. This can take the form of a counsellor suggesting to a doctor to change patterns of practice which amount to over-servicing, or the possibility of increased physical checks by customs officers of a customs agent's shipments if the agent's performance in the entry of goods has been poor. Negotiation over the complex and disputed facts of corporate tax returns is also the only way the Taxation Office can manage its enormous volume of work. We were told when a large transnational company submits a transfer price on intra-corporate sales which reduce taxable profits, the Taxation Office would usually:

Sit down with the company and say, 'Look, we think the arms length price is this . . . Look at this range of prices we have from other companies dealing in the same kinds of goods under what we think are the same kinds of conditions. Are there any special conditions attached to your import or sale? . . . They would then so argue. We will either accept their representation or we won't. We will then say, well you haven't convinced us. We generally raise the assessments and again a consultation process goes on. They'll come back and we'll still talk after the assessments have been raised and if we still can't reach agreement, its up to the courts to decide.

Such negotiation is the real stuff of this, and in fact most, domains of business regulation.

Postscript: A Backdown on Medifraud?

In March 1985 the Commonwealth Minister for Health heralded a significant change in strategy regarding medical benefits abuses. He announced the transfer of all existing surveillance and investigations functions of the Commonwealth Department of Health to the Commonwealth Health Insurance Commission, the statutory authority responsible for processing Medicare claims and dispensing benefits.

Whilst the minister sought to justify the transfer in terms of administrative efficiency, he referred explicitly to a 'new approach to addressing the abuses of the medical benefits arrangements' (Blewett, 1985). A report on which his decision was based recommended the abandonment of an aggressively prosecutorial approach to medical benefits fraud (Field, 1984).

Although the future dimensions of medical benefits regulation remained unclear, the general manager of the Health Insurance Commission referred to: 'a strong emphasis on the development and maintenance of liaison and rapport with medical representative bodies, such as the AMA, and with the medical practitioners themselves and to the elimination of the central investigations task force and other similar "flying squad" tactics' (Wilcox, 1985, 6).

Within days after the announcement of these proposed changes, federal cabinet approved a number of other measures, including increased remuneration for doctors, designed to resolve an ongoing dispute with the medical profession which had disrupted public hospital services in New South Wales for the previous three months.

It seemed likely that the transfer of medifraud investigations to the Health Insurance Commission would lead to an abandonment of the aggressively adversarial and prosecutorial regulatory regime which briefly characterized the health department, and to a reduction of about forty in the staff devoted to medifraud enforcement.

By contrast, the commonwealth government recently appeared ready and willing to use the criminal process against its own officers. Within hours of the unauthorized publication of statistics on doctors' incomes from the medical benefits programme, the Commonwealth Minister for Health called in the Australian Federal Police to investigate. The Secretary for Health assured the medical profession that:

If the investigation shows that there was such a disclosure, action will, of course, be taken against any person or persons identified as being responsible (*Sydney Morning Herald*, 3 May 1985, 26).

This rhetoric is certainly unfortunate since it gives the impression, perhaps false, that the authorities concerned with health administration are more vigorous in their defence of the principle of confidentiality of doctors' incomes than in their efforts to ascertain how those incomes, derived from the public purse, were actually earned.

References and Recommended Reading*

Australian Audit Office (1984a), 'Processing and Assessment of Income Tax Returns', *Reports of the Auditor-General on Efficiency Audits*, Australian Government Publishing Service, Canberra.

—— (1984b), 'Collection of Sales Tax by the Australian Taxation Office', *Reports of the Auditor-General on Efficiency Audits*, Australian Government Publishing Service, Canberra, 85-112.

Australian Customs Service (no date), *Australian Customs Service Manual*, Commonwealth Department of Industry and Commerce, Canberra.

Blewett, N. (1985), 'Covering letter to Senator G. Georges', *Papers Relating to Location of Surveillance and Investigation Functions in the Health Portfolio*, Commonwealth Department of Health, Canberra.

Commonwealth Commissioner of Taxation (1984), *Sixty Third Report, 1983-84*, Australian Government Publishing Service, Canberra.

*Costigan, F. (1982a), *Royal Commission on the Activities of the Federated Ship Painters and Dockers Union, Interim Report No. 3*, Australian Government Publishing Service, Canberra.

—— (1982b), *Royal Commission on the Activities of the Federated Ship Painters and Dockers Union, Interim Report No. 4, Volume 1*, Australian Government Publishing Service, Canberra.

Crough, G.J. (1981), *Taxation Transfer Pricing and the High Court of Australia: A Case Study of the Aluminium Industry*, Transnational Corporations Research Project, University of Sydney.

Draft White Paper (1985), *Reform of the Australian Tax System*, Australian Government Publishing Service, Canberra.

Field, G. (1984), *The Respective Involvements of the Health Insurance Commission and the Department in Combatting Abuse of the Medical Benefits Arrangements*, Commonwealth Department of Health, Canberra.

Gyles, R. (1984), *Report to the Attorney-General for the Year Ended 30 June 1984*, Australian Government Publishing Service, Canberra.

*Joint Committee of Public Accounts (1982), *Medical Fraud and Overservicing Progress Report (Report 203)*, Australian Government Publishing Service, Canberra.

Medical Practice (1983), 'AMA Accepts Government Estimate of $100 Million', *Medical Practice*, 7, 12-13.

McCabe, P. and La Franchi, D. (1982), *Report of Inspectors Appointed to Investigate the Particular Affairs of Navillus Pty Ltd and 922 Other Companies*, Government Printer, Melbourne.

McCathie, A. (1985), 'Tax Man Takes Fresh Look at Business', *Financial Review*, 15 March, 3.

Parsons, R. (1984), 'Reforming the System: A Lawyer's View', in D.J. Collins (ed.), *Tax Avoidance and the Economy*, Australian Tax Research Foundation, Sydney.

Redlich, R. (1983), *Annual Report of the Special Prosecutor 1982-83*, Australian Government Publishing Service, Canberra.

—— (1984), *Annual Report of the Special Prosecutor 1983-84*, Australian Government Publishing Service, Canberra.

*Rupert Public Interest Movement (1984), *Medifraud: A Professionally Induced Cancer*, Rupert Public Interest Movement, Canberra.

Wilcox, C. (1985), 'Medical Fraud and Overservicing', *Health Insurance Commission Minute 85/209 (21 March)*, Health Insurance Commission, Canberra.

13
Miscellaneous Regulatory Agencies: Fisheries, Patents, Arbitration, Building, Media

Fisheries Regulation

Although the waters surrounding Australia have low nutrient content, fish stocks have been kept in good condition by regulation of fishing. Recent years have seen increased market demand for rock lobsters, prawns, and abalone. Were no strict controls placed on the exploitation of certain species, stocks would become severely depleted. Only limited supplies would be available to the public, and at great cost.

The goal of fisheries regulation in Australia is to restrict access to these resources in a manner which ensures their optimal exploitation and survival. The beneficiaries of regulation are those commercial interests who enjoy access to fisheries, people who fish for recreation, and the Australian consumer who gets an abundant supply of seafood.

Fisheries regulation does not extend to matters of quality control. The inspection of fish for export is the responsibility of the Export Inspection Service (EIS) of the Commonwealth Department of Primary Industry. The hygiene status of fish for domestic consumption is occasionally monitored by state and local health authorities. Whether fish sold as barramundi are in fact something else remains a matter for consumer affairs agencies and food inspectorates in state health departments.

The organization of fisheries regulation varies significantly across Australian jurisdictions. In some states, such as South Australia and Western Australia, the functions of management (including research and technical assistance) and enforcement are combined in a fisheries department. Elsewhere, however, management and inspectorial functions are separate. In Queensland, enforcement is the responsibility of the Boating and Fisheries Patrol, which is part of the Department of Harbours and Marine. Fisheries research and administration remain the responsibility of the Queensland Department of Primary Industries. The Tasmanian fisheries inspectorate was actually integrated into the state police force in 1985. Research and technical assistance in Tasmania is provided by separate Departments of Sea Fisheries and Inland Fisheries.

The basic instrument of commercial fisheries regulation common to all Australian jurisdictions is the licence. A variety of conditions may be attached to a licence; right of access may be limited to a specific fishery, to a certain species, during a defined period.

The entitlement conferred by a fisheries licence may be lucrative indeed. Because of this, and because the number of active licences is stringently controlled, licences are costly. The value of a rock lobster licence in Western Australia or of a prawn fisheries licence in South Australia can approach $500,000.

Enforcement of fisheries regulation occurs primarily through patrol. Inspectorates are equipped with high speed boats and aircraft; inspectors may be assisted in detecting illegalities by law abiding fishing crews who stand to be disadvantaged financially by the predation of their competitors. In most jurisdictions police are also available to assist in enforcement.

Sanctions available to fisheries authorities are numerous and varied. The mildest response involves informal and formal warnings. Criminal prosecution, the most commonly used formal sanction, may result in a monetary fine. A much greater deterrent threat resides in the power to confiscate a catch, or to suspend or cancel a licence. Because of the value of these entitlements, suspension or cancellation constitutes the most severe penalties imposed in fact. Confiscation of equipment, or of an entire vessel may also occur, if only rarely.

In most jurisdictions, penalties awarded subsequent to conviction on criminal charges are relatively low. Recent amendments to the South Australian Fisheries Act raised the maximum fine available from $200 to $10,000, which approximates the gain which might be derived from an unfair early start on the prawn season.

Patent Regulation

In most western societies, a common means of encouraging invention and technological innovation is to grant the inventor a patent: a proprietory right in his or her invention. Without such ownership, it is argued, creations could be appropriated at will, with neither attribution nor remuneration flowing to the inventor. The incentive to create and invent would thus be significantly diminished.

The Australian Patents Trademarks and Designs Office seeks to encourage Australian innovators, and thereby to foster Australian industry and commerce by registering inventions and conferring proprietary rights. The basic function of the Patents Office is the processing of applications and the registering of trademarks and patents. These administrative tasks are not insignificant, as some 30,000 applications for patents, trademarks, or designs are lodged with the office each year. The office does not police the marketplace to determine whether a patent has been infringed, nor does it take legal action in the event of an infringement. Rather, sole responsibility for enforcing these rights rests with the patent holder. In the course of our interview, one respondent compared the role of the Patents Office with that of a land titles office. The Patents Office will register a 'title' as it were, but is not responsible for defending the rights of the patent holder. Just as a lands registry would be unconcerned with trespass upon land or with illicit exploitation of land, so too is the Patents Office unconcerned with violations of patents. The inventor fends for him or herself.

Civil remedies are available, of course, to the patent holder whose rights are infringed. The Patents Office does not see it as its role to provide legal advice or legal assistance, beyond some very general advice on how to protect a patent.

Despite the presence of numerous penalty clauses in the acts which it administers, it does not prosecute. The office reported only two convictions under the Trade Marks Act since federation, both occurring in 1976. Both of these were for falsifications of a trade mark, and in each case, investigation and prosecution was undertaken by the Commonwealth Police and the Attorney-General's Department.

Thus, the Patents Office is unique among the regulatory agencies we visited in that it confers rights which it leaves others to protect.

Arbitration Inspection

The Arbitration Inspectorate in the Commonwealth Department of Employment and Industrial Relations is a significant regulatory agency, with a total staff of 135. Its function is to ensure observance of all awards made pursuant to the *Conciliation and Arbitration Act* 1904, and to enforce rights and duties provided for in the act (e.g. the duty of employers to allow employees to exercise their right to join a union). State departments of labour all have much smaller inspectorates to enforce compliance with state industrial awards.

All inspectorates share an enforcement strategy of using litigation as a last resort; the goal is to persuade employers who underpay their workers to make good the short-fall. Offences are detected by inspections. The Commonwealth Arbitration Inspectorate estimated that 'up to 90 per cent' of prosecutions would have been initiated by a complaint (usually from a worker or union). Nevertheless, most inspections are part of a programmed approach to checking all award respondents periodically. Most employers react positively to requests by inspectors to rectify offences. In the ten months to 30 April 1984, 19,195 of 19,569 breaches of federal awards detected by inspectors were voluntarily rectified.

In the ten years to 30 June 1983, 127,330 award breaches and other offences were detected by the Commonwealth Arbitration Inspectorate. Only 413 of these resulted in convictions of employers for average fines of $114. These data relate to fines per charge, and defendants commonly face as many as ten charges. Moreover, it is usual for much larger amounts than the fines to be ordered by the court to be paid to workers.

Even so, the total amounts recovered from employers by federal arbitration inspectors are relatively small. Adding both voluntary payment of extra wages, and fines and payments ordered by courts following conviction, the total amount extracted by the inspectorate and the courts from non-complying employers in 1982-83 was $2,309,825. This compares with running costs for the inspectorate of $6,226,400 in the same year. It must be pointed out, however, that about a third of enforcement activity relates to non-monetary breaches.

The enforcement strategy of the Commonwealth Arbitration Inspectorate is relatively simple. There is no resort to adverse publicity against offenders or to fostering industry self-regulation. There is no negotiation over compliance; the standards in the awards and the act are regarded as non-negotiable. If the employer will not voluntarily put things right, then he or she is prosecuted, fined, and ordered to make restitution. Notwithstanding its widespread success in securing voluntary compliance, the inspectorate is, comparatively speaking, a relatively prosecutorial agency. Unions also from time to time prosecute employers on behalf of members.

We conducted interviews on arbitration inspection in only three of the states. Nevertheless, we feel confident enough to say that in most states arbitration inspection is also a relatively prosecutorial matter when compared with the use of prosecution by other agencies in this study. The South Australian Department of Labour, for example, has averaged seven such convictions a month between 1977 and 1984. There were 159 in New South Wales during 1983-84. The Queensland Industrial and Factories and Shops Inspectorate is probably the extreme case, launching 364 Industrial Conciliation and Arbitration Act prosecutions (excluding trading hours prosecutions) in 1982-83 and 566 in 1983-84. But as with the federal inspectorate, at least half the prosecution proceedings commenced are withdrawn when the defendant settles.

Building Regulation

The skylines of all Australian cities have changed dramatically over the past two decades, in a manner which has delighted some but repelled others. What is less subject to debate are the problems posed by structural unsoundness, hasty workmanship, and premature deterioration of building materials: conditions which are more prevalent than one would expect from a quick glance at a stately high rise building.

The issues are not trivial, as the recent collapse of relatively new buildings in Europe and North America would attest, as would the collapse of the West Gate bridge in Melbourne which killed thirty-five workers as a result of design inadequacies and safety margins which were much too low (Report of the Royal Commission, 1971). Then there are the economic costs. One CSIRO estimate of the annual maintenance expenses arising from high rise building deterioration in

Australia (such as the notorious 'concrete cancer' on the Gold Coast) is set at $3 billion per year (McDonald, 1984, 50).

The responsibility for ensuring good workmanship and structurally safe construction at most building sites in Australia rests with local government. In the course of our research, we visited four of the largest councils in Australia, the city councils of Sydney, Melbourne, Brisbane, and the Gold Coast.

The Australian Model Uniform Building Code, adopted throughout the nation, provides basic building standards. These include such items as protection of steelwork against erosion, provisions for reinforced concrete, and the bearing capacity of foundations. The enforcement of these standards is the task of each local council inspectorate.

In addition to the more common regulatory tools of warning and prosecution, councils wield the formidable threat of refusing to grant final clearance or to issue certificates of occupancy for a building. In extreme cases, councils may actually make their own modifications and bill a delinquent builder for costs; ultimately they may even order a building's demolition. There have been occasional instances of councils demolishing illegal structures themselves.

Most local authorities undertake only a few building prosecutions each year. The building inspectors to whom we spoke expressed reluctance to use the criminal process for a number of reasons. First among these is the common argument that the penalties available constitute an insufficient deterrent.

If I were paying $80,000 per month interest on a $20 million dollar loan, a fine of $500 wouldn't stop me.

The risk of defeat, and even humiliation, may also enter into a decision:

We wouldn't want to go to court because we wouldn't win. We'd get hopelessly swamped because the courts are opposed to us in the first place. We know that when we go into court . . . you feel the judge is almost laughing up his sleeve at you anyway for going to court over an issue which he thinks should be resolved in the first place.

Perhaps the most significant impediment to prosecution by local governments is political. Most councils pass judgement upon all recommendations to prosecute. This decision is delegated to the town clerk in the larger cities such as Brisbane and Melbourne, where thousands of building applications are processed annually. The Sydney City Council still makes the final decision on matters before it, however.

In discussing the disinclination to prosecute, one official told us:

It depends a lot on the elected representatives because I've seen it here, in the building area, where we have had builders as aldermen. My God, you talk about a hands-off sort of situation! Well, we wouldn't undertake more prosecutions, or we wouldn't make a determined effort to undertake more prosecutions unless instructed to by our superiors, the town clerk and aldermen. They would have to say that we detect from political considerations that the public is unhappy. . .

Indeed when we asked the head of one building inspectorate what the objectives of his agency were, he replied:

To promote the image of Council . . . and to ensure public safety.

Another chief inspector advised:

We don't do anything that will bring the council unfounded criticism.

Despite the uniform laws governing building regulation in Australia, some significant differences remain. The Gold Coast City Council, for example, does not require structural inspection of reinforced concrete. By contrast, an inspector must be present for every concrete pour in North Sydney. Power to require retrospective upgrading of a building exists in some jurisdictions, but not in others:

Say we have got an old building, built lawfully at the time, even though we may consider, because of a change in philosophy of fire safety, that the building is now quite dangerous to the occupants. In the Queensland legislation we have no authority to move in and upgrade that building. New South Wales does; Queensland doesn't.

Otherwise, strategies of building regulation appeared consistent across the four inspectorates we visited. Each devoted considerable resources to providing technical advice to builders. Each expressed a preference for a co-operative rather than an adversarial approach to building regulation. Each exhausted a very long string of warnings, notices to comply, and threats to prosecute before ever using the criminal process.

The Sydney City Council was unique amongst the building inspectorates we visited in providing a detailed set of inspection and enforcement instructions for its officers. The instructions list those aspects of a building site requiring inspection, provide explicit guidance on the service of notices to comply in the event a violation is detected, and set out procedures for follow-up inspections.

A common feature of the building inspectorates we visited was their willingness to bluff; that is, threaten to invoke powers that they don't really have.

People get a printed form, assuming that we can take action on it, but we can't.
Even the people in private business aren't too sure what we can do and what we can't do . . . You'll find that in many, many cases we use the Bluff Act, and we just tell people that we've got the power to do this, and we wouldn't have a clue. We wouldn't know whether we could or not. We don't care too much as long as we get done what we want to get done.

The other side can play their own game of bluff by insisting that their development has aldermanic support. After all, the most distinguishing characteristic of building inspection is the sensitivity of regulatory officials to the political process.

The Tangled Web of Media Regulation

The Australian Broadcasting Tribunal (ABT) is the only government regulatory agency devoted to media regulation. Australia entrusts most media control to a variety of self-regulatory mechanisms, and to private interests asserting their rights under state copyright and defamation laws, or the Trade Practices Act. The Trade Practices Commission and, to a lesser extent, state consumer affairs agencies, have a role in occasional enforcement action against misleading advertising claims. Under section 100 of the *Broadcasting and Television Act* 1942, the Secretary of the Commonwealth Department of Health has a role in approving all radio and television advertising of medicines. State and commonwealth censorship boards, privacy committees, and anti-discrimination agencies (see Chapter 11) also have some involvement in regulating the mass media.

Print media, the Australian Broadcasting Corporation (ABC), and the Special Broadcasting Service (SBS) are not subject to regulatory oversight by a specialized agency, the ABT being limited to non-government radio and television. Unsatisfactory resolution of complaints against the ABC and SBS occasionally leads to recourse to the Commonwealth Ombudsman. With print media, complaints about accuracy, denial of right of reply, and the like, can be lodged with the Australian Press Council. This is a voluntary industry body with the only sanction available to it being the power to require members to publish council determinations in favour of complainants. The Murdoch newspapers are not members.

The Media Council of Australia, the focal point of media self-regulation, is a trade association of virtually all of the private media proprietors in Australia. It promulgates a variety of voluntary advertising codes on topics ranging from alcohol advertising to slimming preparations. The Council seeks authorization of these codes from the Trade Practices Commission, which holds conferences with interested parties to help assess whether anti-competitive aspects of codes are outweighed by public benefit. Enforcement of the codes is by an industry-run Advertising Standards Council.

Below these bodies are a number of advertising approval organizations: the Commercials Acceptance Division of the Federation of Australian Commercial Television Stations, the Federation of Australian Radio Broadcasters which approves radio advertisements in advance of broadcast, and the Australian Publishers' Bureau which requires advertising agencies to submit draft print advertisements to which the Media Council's codes apply. Between them, these bodies approve in advance a significant proportion of advertisements which appear in Australia, though they achieve much less than majority coverage. The most anti-competitive kind of self-regulation is by the Joint Committee for Disparaging Copy, in which media, advertising, and advertising agency representatives can veto advertisments which contain a 'specific and identifiable disparagement of a particular product or service advertised by a rival'.

The Australian Broadcasting Tribunal

Functions

While none of the foregoing self-regulatory institutions came into existence as a result of any policy of fostering them by the ABT, the ABT has been given a role very much designed to mesh in with this self-regulatory apparatus. Day to day enforcement of standards is essentially entrusted to self-regulation, while the ABT concentrates on assessing the fitness of radio and television licence holders to have these renewed every three years.

The Commonwealth Department of Communications advises its minister on how many licences of different types should be issued; the ABT decides on public interest grounds which applicants will get licences. Licensing is necessary because the electro-magnetic spectrum is a scarce resource. There are 438 television and radio stations in Australia, and while the airwaves could carry many more, there are some technological limits. The main beneficiaries of licensing are the licence holders who have their profits protected from further competition.

Nevertheless, licence hearings also become occasions for asserting consumer interests in the service they get from broadcasters. The ABT is empowered to promulgate programme and advertising standards. Such standards cover, *inter alia*, the frequency of advertising, children's programmes, violence and obscenity, and set down minimum requirements for Australian content and frequency of broadcasting religious programmes. At licence renewal hearings, broadcasters are called to account over their compliance with these standards.

The ABT also has responsibility for approving or disapproving share transactions which create or increase prescribed interests in licences (Harding, 1984). It has a power (which it has never used) to order divestitures. The tribunal has the function of enforcing the ownership provisions of the Broadcasting and Television Act in a way which protects the public interest against the dangers of further concentration of media ownership and against takeovers by companies which are not 'fit and proper persons' to hold licences (ABT, 1984).

Regulatory Strategies

Violations of standards written by the ABT are offences under the Broadcasting and Television Act. Since the ABT was established in 1977, neither the ABT nor the Minister for Communications has ever launched such a prosecution. At the time of writing, however, a private prosecution under the act is before the courts; it was launched by a member of the non-smokers movement against Channel 10 for alleged cigarette advertising during the 1984 Sydney rugby league grand final telecast. The tribunal does not see it as its role to recommend prosecutions to its minister, though it does report breaches of the act to the minister.

The tribunal does not go so far as engage in systematic monitoring of radio and television programmes to assess compliance. Its predecessor, the Australian Broadcasting Control Board, did sample about 10 per cent of programmes for monitoring, and in its first year of operation the tribunal recommended that a Broadcasting Information Office be established within the tribunal to conduct, *inter alia*, 'random observation of programmes and advertisements and the checking of station logs and videotape records' (ABT, 1977, 18-19). This proposal was rejected by the government of the day, and in any case the chairman at the time of our interview was not in favour of random monitoring:

We just haven't got the resources to do any extensive monitoring, and personally, I'm not in favour of it anyway, quite frankly. As a technique, its a sort of 'big brother' arrangement.

Monitoring occurs selectively, almost entirely in response to complaints. Even then, the tribunal does not normally view or listen to tapes of the offending broadcast (which the station is required to keep for six weeks). For example, a complaint about excessive advertising during a programme will be dealt with by requesting the station to provide the tribunal with details of the advertising schedule for the programme.

The station may have given incorrect information. We accept that might be so. But the view we take based on our experience is that it's pretty unlikely that a station would stoop to dishonest conduct — say, giving us false information about the advertising schedule — because the consequence of that being detected could be very horrendous in terms of whether they are fit and proper persons to hold a licence.

The problem is, however, that no station has ever suffered this draconian consequence. What has happened on occasion is that staff, held to be responsible by the station, have been sacked. This approach to regulation brings a danger of scapegoating employees who commit an offence on behalf of a company which then sanctions them without any necessary regard for natural justice.

We had one recent example, where, with a television station, we put a condition on its licence about getting us information about advertising. And they gave us some information, and we had some other information available through some schedules for the same period. We looked at them and they didn't stand up. In the end it was ascertained that we were not being given correct information through the deficiencies of one of their staff who subsequently got sacked on the spot.

When the ABT has engaged in direct monitoring, the results have not encouraged trust in the stations. In 1983, the tribunal received complaints that radio stations were artificially loading Australian content in sample weeks, and confining Australian music to unpopular time slots. When it monitored nineteen commercial radio stations from around Australia, it found that eight did not comply with the 20 per cent Australian music content standard (*National Times*, 2-8 March 1984, 32). The station with the worst level of non-compliance was warned, and when re-monitored a month later (20 January 1984), was still found to be out of compliance.

Random monitoring has on occasion been undertaken by complainants. The Australian Consumers' Association (ACA) surveyed 902 Sydney television advertisements during one week in 1981 (ACA, 1982). It claimed that 127 of these had been judged by a panel of six persons trained in broadcasting law to violate either an ABT standard or a Media Council of Australia Code. After reviewing these allegations, the ABT concluded that only fourteen of the advertisements breached their standards or Media Council codes (ABT, 1983). No warnings were issued or other action taken by ABT on the fourteen complaints they upheld:

They'll be taken up with the stations at renewal of their licences. But they weren't of such magnitude that would warrant us taking any action in the meantime.

Thus, the entire enforcement strategy of the ABT rests on licence renewals. Yet, as we have already said, no licence has ever been revoked or suspended for failure to comply with ABT standards. However, five radio stations have suffered the sanction of having their licences extended for only one year instead of the maximum three, and one television station has had its licence extension shortened by six months. There have also been several cases where special conditions have been imposed on licences. For excessive advertising breaches, at least two stations have been required to provide monthly schedules of advertising to the tribunal. Another radio station was detected to be improperly conducting competitions; it was required to provide full details of all its competitions to the tribunal.

In addition, the tribunal also has the power to direct that certain personalities be taken off the air; it also has the power of censorship (section 101). In practice, the latter is applied after the event to stop an offensive programme from being repeated, or subsequent episodes in the same series from going to air.

When licences are issued, licensees give 'programme undertakings'. But again, as with the standards, there are no real sanctions if the undertakings are ignored. There is no power to put a station off the air for a short time without full-blown licence revocation hearings, nor is there any capacity to sanction an excessive advertising offence by cutting the permissible periods of advertising for a specified period, or to sanction an Australian content offence by requiring additional Australian content.

Conclusion

The enforcement strategy of the Australian Broadcasting Tribunal turns almost entirely on fostering a network of self-regulatory institutions and carpeting stations which breach standards at licence renewal hearings. Imposition of minor conditions on licences and limitation of licence terms are the only sanctions used. The regulatory regime is almost entirely reactive to complaints, licence applications, and requests for approval of ownership changes, there having been an explicit rejection of the more proactive appoach of the tribunal's predecessor, the Australian Broadcasting Control Board.

References and Recommended Reading*

*Armstrong, Mark, Blakeney, Michael, and Watterson, Ray, (1983), *Media Law in Australia*, Oxford University Press, Melbourne.

Australian Broadcasting Tribunal (1977), *Self-Regulation for Broadcasters*, Australian Government Publishing Service, Canberra.

—— (1983), *Report Re Complaint by the Australian Consumers' Association Concerning Various Television Advertisements*, Australian Broadcasting Tribunal, Sydney, 20 December.

—— (1984), *Fit and Proper Person*, (POS 09), Australian Broadcasting Tribunal, Sydney.

Australian Consumers' Association (1982), *Report on Law and Self Regulation of Advertising*, Australian Consumers' Association, Sydney.

Barnes, Shenagh and Blakeney, Michael (1982), *Advertising Regulation*, Law Book Company, Sydney.

*Harding, Richard (1984), 'Regulation of the Media Industries', in R. Tomasic (ed.), *Business Regulation in Australia*, CCH Australia, Sydney, 197-206.

McDonald, W. (1984), 'The Cancer that is Eating our High Rise Buildings', *Bulletin*, 4 September, 50-4.

Report of the Royal Commission into the Failure of the West Gate Bridge, (1971), Government Printer, Melbourne.

14
Variation in Regulatory Behaviour

In this chapter, we seek to describe variation in regulatory behaviour across all the agencies discussed above. This chapter is divided into two sections. First, we consider each of the major types of enforcement employed: self-regulatory enforcement, economic incentives, encouraging civil litigation, disclosure, pre-marketing clearance, licensing, prosecution, injunctions and directives, seizure, and adverse publicity.

Second, we address a number of key issues in regulatory variation: approaches to monitoring the costs of regulation, to regulatory accountability, to dealing with corruption, to the dangers of 'capture', to public involvement in the regulatory process, and to co-ordination between regulatory agencies.

Types of Enforcement
Self-Regulation and Co-Regulation
The first type of enforcement is really non-enforcement; it is the strategy of relying upon or encouraging business to regulate itself. No agency relied exclusively on self-regulation, but for fifty-seven (59.4 per cent) of them, self-regulation was described in interview as an important part of their regulatory strategy.

This can occur by negotiating agreements with industry associations for the writing of voluntary codes or guidelines. Sometimes the agreement will include provision for enforcement of compliance by the industry association and/or monitoring of compliance by the government. Where the latter occurs, many agencies prefer the term co-regulation to self-regulation.

Self-regulation is often encouraged on the basis that unless the industry makes a good fist of self-regulation, they can expect government command and control of some kind. However, such a social contract between government and industry is rarely explicit and, in many cases, self-regulation is entered into with total trust that self-regulation is the best strategy for the area concerned, and that no contemplation of regulatory escalation is required.

With some agencies, notably a number of general occupational health and safety inspectorates, there was a distrust of self-regulation. As one respondent put it: 'If self-regulation worked, Moses would have come down from Mt Sinai with the ten guidelines'.

The Economic Incentives Approach

Economists are continually urging that prescriptive regulation be abandoned in favour of imposing taxes on the harm which regulation is intended to control (Anderson *et al.*, 1977; Baumol and Oates, 1971; Kneese and Schultze, 1975). Thus, safer car design would not be encouraged by mandatory design standards but by imposing sales taxes which increased as the crashworthiness of the vehicle declined; pollution would not be outlawed, but polluters would pay an effluent charge for each quantum of pollution discharged from their pipes or stacks. There are two main advantages of this approach. First, when regulation mandates a specific technological fix to a problem, there is no incentive for companies to experiment with new control technologies which may prove superior. Second, penalizing the output of harm, rather than enforcing a prescribed means of preventing the harm, allows industry more scope to find the least cost method of reducing the harm: higher pollution from one outlet which is costly to control might be offset by extraordinarily low pollution from a second outlet where control is cheap.

No Australian business regulatory agency has adopted as part of its regulatory strategy an economic incentives approach to regulation. The only agencies where serious consideration has been given to the economists' preferred regulatory model are in the environmental area. With every Australian environmental protection agency, however, after such deliberation, the incentives model has been firmly rejected. A variety of reasons were given for this, but the most fundamental one was that it was simply impracticable with present regulatory resources. Monitoring the level of output of a harm like pollution in a way sufficiently reliable to provide the basis for tax rates would require enormous increases in inspectorial resources. Checking that a mandated pollution control device is properly installed on a smokestack takes a matter of minutes; testing the level of emission from a stack takes three days by the time scaffolding is erected and a suitable number of traverses completed.

While all of our regulatory agencies either rejected or had never considered an economic incentives approach as part of their regulatory strategy, there are areas of government policy beyond the direct control of regulatory agencies where economic disincentives against perpetrating harms have been installed. Tax policy is the most important one: cigarettes are subject to steep excise to discourage consumption; fruit juice is subject to lower sales tax than other soft drinks, in part, to foster consumption of the healthier product and to encourage manufacturers to use more real fruit in their products. As Chapter 11 showed, the commonwealth has fostered anti-discrimination goals by giving cash rebates to employers in certain trades who take on female apprentices. Some workers' compensation schemes give substantial rebates to companies with low accident rates, though this is done by insurers to cut workers' compensation costs, rather than as a regulatory policy for occupational health and safety.

These are isolated examples which are becoming increasingly isolated as governments try to grapple with making their tax systems simpler by eliminating exemptions and special tax rates which can worsen problems of avoidance and evasion. And fundamentally, Australian regulatory agencies do not foster economic incentives approaches to their responsibilities because they have little practical capacity to influence the tax system.

Encouraging Civil Litigation

Posner (1977) and other devotees of the economic analysis of law see civil litigation by victims against companies which do them harm as a more efficient way of controlling the abuses of corporations than command and control regulation (Landes and Posner, 1984; cf. Cranston, 1977). Like the economic incentives approach, this strategy has no support among Australian regulatory agencies. They have not significantly involved themselves in campaigns for law reforms to make civil litigation by citizens against corporations more possible, such as through facilitating class actions.

Only fourteen of the agencies had ever provided active assistance for civil litigants against alleged corporate offenders. Most of the consumer affairs agencies have the power to take civil action on behalf of aggrieved consumers, and to provide financial assistance in such cases. In practice, this is only done with occasional test cases of particular interest to the agency.

The Patents, Trademarks, and Designs Office is the only agency in our study which relies predominantly on controlling corporate malpractices by establishing a framework and an information base which enables aggrieved parties to pursue their own interests in the courts.

Disclosure

The fourth minimal intervention kind of regulation is to require companies to disclose certain facts, and then let potential victims of the harm concerned take note of those facts and take care of themselves. This philosophy is strongest in corporate affairs through prospectus requirements to disclose the financial state of a company, and takeover rules to ensure that small investors are not kept out of the picture. Ingredient labelling and date stamping requirements for food are also classic examples, as are a variety of consumer affairs provisions for care labelling of clothing, disclosure of interest rates calculated according to uniform rules, and disclosure of fuel consumption rates for motor cars calculated according to standard rules.

There is no area of business regulation where disclosure requirements do not play an important role, but with the exception of corporate affairs, in no area are disclosure rules the central plank of the regulatory regime.

Pre-Marketing Clearance

In Chapters 8 and 9, we saw that in both drug and transport safety regulation, the core strategy is not to allow products on the market until they are approved. That is, each new kind of drug, car, ship, or aircraft cannot legally be used until it is granted a particularistic approval for use. This is distinguished from the usual regulatory arrangement where any product can be brought onto the market without approval, but if the product is found after marketing not to comply with a universalistic mandatory standard, enforcement action can be taken.

In addition to drugs and transport safety, pre-marketing clearance is applied to most electrical goods by state electricity authorities. There are also current moves to apply pre-marketing clearance to some types of industrial and agricultural chemicals. The relatively narrow range of areas where this strategy is used undoubtedly reflects the costs of a particularistic assessment of each new type of product before it can be used. Considerable resources are needed to ensure that massive backlogs in approvals do not accumulate, thereby holding up the diffusion of product innovation.

Environmental impact statements followed by government approval of projects or processes are a functional equivalent of pre-marketing clearance of products. Similarly, planning approvals are central to land-use regulation. These too are strategies of particularistic assessment aimed at preventing harm before an economic activity begins, as opposed to correcting it after the event.

Licensing

An alternative to approval of a product, project, or process prior to production and marketing is prior approval of the person or organization who will be responsible for the economic activity. This is licensing. For example, instead of requiring prior government approval of each type of insurance policy which can be written by an insurance company, the government simply issues licences only to those companies with the reserves, prudential controls, and managerial competence to be trusted to design their own policies for the public. Instead of requiring government approval of each blasting operation in a mine before it can go ahead, the requirement is that blasting can only be undertaken under the supervision of a person with a certificate of competency as a shot-firer.

Only seventeen of the agencies in this study did not have effective access to action against the licence of a person or company which flouted their requirements. Anti-discrimination is the only major area of regulation covered in this book where licensing is not an important tool of regulatory strategy. At the same time, it is remarkable how rarely action is taken to remove or suspend licences in most cases. The area where such action is most common is with respect to the registration of tax agents where there were seven cancellations in 1984 and nine in 1983 for 'neglect, misconduct, preparation of a false return, or lack of fitness to remain registered as a tax agent' (Commonwealth Commissioner of Taxation, 1984, 77). As with the Tax Agents' Board, licensing actions are often in the hands of an independent board, though in these cases it is usual for most actions against licences to be initiated by the relevant regulatory agency. Twenty-five of the seventy-five agencies which had effective access to taking licencing actions never used this sanction.

Licence cancellation is rarely resorted to, because it is such a severe sanction; it can take away a company's or an individual's ability to earn a living, thereby dealing a more severe economic blow than prosecution ever could. On the other hand, licence suspension for a short period is not so catastrophic a sanction, and one wonders why, with the enormous proliferation of types of licences in Australia, this sanction is also used very rarely.

Sixty of the agencies (62.5 per cent) used conditions of licence as a regulatory tool. That is, instead of relying on universalistic rules, in part, they rely on particularistic rules specified as a condition of licence. The most detailed sets of licence conditions are to be found with environmental regulation. Some Victorian Environmental Protection Agency (EPA) licences run to over 300 pages of conditions to cover every point of pollution discharge in a plant. Prosecutions for breach of licence conditions, as opposed to breach of universalistic standards, are common with the Victorian EPA.

In some ways, use of indentures or other legally binding compliance contracts, as illustrated by the Roxby Downs Indenture Agreement (Chapters 3 and 5), are functionally equivalent to imposing conditions upon licences. Fourteen of the agencies in this study had used such contractual instruments as a route to tailor-made standards for a particular project. However, the difference from the Victorian EPA model of licence conditions is that the company cannot be prosecuted for failing to meet one of the conditions; civil action for breach of contract is all that is possible.

Another alternative to licence conditions for achieving particularistic standards is simply to have universalistic standards, but to make liberal use of exemptions from them. Seventy-nine of the agencies (82.3 per cent) had some provisions in their legislation for granting waivers or exemptions. Yet another alternative is to provide for special rules to be written to cover a particular site (e.g. a mine). Thirty-six agencies have this tool; mine safety agencies make the greatest use of it.

An alternative to licensing being developed by the South Australian Commissioner for Consumer Affairs is negative licensing. Instead of requiring all traders in an industry to be licensed, the commissioner is empowered to apply to a tribunal to withdraw the right of an unscrupulous trader to operate in the industry concerned. This approach cuts the costs of administering a licensing system and avoids the anti-competitive effects of erecting barriers to entering an industry. It has also been applied under the New South Wales Pure Food Act (Chapter 7).

Prosecution

Prosecution is both the best known regulatory tool, and the most widely used of all the formal regulatory actions. Nevertheless, a third of the agencies had not launched a prosecution in the most recent three years for which data were available. The most prosecutorial agencies (with over 500 convictions during the three years) were the Corporate Affairs Commissions of Victoria, New South Wales, Queensland, and South Australia; the New South Wales and Queensland food inspectorates; the Queensland Industrial and Factories and Shops Inspectorate; the Brisbane City Council building inspectorate; the Australian Customs Service; and the Australian Taxation Office.

Only two agencies set themselves a target number of prosecutions to be achieved for the year: the Victorian Ministry of Consumer Affairs and the Surveillance and Investigation Division of the Commonwealth Department of Health (responsible for medical benefits fraud and over-servicing). In the case of the former, the target is not a central part of departmental strategy, being one element of a programme budgeting exercise. In the case of the latter, the division was abolished and its functions given to the Commonwealth Health Insurance Commission, in part, because of its 'numbers' approach to prosecutions (see Chapter 12). Only six of the agencies indicated that they would be concerned if they had fewer prosecutions than the previous year, though twenty-three others that said they might be concerned, depending on the circumstances.

Only eighteen (18.8 per cent) of the agencies had a written enforcement policy which specified the circumstances in which prosecution would be the most likely result. In descending order of being mentioned by our respondents, the most important written or unwritten guidelines affecting the likelihood of prosecution were: seriousness of the offence or harm to the victim (51 per cent); failure to rectify the offence after warning (46 per cent); repeat offender (42 per cent); the presence of intent on the part of the offender (32 per cent); and public pressure for a prosecution (20 per cent). The finding that intent was often important provides some support for Hawkins's (1984, 61-3) conclusion that, ironically, agencies which administer predominantly strict liability laws are widely guided by conceptions of *mens rea* in decisions to prosecute.

Approximately equal numbers of agencies gave the following as the main obstacles to initiating more prosecutions: inadequate resources, deficiencies in the law, delays in the criminal process, and low fines do not make prosecutions worthwhile. Twenty-nine of the agencies had engaged in prosecution crackdowns on a particular aspect of the law; sixteen had engaged in single showcase prosecutions with maximum publicity, and thirty had targeted single repeat offenders.

Prosecutions are overwhelmingly directed at companies rather than at individuals who acted on behalf of the company. Only twenty of the agencies had a policy or preference for prosecuting individuals rather than companies, mostly in the mining and marine areas where mine managers and ships' captains were viewed as preferred targets. Mine safety regulation is notable for fostering individual accountability through statutes which nominate in some detail the responsibilities of individuals who fulfil various roles in the organization.

Half the agencies which initiated prosecutions secured convictions more than 90 per cent of the time, and only one agency lost more cases than it won.

For more than half the agencies which do prosecute, the average fine is under $200. The Trade Practices Commission stands out as the only agency which achieves more than flea-bite fines on companies, with its average fines since inception ($16,630) being more than ten times as high as the average obtained by any other agency. While 60 per cent of the agencies have statutes which provide for imprisonment of offenders, apart from one case involving aviation safety, only the agencies dealing with financial fraud (corporate affairs, tax, customs, and medical benefits) engage in enforcement which leads to imprisonment, and then rarely.

Injunctions and Directives

Only twenty-two (22.9 per cent) of the agencies had ever sought an injunction in a court of law, and for most of these an injunction proceeding was a very unusual event. However, 49 per cent of the agencies do not need to have recourse to injunctions, because their inspectors have the power to order that behaviour not specifically covered by their legislation cease or be changed, with failure to comply constituting an offence.

Fifty-one (53.1 per cent) of the agencies have a specific power to order production to cease in a workplace, to order that a machine no longer be used, or to close down a workplace. These powers are used most widely in the occupational health and safety, radiation safety, and food standards areas. However, even in these areas, as the relevant chapters show, use of this very potent enforcement tool is infrequent.

Seizure

Seizure of assets such as a catch of fish, an X-ray machine, explosives, or a batch of mislabelled food or drugs, is also a powerful sanction. There have been food seizures in recent years where up to $200,000 worth of product has been taken. Twenty-eight of the agencies (29.2 per cent) reported having seized assets of regulated companies at some time. Food and fisheries regulation are the only areas where this enforcement tool is regularly used, and voluntary recall of contaminated or mislabelled food is much more widely relied upon than seizure.

Adverse Publicity

Forty-six (47.9 per cent) of the agencies reported that they used adverse publicity in some way as a regulatory tool against non-compliant companies. Twelve had issued a press release following the conviction of a company; twenty had named offending companies in their annual report. Some agencies employed journalists to maximize the impact of such activities. More commonly, though, the respondent would admit, often off the record, that they would direct adverse publicity at corporate offenders by confidentially tipping off journalists about scandals or by advising journalists that it might be worth their while to sit in on a particular court case.

Mine safety, radiation safety, and prudential regulators were unusually reticent about using adverse publicity. Some health departments were of the view that publicity could, on occasions, be counterproductive in promoting the activities of purveyors of quack medicines or slimming preparations. On the other hand, it is health departments which have given us the placarding of pubs convicted for selling watered-down beer, and the requirement that signs be posted in the surgeries of fraudulent doctors with warnings that they are not eligible to participate in the Medicare programme.

The Real Stuff of Getting Compliance

Any reader who has ventured this far and bothers to go no further will have missed the important finding of our research. The fact is that none of the above enforcement tools are regularly used on a day to day basis in any but a handful of the agencies. In fact, most of the agencies do not see themselves as primarily concerned with enforcement of their act(s). Only fifteen (15.6 per cent) of the respondents said that law enforcement was the most important function of their agency. Seventy-eight (81.3 per cent) said education and persuasion were more important functions for them than law enforcement.

The enforcement tools we have listed and described above are important as bargaining chips in the real substance of day to day business regulation. Licences might rarely be revoked, workplaces rarely shut down, and prosecutions rarely initiated, but these infrequent moments of adversary enforcement are part of the background against which co-operative negotiation of improved compliance is understood by companies to be something they cannot totally avoid.

Most regulatory action begins with an inspector or other compliance officer noticing some substandard practice by a company. Whether or not this substandard practice constitutes an offence was not generally a question of much interest to our respondents. Having become aware of the sub-standard practice, be it insufficient reserves by an insurance company or dangerous dust on a production line, the almost universal policy preference was for the front-line person to take the initiative to persuade the company to correct the problem. If the company was intransigent, then it would be reminded with diminishing degrees of subtlety that one of the types of enforcement action discussed above might ensue.

Australian business is not litigious in its relationships with regulatory agencies in the way American business is, though it is hardly as deferential to government as is Japanese business. Generally then, Australian business regulatory agencies operate on assumptions that business will respond to a reasonable request from them without any need to threaten enforcement action, let alone use it. If a company is recalcitrant, harassment in the form of follow-up inspections will often be preferred to the adversarial measure of threatening enforcement. Such harassment often leads to compliance simply so the company can be free of the inspector.

The data on attitudes of the top regulatory officials in Table 1 confirm all of this. Their manners are indeed gentle: they overwhelmingly reject a law enforcement ideology; they trust business as socially responsible and anxious to be law abiding; and they reject adversariness in favour of a co-operative ideology. On the other hand, there is a strong attachment to the rulebook (item 3); and even if they do not believe in *using* the stick, most think it crucial that they *have* the stick (item 8).

Field personnel of regulatory agencies do a lot of things: they educate, they offer technical assistance to solve problems, and they try to get compliance. The latter is fundamentally seen as a matter of persuasion, negotiation, or simply tapping people on the shoulder to remind them to do what they know they should do. Not only the use of enforcement, but even the threatened use of the enforcement tools described above, is generally viewed as an adversarial breakdown indicative of failure by the regulatory agency. The enforcement tools are seen as important primarily as a background which gives the agency authority; secondly, they are seen as bargaining chips in negotiation for compliance when faced with resistance; thirdly, and least importantly in the eyes of Australian regulatory managers, they are seen as tools to achieve specific or general deterrence. Twice as many agencies see specific deterrence as more important than general deterrence. This was tapped by the question: 'Do you see your prosecution policy aimed mainly at deterring subsequent misconduct by the particular offending company [specific deterrence], or as an example to all firms in the industry [general deterrence]'.

Table 1

Regulatory Attitudes Questionnaire Completed by the Most Senior Respondent to Reflect 'Your Agency's Position'

(n = 87)

	Strongly Disagree %	Disagree %	Inclined to Disagree %	Inclined to Agree %	Agree %	Strongly Agree %
1 It is better to seek to persuade companies to comply with regulations voluntarily even at the risk of being considered 'soft'.	2	9	10	29	39	10
2 A large number of prosecutions is a sign that a regulatory agency is failing in its job of achieving compliance by more efficient means.	5	18	18	26	24	8
3 It is best for regulatory agencies to adopt clear interpretations of the law and stick by them.	0	3	10	21	49	16
4 Most companies are sincerely interested in conforming to regulatory standards.	0	6	8	43	40	3
5 Most companies are law abiding; they try to follow the standards simply because a government agency has issued them.	0	13	22	29	36	0
6 A large number of prosecutions is a sign that a regulatory agency is doing its job.	3	58	26	8	5	0
7 Most companies are mainly out to 'make a buck' and will avoid conforming to regulatory standards if at all possible.	6	35	37	17	5	1
8 Without the penalty imposing powers your agency has, many companies would simply ignore your regulatory standards.	1	18	16	26	30	8
9 It is best to obtain compliance with the law by advice and encouragement rather than prosecution.	0	0	6	10	67	17

Table 1 (Continued)
Regulatory Attitudes Questionnaire Completed by the Most Senior Respondent to Reflect 'Your Agency's Position'
(n = 87)

	Strongly Disagree %	Disagree %	Inclined to Disagree %	Inclined to Agree %	Agree %	Strongly Agree %
10 It is best for regulatory agencies to be flexible in interpreting the law.	5	18	15	22	38	2
11 It is better to be a tough enforcer of regulations, even at the risk of being considered punitive.	5	35	29	21	11	0
12 Businesses more often than not ignore requests or directions from your agency.	14	66	18	1	1	0
13 Businesses usually do what your agency asks of them.	0	1	3	29	62	5
14 Enforcing the letter of the law is the best way to deal with business.	9	37	35	15	4	0
15 The relationship of my agency to the businesses which we oversee may best be described as adversarial.	21	55	10	12	2	0
16 Businesses always place profit ahead of the welfare of the community.	5	30	23	35	7	0
17 I expect my officers to use common sense by applying the law in a way that is not dogmatic or legalistic.	0	0	2	14	64	20
18 The relationship of my agency to the businesses which we oversee may be characterised as based on negotiation, mutual accommodation, and compromise.	2	13	16	34	30	5
19 Businesses in general are socially responsible and most of their decisions are made in the public interest.	2	24	30	35	10	0

In short, the policy of most Australian regulatory agencies is all about getting companies to 'do the right thing' by as informal and non-confrontationist a means as possible. The concern is to solve each problem as it comes up; using enforcement tools to foster general deterrence is foreign to the thinking of most top regulatory officials in Australia.

Key Issues in Regulatory Variation
The Costs and Benefits of Regulation

In 1980 the Confederation of Australian Industry put the cost of business regulation on the Australian political agenda, with a survey which concluded that in 1978-79 regulation cost industry $3,720 million and tied up 54,400 private sector employees full-time (*Canberra Times*, 6 August 1980, 20; see also Gayler, 1980). This was a global study of dubious methodology. In our study we asked all agencies if industry had undertaken any cost-benefit analyses or systematic cost of regulation impact studies. There were a few minor studies of the economic impact of environmental reg ulations on specific development projects, one study of the impact of certain occupational health and safety regulations in Victoria (Crow, 1981), and some work on the costs imposed by broadcasting regulation and pharmaceuticals regulation. These were the only examples of cost-of-regulation impact studies which regulatory agencies were able to tell us had been put to them by industry. None of the studies could be described as cost-benefit analyses in the sense of putting a monetary value on the benefits as well as the costs of regulation.

As for the agencies themselves, the two fisheries departments we visited had both done studies which could be described as cost-benefit analyses of fisheries regulation, and the Trade Practices Commission (Grant, 1984) had also done some work which approached this description. None of the other agencies had undertaken anything approaching even a cost-of-regulation impact study. As with the indifference of Australian regulators to the economistic theorizing about incentives and tort liability as alternatives to government command and control, the enormous volume of academic writing on the need for cost-benefit analyses of regulation has had little practical impact on either the regulators or even the regulated industries.

Most respondents were very concerned to be sensitive to the costs which their regulatory activities imposed on industry. They were, however, just averse to the 'academic impracticality' of conducting systematic research on the question. They could see no sensible way of assigning values to intangible things like preserving rainforests or saving human lives. Moreover, they were not sufficiently persuaded that the benefits of cost-benefit analysis exceeded its costs to spend scarce resources on it.

Regulatory Accountability

Accountability to the Australian community is confronted in very different ways by Australian regulatory agencies. A number of the agencies do not even produce annual reports to inform the community about their activities. Most of the states do not have the freedom of information and administrative appeals legislation which exists at federal level. Even in the jurisdictions which have freedom of information acts (the commonwealth and Victoria), secrecy can be, and is, easily protected by a spate of statutory exemptions. We have already seen how most agencies which engage in prosecutions do not publish any prosecution guidelines, nor for that matter any publicly available material on the proper boundaries for the exercise of their administrative discretion. As a Victorian judge said recently: 'The people may have to dance to the bureaucracy's tune, but they are entitled to a copy of the music' (Lazarus, J. in *Pennhalluriack* v. *Department of Labour and Industry*, County Court, unreported, 19 December 1983).

Some agencies do make copies of the music freely available. The Trade Practices Commission and the Australian Broadcasting Tribunal are agencies which, at least in relation to some of their activities, disclose reasonably detailed information to the public on how their officers exercise discretion. The media which they employ include regular reports and newsletters, publicly available staff manuals and enforcement guidelines, and public registers.

On the other hand, Chapter 3 discussed some staggering examples of regulatory secrecy in the form of the statutory limitations on disclosure of information by the Office of the Supervising Scientist, the secrecy of the deliberations of the Queensland Water Quality Council, and the fact that, in Queensland, the contents of environmental impact statements are confidential except at the discretion of the developer.

The worst examples of secrecy are found in many occupational health and safety statutes which are interpreted as preventing inspectors from divulging the result of an inspection even to a worker whose complaint led to the inspection (Braithwaite and Grabosky, 1985, Chapter 8).

An ironic testimony to the commitment of Australian governments to regulatory secrecy is the fact that some statutes provide for much harsher penalties for public servants who breach secrecy concerning corporate offenders than they provide for the corporate offenders! For example, the only provision for imprisonment under the *Tasmanian Environment Protection Act* 1973 is for unauthorized disclosure of information (section 53). In the Northern Territory, a public servant may be imprisoned up to three years, five years if the disclosure is done for the purpose of gain (Northern Territory Criminal Code, section 76).

There are, of course, other paths to accountability besides openness to the general public. Parliamentary public accounts committees have been responsible for some outstanding examples of revealing the internal machinations of regulatory bodies to public view. Leading recent examples are the exposure by the Commonwealth Parliament's Joint Committee on Public Accounts (Chapter 12) of inadequacies of medical benefits fraud enforcement, and the appalling neglect of workers' health by the New South Wales mines inspectorate revealed by the report of the House of Representatives Standing Committee on Aboriginal Affairs (House of Representatives, 1984).

Royal Commissions have, on occasion, performed important regulatory accountability functions. In the aftermath of the 1981 meat substitution scandal, the Woodward Royal Commission called attention to maladministration and corruption in meat inspection (Chapter 7). The Costigan Royal Commission commented critically upon the adequacy of company law enforcement by various state corporate affairs agencies (Costigan, 1984, 271). Independent prosecutors external to the regulatory agency have also, in at least one case, drawn public attention to alleged regulatory inadequacies. As we saw in Chapter 12, Special Prosecutors Gyles and Redlich made some scathing attacks on enforcement practices of the Australian Taxation Office. The Commonwealth Deputy Director of Public Prosecutions has heralded that his office is prepared to play a similar role (Potas, 1985, 229).

Of course the ultimate form of accountability in a democracy is accountability to the elected representatives of the people. With business regulation, however, the question of how independent the regulatory process ought to be from the political process is a vexed one. Mostly off the record, we were told some disturbing stories of ministers, for what would seem to be reasons of political favouritism, ordering that enforcement actions be stopped. There have been occasional instances of such allegations being made on the public record (Bacon, 1984, 14; Venturini, 1980, 346). In our study, we were told of instances of political interference in enforcement by twenty-six of the agencies we visited.

We found an amazing variety of philosophies and practices which exist toward political involvement in Australian business regulation. At one extreme is business regulation by local government. There, the norm, particularly with the smaller councils, is that all recommendations for enforcement action be approved by a full meeting of the council. This is a strange procedure because council meetings are open to the public. Thus, a decision can be made by aldermen not to prosecute because of insufficient evidence, yet the details of this insufficient evidence, the hearsay, the innuendo, is discussed openly in front of journalists who might attend the council meeting. Whatever the merits of the approach, the local government norm in most states is one of unashamed and unquestioning vesting of prosecutorial discretion in the hands of elected aldermen.

There are other acts, state and commonwealth, where ministerial approval is required, and always sought, to launch prosecutions. For example, all criminal prosecutions under the Trade Practices Act must be approved by the minister. More commonly, ministerial authority to approve prosecutions is delegated to a public servant, or the statute explicitly makes a public servant responsible. In these circumstances, practices also vary enormously. Some agencies scrupulously avoid any communication with ministers about prosecutions lest the minister be 'opened up to accusations of political favouritism', and they reported that their ministers welcomed this arrangement. Others prefer to keep their minister informed of all prosecutions so he or she can be ready when the flak comes from powerful corporations, but they say they do so for information only, and not to invite any intervention by the minister. Others take this a step further: 'I think the minister should be able to inquire, but shouldn't be able to direct any regulatory function, because if he does, he is opening himself up to criticism'.

In short, there is no predominant solution in Australia to the question of political accountability for regulatory enforcement. After our interviews, however, we are sceptical enough to suggest that where ministerial intervention occurs, it may not always be the broader interests of the community which the interventionist minister attempts to assert. In his or her public role, the minister in a democracy must be responsive to broad public interests; in secret roles such as those of a censor of enforcement against powerful interests, the incentives to defend broader interests are not so profound. If ministers are to make the determination that a case shall not proceed, it seems appropriate that this decision, at the very least, should be published in the appropriate government gazette.

Dealing With Corruption
It was again primarily off the record that we learned of instances of alleged corruption in nineteen of the agencies we visited. Most of these were dealt with quietly by dismissing the inspector or other officer believed to be 'on the take'. The folklore of Australian politics is that local government has a lot of corruption, followed by state government (particularly in New South Wales and Queensland), with commonwealth government administration being relatively free from corruption. But, in fact, some of the best documented instances of regulatory corruption have been in the commonwealth jurisdiction, particularly with meat inspection (*Australian*, 5 October 1982) and customs (Delaney, 1979).

By no means did our interviews create the impression that Australian business regulation is a hot-bed of corruption, but they did suggest that corruption was an occasional problem in most of the regulatory domains covered in the book. This is in fact surprising, given the minimal severity of the sanctions imposed by Australian business regulatory agencies. The economic rationality of Australian business is called into question by the car dealer who offered a consumer affairs investigator $1,000 to drop his case; the reader will recall (page 87) that the investigator ignored the offer and the dealer was fined $200 for the original offence!

Notwithstanding the fact that attempts to corrupt regulators do occur from time to time, only twenty-three (24 per cent) of the agencies could describe any administrative counter measures they had against corruption. Mostly these consisted of spot audits of inspections, rules that certain types of meetings with business require two officers to be present, or that staff be rotated geographically or into a different type of work at regular intervals to ensure that ongoing relationships could not develop with companies. Some other agencies aggressively rejected the latter counter-measure as undesirable because ongoing relationships of familiarity with business are the very stuff from which effective regulation is made. The Customs Service is the only agency with a tiny internal affairs unit having the specific function of guarding against corruption.

Dealing With 'Capture'
The concept of 'capture' is a more subtle one than corruption. It is the prediction that, over time, regulators come to be more concerned to serve the interests of the industry with which they are in regular contact, than the more remote and abstract public interest. Capture is assumed to be exacerbated by the revolving door: a situation where either regulators are tempted from time to time with plum jobs in the regulated industry (thereby giving them an incentive to be sympathetic to industry in the hope of such an offer), or where most regulators are recruited from the regulated industry. The first type of problem is not widespread in Australia. Only nine agencies reported that they had the problem of their best people being 'poached' by the regulated industry. This is primarily a problem of lawyers and accountants being recruited from agencies which regulate commercial matters, such as corporate affairs, trade practices, and tax.

The second problem, if it is a problem, is more widespread. For thirty-one (42.7 per cent) of the agencies, a majority of inspectors, investigators, and complaints officers were recruited from industry. In areas such as mine safety, all inspectors, as a matter of law, are required to have had extensive mining experience. The mining example points out the advantages of recruitment from industry: you are more likely to get people with intimate knowlege of processes and procedures, who know how corners are cut, and where to look to find the bodies buried; people who have expertise which makes them better at their job and which commands respect from industry; and people who can exploit an industry old boy network to get changes made expeditiously. On the other hand, with this familiarity comes the risk of capture.

A move in 1985 by Mr Kerry Packer's Channel 9 television network to recruit a recently retired senior officer of the Australian Broadcasting Tribunal was delayed under the commonwealth government's Code of

Official Conduct. The tribunal, which is sensitive to the issue of the revolving door because of past appointments into top positions from the television industry, has unusually strong policies about meetings with industry being on the record, with copies of the minutes of such meetings being available for public inspection.

Conflict of interest provisions are also important. The strictest provision we encountered may be found in the South Australian Fisheries Act which prohibits officers of the Department of Fisheries from holding any financial interest whatsoever in the fishing industry. The only other outright pecuniary interest prohibition we encountered was also from South Australia, and applied to radiation control officials in the Health Commission.

Short of outright pecuniary interest prohibitions, a number of jurisdictions have introduced financial disclosure requirements of various kinds. Top executives of the Victorian and commonwealth public services must advise their ministers of their financial holdings. Northern Territory public servants are required by general order to declare any direct or indirect pecuniary interest that conflicts, or appears to conflict, with their public duty. The Code of Conduct and Ethics of the New South Wales Public Service requires that:

Officers and employees shall disclose in writing to a senior officer any pecuniary or other definite interest held by them immediately on becoming aware that a potential conflict between personal interest and official duty, whether real or apparent, has arisen or is likely to arise. In the case of senior officers, propriety may require the disclosure of pecuniary interests regardless of whether or not there is an immediate real, or potential, conflict of interest.

There are some areas of regulation in Australia which have very limited conflict of interest controls and which have been documented as areas of massive abuse in other countries. A notable example is drug regulation (Braithwaite, 1984). Members of the Australian Drug Evaluation Committee, which recommends to the health minister whether drugs should be allowed on the market, are not prohibited from holding shares in drug companies, nor are they required to declare any such pecuniary interests. Some members are in receipt of large research grants and have accepted overseas trips to conferences funded by pharmaceutical companies on whose products they make recommendations. They are not required to disclose these interests, though we were assured that the health department has the highest 'faith in the calibre of the people involved'. Moreover, we were told that when a member of the committee has conducted one of the studies for a company, 'quite often . . . they will say little, or merely answer questions, when the committee is deciding what they do with a particular drug'.

Public Involvement in the Regulatory Process

Chapter 4 showed that an increasing feature of occupational health and safety regulatory strategy is the involvement of workers in regulation through workplace safety committees and elected safety representatives. We saw how in mine safety regulation, in some jurisdictions, full-time union safety inspectors have their salaries subsidized or completely supported by state governments. The permanent location of a record book at the mine in which both government and union inspectors write their reports, and management indicates what action has been taken in response, is an interesting innovation in participation because the record book is available for inspection by all who work in the mine.

Beyond occupational health and safety, the only significant attempts at multiplying regulatory presence by involving the public were the use of a network of volunteers from the consumer movement to discover hazardous products on the market, by the New South Wales Department of Consumer Affairs (Chapter 6); the use of volunteers to monitor the state of beaches, by the Queensland Beach Protection Authority; and the use of voluntary wardens in South Australia to watch over historic shipwrecks (Chapter 3). Involvements of third parties in self-regulatory schemes, such as the stock exchanges and auditors in corporate affairs, licensed actuaries in insurance regulation, or monitoring of compliance with voluntary product standards by the Standards Association of Australia, amount to a very limited form of public involvement.

Co-ordination Between Regulatory Agencies
We could go into endless detail about how different regulatory agencies co-ordinate their overlapping responsibilities in a federal system. In all areas, much time is devoted, with variable success, to attempting to sort out common regulatory approaches with agencies from other parts of Australia. Beyond formal ministerial councils, all manner of *ad hoc* arrangements exist, such as an enforcement agency liaison group in Victoria where officers of the Victorian Ministry of Consumer Affairs, the Commonwealth Trade Practices Commission, state Corporate Affairs, the Stamps Office, and the Police Fraud Squad meet to swap notes on enforcement work involving the same targets.

The most widely quoted co-ordination problems were between agencies and crown prosecutors. Only nine of the agencies always did their own prosecutions, with another nine sometimes conducting their own. Most of them referred prosecutions to their state Crown Law Office or, in the case of commonwealth agencies, to the Director of Public Prosecutions. Those who relied on prosecutors outside the agency were equally divided between agencies who were more or less satisfied with the service, and those who were dissatisfied. The most common complaints were the failure of prosecutors to understand technical problems, according low priority to regulatory work compared to 'cops and robbers' cases, entering into plea bargains without consulting the agency, delays, and failure to come to grips with the regulatory strategy of the agency.

Some of the commonwealth agencies which relied on the Australian Federal Police for their investigative legwork made very similar criticisms of them. Medical benefits fraud (Field, 1984, 18) and meat substitution fraud (*Australian Financial Review*, 3 September 1981) have been areas where mutual recriminations between the Australian Federal Police and regulatory bureaucracies for failed enforcement have become public.

Powers of the Agencies

If Australian regulatory agencies are of manners gentle, it is not because they lack the powers to be otherwise. Consider, for example, the powers of the Reserve Bank to march in and take over the running of a bank, to seize its gold, or to impose enormous financial penalties. Consider the ability of the National Companies and Securities Commission to declare the Companies (Acquisition of Shares) Act as if modified, and to freeze or reverse trading in shares. The particularistic rulemaking capacities of many agencies discussed earlier in this chapter similarly confer enormous power on the regulator.

One-third of the agencies have the power to force people to answer questions even if such answers may be incriminating; another 24 per cent have the power to compel incriminating answers, but such incriminating answers may not be used in proceedings against the person; and another 11.5 per cent have the power to compel answers to questions except where the answers would be incriminating. The powers are even stronger with respect to company records: 57.3 per cent of the agencies had the power to demand to see company records even if such records were incriminating, and without any prohibition against use of such evidence in proceedings. Such powers go far beyond those available to the police.

Similarly, 77.1 per cent of the agencies in our study had power to inspect private premises without warrant, something the police do not have. Fifty-eight (60.4 per cent) of the agencies work with principal statutes in which strict liability offences are dominant; that is, generally they need not prove intent in order to secure a conviction. Twenty-nine of the agencies have a major statute with a 'general clause' which permits them to take enforcement action against any other activity not specifically forbidden in the act, but which is judged to compromise the goals of the legislation. Inspectors in forty-seven (49 per cent) of the agencies have the power to order that behaviour not specifically covered by their legislation cease or be changed, with failure to comply being an offence. Forty of the agencies (41.7 per cent) have statutes which include at least some provisions which reverse the onus of proof: the burden is placed on the defendant to prove innocence in these circumstances.

This means that the gentle manners of Australian regulatory agencies cannot be explained by inadequate powers which are holding them back from tough enforcement. Their conciliatory style is not something forced upon them, but something that, in general, they freely choose and prefer.

References

Anderson, F., Kneese, Allen V., Reed, Phillip D., Stevenson, Russell B., and Taylor, Serge (1977), *Environmental Improvement Through Economic Incentives*, John Hopkins University Press, Baltimore.

Bacon, Wendy (1984), 'Charges Dropped over Sale of Protected Birds', *National Times*, 3-9 May, 14.

Baumol, W.J. and Oates, W.E. (1971), 'The Use of Standards and Prices for Protection of the Environment', in P. Bohm and A.V. Kneese (eds), *The Economics of Environment*, Macmillan, London.

Braithwaite, J. (1984), *Corporate Crime in the Pharmaceutical Industry*, Routledge and Kegan Paul, London.

Braithwaite, J. and Grabosky, P. (1985), *Occupational Health and Safety Enforcement in Australia: A Report to the National Occupational Health and Safety Commission*, Australian Institute of Criminology, Canberra.

Commonwealth Commissioner of Taxation (1984), *Sixty Third Report, 1983-84*, Australian Government Publishing Service, Canberra.

Costigan, F. (1984) *Royal Commission on the Activities of the Federated Ship Painters and Dockers Union, Final Report, Volume I*, Australian Government Publishing Service, Canberra.

Cranston, R. (1977), 'Creeping Economism: Some Thoughts on Law and Economics', *British Journal of Law and Society*, 4, 103-15.

Crow, J. (1981), *Government Regulation of Industry – The Impact of Government Regulation on the Foundry Industry in Victoria*, Victorian Chamber of Manufactures, Melbourne.

Delaney, B. (1979), *Narc! Inside the Australian Bureau of Narcotics*, Angus and Robertson, Sydney.

Field, G. (1984), *The Respective Involvement of the Health Insurance Commission and the Department in Combatting Abuse of the Medical Benefits Arrangements*, Commonwealth Department of Health, Canberra.

Gayler, D. (1980), *Deregulation: A Plan to Rationalise South Australian Legislation*, Government Printer, Adelaide.

Grant, John (1984), 'The Economic Benefits and Costs of the Australian Trade Practices Legislation', in R. Tomasic (ed.), *Business Regulation in Australia*, CCH Australia, Sydney, 325-50.

Hawkins, Keith (1984), *Environment and Enforcement: Regulation and the Social Definition of Pollution*, Clarendon Press, Oxford.

House of Representatives Standing Committee on Aboriginal Affairs (1984), *The Effects of Asbestos Mining on the Baryulgil Community*, Australian Government Publishing Service, Canberra.

Kneese, A.V. and Schultze, C.L. (1975), *Pollution, Prices and Public Policy*, Bookings Institution, Washington.

Landes, W.M. and Posner, Richard A. (1984), 'Tort Law as a Regulatory Regime for Catastrophic Personal Injuries', *Journal of Legal Studies*, 13, 417-43.

Posner, R. (1977), *Economic Analysis of Law*, Little Brown, Boston.

Potas, I. (ed. 1985), *Prosecutorial Discretion*, Australian Institute of Criminology, Canberra.

Venturini, G. (1980), *Malpractice: The Administration of the Murphy Trade Practices Act*, Non Mollare, Sydney.

15
Explaining Regulatory Behaviour

The previous chapters have described how Australia's business regulatory agencies differ in their approaches to the task of regulation. Our purpose in this chapter is to explain why such differences occur. Is there something about the structure of an agency which influences its enforcement strategy, or does the key lie in the nature of the industry itself? Alternatively, what role do political factors play?

These and other plausible explanations were tested in a quantitative analysis of variations across the ninety-six agencies under study. This analysis supports the conclusion that when regulatory agencies have close relations with a small number of regulated companies or regulated industries, they are less punitive, and when regulatory agencies confront big business, they are less punitive.

Variables
For each of the ninety-six agencies, 127 variables were coded. These addressed seven dimensions:

1. Structural variables relating to the agency, for example:
   - size of staff
   - percentage of staff in enforcement roles
   - centralization of decision making
2. Structural variables relating to the industry regulated by the agency, for example:
   - number of firms
   - size of firms
   - diversity of firms
3. Policy variables, for example:
   - agency functions accorded greatest importance
   - extent of reliance on industry self-regulation
   - encouragement of private civil litigation

4. Behavioural variables, for example:
   - use of prosecution
   - use of licence revocation
   - targeting of repeat offenders
5. Statutory powers, for example:
   - imprisonment
   - search without warrant
   - maximum fine available
6. Attitudinal variables, for example:
   - strict legalism preferable to flexibility
   - companies regarded as socially responsible
7. Miscellaneous variables, for example:
   - date of agency's founding (pre or post 1970)

We employed, as our basic measure of enforcement activity, the total number of convictions obtained by each agency during the three years to 1 July 1984, or the nearest date for which data were available. Our choice of total convictions, as a variable to be explained, was governed by a number of considerations. First, prosecution is the most stigmatic, if not the most potent, enforcement response by a regulatory agency. Second, it is by far the most widely used formal sanction. Moreover, the data revealed that those agencies which use other formal 'sanctions', such as licence revocation or court injunctions, are also more inclined to prosecute. We were unable to obtain reliable data on the number of occasions each of these alternative sanctions was used over the three year period; where we were able to do so, their numbers were so small as to minimally change the totals for convictions alone. Overall, the total number of convictions is the most precise and informative statistic available.

The initial decision to use the total number of convictions rather than a rate weighted by population size, agency size, or number of companies regulated was a conscious one. It became apparent to us that all agencies under review, from the two Australian Capital Territory weights and measures inspectors, to the 15,000 strong Australian Taxation Office, are confronted by an overwhelming number of corporate offences. One survey, for example, found that 32 per cent of the petrol pumps in the Australian Capital Territory gave short measure petrol to motorists (*Canberra Times*, 13 January 1981, 1). Hence, it is not unreasonable to conceive that even the smallest of agencies has an approximately infinite number of offences against which it could choose to take enforcement action.

Controlling for population as an indicator of the available number of offences or offenders is therefore unnecessary. It is also misleading where there are overlapping commonwealth, state, and local government jurisdictions. There is no sense in comparing New South Wales Department of Consumer Affairs prosecutions per 100,000 population in New South Wales, with Trade Practices Commission prosecutions per 100,000 population in Australia. Moreover, if one considers a domain such as environmental regulation, using either population or number of regulated companies (to the extent that this can be reliably known) as a denominator, is misleading, because while the Australian Capital Territory might have more people and more companies subject to environmental regulation than the Northern Territory, there is more environment to degrade, and more activities of a degrading nature (e.g. uranium mining), in the Northern Territory. Variation in prosecutorial activity is less a function of opportunity than of policy. All these things considered, the most reasonable course was the simplest one: to take the raw number of convictions as the dependent variable, and to treat jurisdiction size, agency size, and number of companies regulated, as independent variables. Such analyses we did using prosecutions *per capita* did not, in any case, suggest conclusions different from those discussed below.

The data provide a uniquely comprehensive description of the most important regulatory agencies in one country. They allowed us to test a wide variety of hypotheses derived from the folklore of Australian politics, from the literature on regulation, and from more general theories of social control. We predicted that states with long histories of conservative government would have less punitive, less enforcement-oriented regulatory agencies. Agencies with centralized decision making structures were expected to be more punitive than agencies which leave field officers free to sort out their own accommodation with industry. We expected that agencies with enormous powers would use those powers to bring about tougher enforcement. We assumed that agencies with a history of political intervention in enforcement would rely on less formal means of achieving compliance. More reactive agencies would be less prosecutorial than agencies which proactively sent inspectors out into the field to find problems. Stand-alone regulatory agencies were expected to be more prosecutorial than agencies which had to account to a larger department of which they were a part. We also tested the hypothesis that new agencies established at the high tide of pro-regulation sentiment in the early 1970s would be more prosecutorial than agencies which were 'old' in the regulatory life-cycle (Bernstein, 1955). There is little point in outlining the deeper theoretical justifications for the above hypotheses, because they all fell by the wayside for the lack of empirical support. It is remarkable how little there is to show for so many cross-tabulations, correlations, factor analyses, and regressions (with which we shall not burden the reader). There was, however, one type of explanation which generated quite strong support, and to this we now turn.

Relational Distance

In our efforts to explain variations in enforcement activity across the ninety-six agencies, we ultimately turned to a general, structural

Table 1
Number of Convictions 1981–84 by Main Function of Agency

	Median	Mean	Range	N
Corporate Affairs	707.5	2318.3	1–9,631	6
Worker Health and Safety	345.0	432.0	5–1,820	7 (1 missing)
Local Government	125.0	267.3	36–641	3 (3 missing)
Consumer Affairs	56.5	83.1	1–225	10
Fraud Against Government	46.0	46.0	46–46	1 (2 missing)
Transport Safety	13.0	9.3	0–15	3
State Food Standards	7.5	311.8	0–1,225	6 (2 missing)
Oil Spill Control	6.5	6.5	0–13	4
Prudential Regulation	5.3	7.0	0–21	3
Environmental Protection	1.0	23.8	0–208	14
Miner Health and Safety	0.6	2.8	0–12	8 (1 missing)
Other	0.5	16.1	0–72	12 (2 missing)
Radiation Control	0.2	0.3	0–1	4
Anti-Discrimination	0	0	0–0	4

Table 2
Number of Convictions 1981–84 by Jurisdiction

	Median	Mean	Range	N
Commonwealth	0.7	9.3	0–51	20 (1 missing)
New South Wales	13.5	517.3	0–2,527	8
Victoria	68.0	1,454.0	0–9,631	7 (2 missing)
Queensland	48.0	322.3	0–1,820	9
South Australia	5.0	119.2	0–980	11
Western Australia	16.0	97.3	0–370	8 (2 missing)
Tasmania	1.0	11.4	0–55	7
Australian Capital Territory	6.0	171.5	0–645	4 (1 missing)
Northern Territory	2.0	6.1	0–25	7
Local Government	51.0	202.0	6–641	4 (3 missing)

explanation rather than one based on attitude, function, or folklore. To be sure, it is worthy of note that mines inspectorates are less likely to prosecute than are consumer affairs agencies (Table 1), or that Victorian agencies prosecute more than those of New South Wales (Table 2). But an explanation based upon the general properties of agencies has more theoretical significance.

One key hypothesis on whether an agency would be more or less enforcement-oriented was based on Black's (1976) general theory of law. From this, one would predict that the greater the relational distance between regulator and regulatee, the greater the tendency to use formal sanctions. Thus, we would predict that an agency with a high percentage of staff drawn from the industries which they regulate would prosecute less than one whose staff were recruited directly from school or from elsewhere in the public service. Similarly, we would predict that agencies which regulate a relatively small number of companies, or companies drawn from a single industry would resort to less formal means of achieving compliance than those which regulate a relatively large number of companies from diverse industries. Moreover, agencies whose inspectors have frequent contact with the same firms may be expected to use less formal sanctions than those characterized by more impersonal contact.

The data summarized in Figures 1 through to 4 reveal strong support for the hypothesized relationship between relational distance and enforcement activity. We have chosen to base our graphical comparison on median levels of prosecution rather than means, because extremely high numbers of prosecutions by a very few agencies render the mean a less useful summary statistic. Means and ranges are also reported as well as the number of agencies in each category.

Figure 1 shows quite strikingly that the larger the number of companies within an agency's regulatory purview, the greater the agency's use of criminal sanctions. Indeed, none of the nine agencies responsible for fifty or fewer companies resorted to prosecution at all.

Figure 2 reveals that agencies whose regulatory activity is limited to a single industry (e.g. mining or insurance) resort to prosecution about one-fifth as often as regulatory bodies which oversee a diverse variety of industry sectors.

Figure 3 indicates even more distinctly that agencies whose inspectors tend to be in relatively frequent contact with the same regulated companies are less formal in their sanctioning response than those whose inspectors are in less frequent contact with the same companies.

Figure 4 suggests that those agencies whose inspectors are recruited predominantly from industry tend to be less prosecutorial than those whose inspectors are without prior industry experience. This relationship is not as strong as the other three, particularly if one looks at the mean as well as median number of convictions. From a different theoretical perspective, this association, weak though it is, can also be

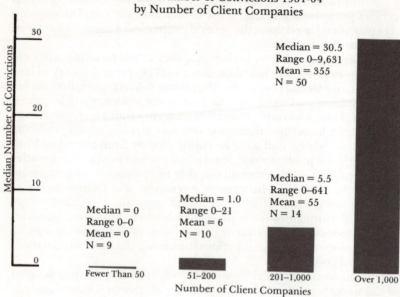

Figure 1
Median Number of Convictions 1981-84
by Number of Client Companies

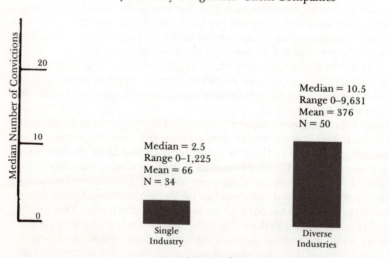

Figure 2
Median Number of Convictions 1981-84
by Diversity of Agencies' Client Companies

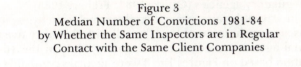

Figure 3
Median Number of Convictions 1981-84
by Whether the Same Inspectors are in Regular
Contact with the Same Client Companies

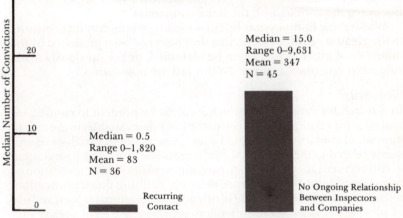

Median = 15.0
Range 0–9,631
Mean = 347
N = 45

Median = 0.5
Range 0–1,820
Mean = 83
N = 36

Recurring
Contact

No Ongoing Relationship
Between Inspectors
and Companies

Relationships with Client Companies

Figure 4
Median Number of Convictions 1981-84
by Proportion of Inspectorate with Industry Backgrounds

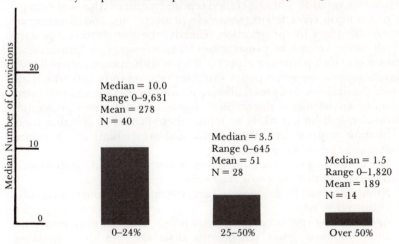

Median = 10.0
Range 0–9,631
Mean = 278
N = 40

Median = 3.5
Range 0–645
Mean = 51
N = 28

Median = 1.5
Range 0–1,820
Mean = 189
N = 14

0–24%

25–50%

Over 50%

Inspectors with Industry Backgrounds

interpreted as support for the thesis of 'capture' when industry penet-rates regulatory agencies (Quirk, 1981; Freitag, 1983).

Multi-way tables also strengthen this conclusion by exploring inter-actions among these variables. The cell with the thirty-five most pros-ecutorial agencies (median convictions = 55.5) in the 16-cell cross-tabulation based on Figures 1 to 3 were agencies regulating over 1,000 companies in multiple industry sectors where the same inspectors were not in regular contact with the same companies.

Whilst these findings may be encouraging, it is important to ensure, to the greatest possible extent, that they have not been produced by the influence of other factors yet to be identified, or not previously made subject to systematic control. To this task we now turn.

Controls

In a search for variables for which it might be prudent to control, we looked at the relationship of each of the 126 other variables in the data to number of convictions. As noted above, one group of variables signifi-cantly related to the number of convictions was those which amounted to enforcement alternatives to prosecutions: use of licence revocation or suspension, injunctions, seizure of assets, shutting down production, formal warning letters, naming of offenders in an annual report, and use of adverse publicity against offenders generally. We have already sug-gested that the use of these sanctions is positively associated with the use of prosecution, but that to add these together with convictions to form a composite measure of punitiveness, would add a deal of error without changing the dependent variable greatly. It would not make sense to enter these variables as controls.

The second group of variables significantly associated with number of convictions has clearly tautologous or artifactual associations with the dependent variable. These included reports by officials that they engage in prosecution crackdowns, showcase prosecutions, and targeting of repeat offenders for prosecution. Clearly, the one-third of agencies which never engage in prosecutions cannot engage in 'prosecution crackdowns on a particular aspect of the law with maximum publicity'. Similarly, there were ten policy variables relating to factors which in-crease the likelihood of prosecution (e.g. whether the offender exhibited intent or knowledge of the offence). Agencies which never prosecute, obviously, will be less likely to report these factors as affecting their inclination to prosecute. These artifactual associations are therefore also inappropriate as controls.

The remaining variables which were statistically significantly associ-ated with a number of convictions were:

1 Number of staff in the agency. Larger agencies obtained more con-victions ($r = .68$).
2 Agencies that regulated companies which were disproportionately large obtained fewer convictions than agencies that regulated

companies which were either disproportionately small, or were a representative cross-section of the mix of small and large companies in the economy.

3 Agencies that normally engage in inspections without giving prior notice of the inspection obtained more convictions than agencies that inspected with warning, and they, in turn, obtained more convictions than agencies that never used random inspections to detect offences (mainly agencies which relied totally on complaints to detect offences).

4 Agencies that had policies and procedures to monitor systematically the productivity of enforcement personnel (e.g. graphs of inspections completed and offences detected) had more convictions.

5 Agencies with some personnel who had undertaken criminal investigation training had more convictions.

6 Agencies that reported in interview that they had had to deal with corruption allegations had more convictions.

7 Agencies that reported administrative counter-measures against corruption had more convictions.

The latter two variables were rejected on theoretical grounds as appropriate controls. We assumed it to be highly implausible that the existence of corruption in an agency would cause it to engage in tougher enforcement. In contrast, it is plausible that agencies which engage in tough enforcement give regulated companies more reason to attempt to corrupt their officers.

Some of the other controls are certainly of dubious merit. It may be that sending officers on criminal investigation courses is a cause of higher convictions but, equally, it may be that causality runs in the opposite direction: agencies which have a lot of prosecutions find it more necessary to send officers on criminal investigation courses than agencies which never prosecute. Nevertheless, in the interests of maximum conservatism in assessing whether the association between relational distance and convictions disappears after introducing controls, it was decided to test the five remaining controls.

First, the size of the agency was controlled by calculating the median and mean number of convictions per 100 agency staff. Entry of this control eliminated the association between convictions and proportion of enforcement officers which came from industry backgrounds. Median convictions per 100 agency personnel were almost identical for agencies where a majority, and those where a minority, of enforcement personnel came from industry backgrounds.

As for the relationships in Figures 1 and 3, these became considerably stronger after controlling for size of agency.

When each of the remaining four controls above was separately added to agency size, as a second control, by looking at median and mean convictions per 100 agency personnel, between cells defined by the control variable categories, only one control produced notable

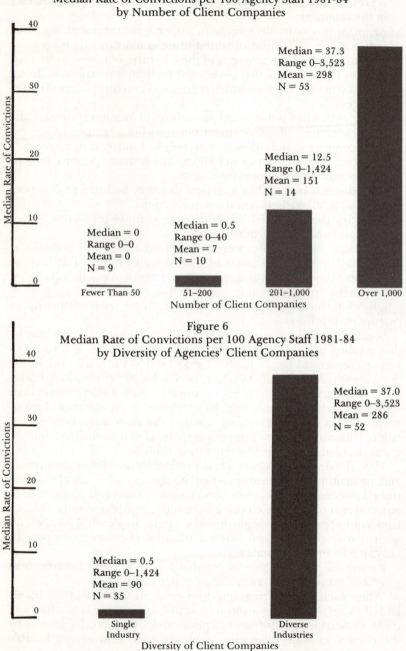

Figure 5
Median Rate of Convictions per 100 Agency Staff 1981-84
by Number of Client Companies

Median = 37.3
Range 0–3,523
Mean = 298
N = 53

Median = 12.5
Range 0–1,424
Mean = 151
N = 14

Median = 0.5
Range 0–40
Mean = 7
N = 10

Median = 0
Range 0–0
Mean = 0
N = 9

Median Rate of Convictions

Fewer Than 50   51–200   201–1,000   Over 1,000
Number of Client Companies

Figure 6
Median Rate of Convictions per 100 Agency Staff 1981-84
by Diversity of Agencies' Client Companies

Median = 37.0
Range 0–3,523
Mean = 286
N = 52

Median = 0.5
Range 0–1,424
Mean = 90
N = 35

Median Rate of Convictions

Single
Industry

Diverse
Industries
Diversity of Client Companies

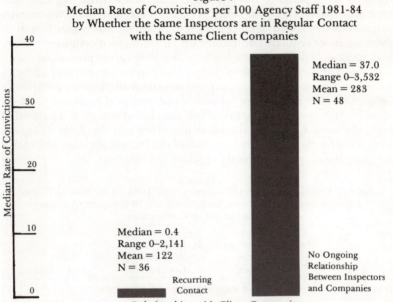

Figure 7
Median Rate of Convictions per 100 Agency Staff 1981-84
by Whether the Same Inspectors are in Regular Contact
with the Same Client Companies

Median = 37.0
Range 0–3,532
Mean = 283
N = 48

Median = 0.4
Range 0–2,141
Mean = 122
N = 36

Recurring
Contact

No Ongoing
Relationship
Between Inspectors
and Companies

Relationships with Client Companies

changes in the relationships. This was the control for the size of regulated companies. The strength of the association between the number of companies regulated by the agencies, and the number of convictions per 100 agency staff, remained substantially undiminished by controlling for the size of the regulated companies. However, Table 3 shows that the relationship between convictions and whether the agency regulates a single industry or multiple industry sectors, is considerably

Table 3
Rate of Convictions per 100 Agency Staff 1981-84 by Size of Client
Companies and Diversity of Industry Sector

	Single Industry	Diverse Industries
Disproportionately Small or Representative Companies		
Median	22.5	37.3
Mean	155	291
Range	0-1425	0-3523
N	20	51
(missing)	(7)	(2)
Disproportionately Large Companies		
Median	0.2	0.00
Mean	2.00	0.00
Range	0-15	0-0
N	15	1

reduced by separating out the sixteen agencies which regulate disproportionately large companies. A considerable part of the reason why single industry sector agencies are less prosecutorial is that fifteen of these agencies regulate companies which are disproportionately large, and agencies which regulate big business very rarely prosecute.

Table 4 shows that the association between conviction and agencies having inspectors who are in frequent contact with the same companies disappears after controlling for size of the regulated companies. There would be no association between low conviction rates and a pattern of regular contacts between the same inspector and the same company were it not for the low conviction rates of the sixteen agencies within this category which predominantly regulate big business.

Table 4
Rate of Convictions per 100 Agency Staff 1981-84 by Size of Client Companies and Whether Inspectors are in Frequent Contact with the Same Companies

	Inspectors in Frequent Contact With Same Companies	Inspectors not in Frequent Contact With Same Companies	No Inspectors
Disproportionately Small or Representative Companies			
Median	35.5	37.0	0.0
Mean	218.9	282.8	0.0
Range	0-2141	0-3523	0.0
N	20	48	3
(missing)	(5)	(4)	(0)
Disproportionately Large Companies			
Median	0.2	—	—
Mean	1.9	—	—
Range	0–14	—	—
N	16	0	0

None of the other controls produced changes in the associations worth reporting. Thus, there is no need for further sub-classifying the medians and means to explore the combined effect of three or more controls.

Summary on the Effect of Controls

Entry of appropriate controls eliminates industry background of enforcement personnel as an explanation of conviction levels. This delivers somewhat of a blow to 'capture' theories of regulatory behaviour. Apart from this, the relational distance explanation is unshaken by all but one of a number of controls. The control which made a difference was the size of the companies being regulated. Controlling for company size still leaves the association with the number of client companies, and the number of industry sectors intact, though the latter is diminished. Thus, challenge by the company size control by no means refutes the relational distance explanation.

Even the association between low convictions and high regularity of contact of the same regulatory officers with the same companies may be due to either a 'relational distance' or a 'big business' explanation. It is difficult to answer whether the fact that the Reserve Bank never initiates prosecutions against the trading banks has more to do with the latter being very powerful adversaries, or whether it is because close ongoing relationships exist between officers of the Reserve Bank and the trading banks (members of the 'banking club'). Similarly, does the Chief Inspector of Coal Mines in Queensland never prosecute companies like Utah because he is afraid of the political consequences? Or is it that inspectors who are professional peers to, and regularly meet with, management of the mines in their district can effectively persuade management to come into compliance without risking the co-operative relationships which achieve this by engaging in litigation? There is probably truth to both explanations, but there is no satisfactory empirical technique for disentangling their relative importance in these data.

The 'Big Business/Weak Enforcement' Explanation

While the control for size of regulated companies does not refute the relational distance explanation, it does present a competing explanation which is worthy of some consideration.

The sixteen agencies coded as having client companies which are disproportionately large were:
Reserve Bank of Australia
Life Insurance Commissioner
Australian Broadcasting Tribunal
Office of the Supervising Scientist for the Alligator Rivers Region
Commonwealth Department of Health, Drug Approvals
National Biological Standards Laboratory
Prices Surveillance Authority
Commonwealth Department of Aviation, Flight Standards Division
Queensland, Chief Inspector of Coal Mines
Western Australia, Department of Mines, Petroleum Division
Tasmania, Department of Mines
Northern Territory, Department of Mines and Energy, Mining Division
Western Australia, Department of Mines, State Mining Engineer
Victoria, Department of Minerals and Energy, Oil and Gas Division
Commonwealth Department of Transport, Office of Road Safety
Commonwealth Department of Transport, Ship Safety Branch

Figure 8 compares the median rate of convictions for these agencies with others.

There is not only a tendency for agencies which deal predominantly with big business to be non-prosecutorial, but our research also found a

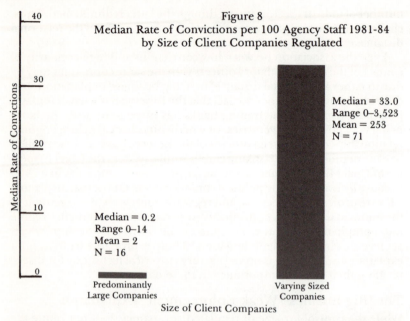

Figure 8
Median Rate of Convictions per 100 Agency Staff 1981-84
by Size of Client Companies Regulated

Median = 33.0
Range 0–3,523
Mean = 253
N = 71

Median = 0.2
Range 0–14
Mean = 2
N = 16

Predominantly   Varying Sized
Large Companies   Companies
Size of Client Companies

reluctance of many agencies which deal with a cross-section of small and large companies to take on major companies. The substantive chapters noted that some of the most prosecutorial agencies have a tendency to net the minnows to the neglect of the sharks. The Australian Taxation Office, the most prosecutorial agency in Australia, has been criticized for this (Chapter 12). So have the other highly prosecutorial agencies: the corporate affairs commissions (Chapter 2), the food inspectorates in New South Wales and Queensland (Chapter 7), and the agencies concerned with fraud against the government (Chapter 12).

The one agency which has maintained a clear policy of assigning top priority to offences by big, rather than small, business, is the Trade Practices Commission. Recently it challenged what it regarded as restrictive trade practices by Australia's largest transport companies. The commission lost the case, then, faced with legal costs which exceed its annual budget, decided not to appeal.

We do not suggest that food inspectorates are more likely to prosecute local butchers than giant retailers, or that the Australian Broadcasting Tribunal is more likely to place limitations on the licence renewal of a community radio station than on a Murdoch or Packer licence, only, or even primarily, for fear of the more formidable adversary. Most Australian regulatory officals genuinely believe big business is more law abiding than small business. Sixty per cent of respondents in our study indicated that the perception was that large companies were more likely to comply with their legislation; only 3 per cent thought small

companies were more likely to comply, and 37 per cent saw no difference between large and small companies.

The reasons the majority gave for the perceived law-abidingness of
big business were generally that large firms are more concerned about
their reputation, and that they have more resources to employ their own
internal compliance staff (e.g. safety, environmental, or equal opportunity officers). These findings are identical with those of an American
study which identified reasons for environmental regulators engaging
in somewhat less punitive enforcement towards large corporations than
small (Lynxwiler *et al.*, 1984).

Whether big business really is more law abiding than small business
in Australia cannot be answered by the data in this study. What we have
shown, however, is that Australian regulatory agencies perceive big
business to be more law abiding. There is some evidence to suggest that,
in general, regulatory agencies adopt less prosecutorial enforcement
policies toward big business compared with small business. This is also
consistent with Black's theory of law which predicts that all else equal
persons or organizations of lower rank or inferior status will be more
subject to punitive sanctions than their wealthier counterparts (Black,
1976, 16-36). In dealings with small business, Australian enforcement
policies sometimes tend to Reiss's deterrence model (see Chapter 1); in
dealing with big business, they overwhelmingly conform to the compliance model.

Implications for Future Research

The data have produced some compelling support for the predictions
from Black's general theory of law that the greater the relational distance
between regulator and regulatee, and the less powerful the regulatee,
the greater the tendency to use formal sanctions. We make no judgement here on whether distance or closeness are desirable in business
regulation. While we have shown some tendencies for closeness to be
associated with a rejection of punitiveness towards industry, it may also
be associated with a superior capacity to achieve substantive regulatory
ends by persuasion or the give-and-take which tend to be part of
ongoing relationships.

The failure to support any of the many other hypotheses concerning
other substantial predictors of conviction levels beyond company size
was surprising, but the importance of relational distance was not. The
tendency for formality to vary directly with social distance has been
observed in a wide variety of contexts, from police–citizen encounters
(Black, 1980), to primitive societies (Levi-Strauss, 1963, 386-7), to collec-
tivities in general (Grabosky, 1984). The present findings thus contribute an important new strand to this body of evidence from the
sociology of law.

In the next chapter, we turn to another contribution which can be
made from a data set such as this: developing a typology of regulatory

agencies. No one before has collected so much data on a number of agencies sufficient to make a credible claim for substantial coverage of all the types of major regulatory agencies in one country. We therefore have the best feasible data set for using multivariate techniques to develop a definitive typology of regulatory agencies.

We will see that two of the groupings in the typology are distinguished by policies of regulators to maintain relational distance from industry (a 'detached', arms-length relationship). Thus, there is a very practical sense in which the findings in this chapter about relational distance matter. Many Australian regulatory agencies have policies which seek to maintain relational distance precisely because they see it as something which changes regulatory behaviour. Looking back to the previous chapter, we discussed policies of rotating staff as an example.

In contrast, only the Trade Practices Commission has a clear policy of directing tougher enforcement at big business than at small business, as a corrective against the other striking tendency which our data reveal. Given the tendency we found for big business to benefit from gentler enforcement, this may be the only way to counterbalance the more general sociological dictum that 'the more the rich and the poor are dealt with according to the same legal propositions, the more the advantage of the rich is increased' (Ehrlich, 1936, 238).

While not wanting to downplay the importance of our findings, we concede that ours is not the only lens through which regulatory behaviour can or should be viewed. Some of the most illuminating explanations of regulatory activity flow from analyses of the historical struggles between interests opposing and supporting regulation, struggles which mould the regulatory stance of the state.

There is little that is inherent in the nature of a regulatory problem which leads inexorably to a particular type of regulation. Some would contend, for example, that a high-stakes area like nuclear reactor safety regulation leads inevitably to a detailed command and control approach, yet in Chapter 5 we saw that a virtual self-regulation approach to this area is adopted in Australia, and that very different regulatory strategies apply in Britain and the United States. With mine safety regulation, we can see similar regulatory problems solved by very dissimilar regulatory strategies when we compare Australia with the United States (Braithwaite, 1985, 119-64).

Further studies of the historical and political context of regulation would complement our work. Intensive studies of particular agencies, which explore the social construction and implementation of agency policy, would further enhance our understanding of how agencies come to have the disparate patchwork of regulatory strategies which we will begin to systematize in the next chapter.

References

Bernstein, M. (1955), *Regulating Business by Independent Commission*, Princeton University Press, Princeton.

Black, D. (1976), *The Behavior of Law*, Academic Press, New York.

—— (1980), *The Manners and Customs of the Police*, Academic Press, New York.

Braithwaite J. (1985), *To Punish or Persuade: Enforcement of Coal Mine Safety*, State University of New York Press, Albany.

Ehrlich, E. (1936), *Fundamental Principles of the Sociology of Law*, Arno Press, New York.

Freitag, P. (1983), 'The Myth of Corporate Capture: Regulatory Commissions in the United States', *Social Problems*, 30, 480-91.

Grabosky, P. (1984), 'The Variability of Punishment', in D. Black (ed.), *Toward A General Theory of Social Control*, vol. 1, Academic Press, Orlando, 163-90.

Levi-Strauss, C. (1963), *Tristes Tropiques: An Anthropological Study of Primitive Societies in Brazil*, Atheneum, New York.

Lynxwiler, J., Shover, N., and Clelland, D. (1984), 'Determinants of Sanction Severity in a Regulatory Bureaucracy', in E. Hochstedler (ed.), *Corporations as Criminals*, Sage Publications, Beverly Hills, 147-67.

Quirk, P. (1981), *Industry Influence in Federal Regulatory Agencies*, Princeton University Press, Princeton.

16
A Typology of Regulatory Agencies

As noted in the previous chapter, our data set is uniquely well-placed empirically to develop a typology of regulatory agencies according to their enforcement policies and practices.

Methods

The first step we took to look at similarities between agencies in their enforcement strategies was exploratory. Correlation coefficients were calculated between each agency and every other agency. Normally, social scientists look at correlations between variables across subject scores. Instead, we looked at correlations between subjects (agencies) across variable scores. This was done because we were interested in developing a typology of agencies rather than a typology of variables.

Initially inter-agency correlation coefficients were calculated for every variable in our data set apart from a number of attitudinal items. This gave us data on 105 variables for each of the ninety-six agencies. The correlation coefficients then told us how similar any two agencies were across these 105 variables. A principal components factor analysis (Q-technique) was then conducted on the matrix of inter-agency correlations (Cattell, 1952, 88-107). In subsequent analyses, the number of variables was culled to thirty-nine, thirty-three, and thirty-one because of a desire to limit the domain to variables representing regulatory policy and practice. Many of the 105 variables in the first analysis, for example, represented aspects of the legislation under which the agencies operate (e.g. whether they have power to enter premises and conduct searches without first obtaining a warrant).

Next, the agencies were classified by means of a hierarchical clustering analysis. Instead of operating on a matrix of correlations between agencies, this technique calculates Euclidean distances between agencies, and the centroids of groups of agencies. In an analysis based on thirty-nine variables, the distance (dissimilarity) between agencies is measured by plotting scores for agencies on the variables in thirty-nine-dimensional space, and measuring distances between agencies in that space. The iterative procedure aggregates agencies into mutually most similar

Figure 1

Typology of Australian regulatory agencies based on hierarchical clustering analysis

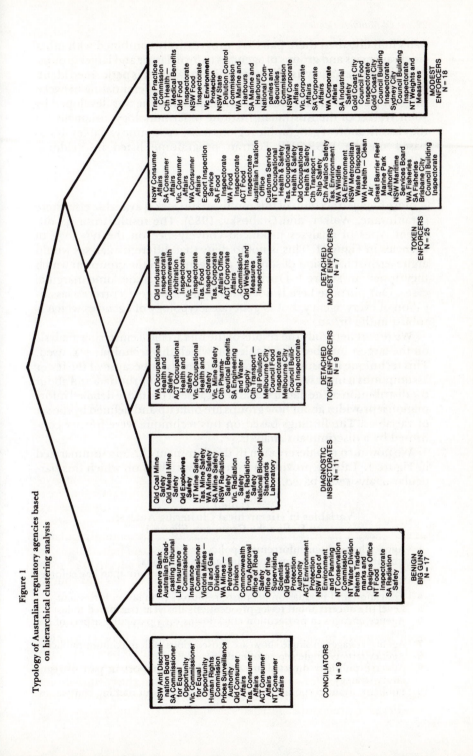

pairs initially; then these pairs are progressively combined with other single agencies and groups of agencies to form larger and larger groups. At each stage, an analysis of between-group variance is performed identifying those variables which contribute most to differentiating between the groups. This hierarchical clustering programme was developed by John Walker of the Australian Institute of Criminology, originally for the classification of geographic regions using economic variables. It was based on the HGROUP Fortran programme listed in Veldman (1965).

The Typology

A more detailed account of this multivariate work is available elsewhere (Braithwaite, Walker, and Grabosky, 1985). The results from six different types of analyses produced convergence on the typology of agencies in Figure 1. This is not to deny that different analyses would argue against inclusion of some of the agencies in the groups in which they appear in Figure 1. Obviously all clusters include some marginal cases. Our purpose here is not to achieve a uniquely 'correct' classification of every agency, but to generate a typology of agencies which is robust in the broad.

We report here only the results of the hierarchical clustering analysis on the largest number of variables on which this technique was used. This technique is vastly superior to factor analysis because of the fewer assumptions it makes about the structure underlying the data and about the distribution of the data itself, and because of the more detailed information it provides about how groups are built up and defined by the set of variables. The findings based on this technique were further confirmed by a discriminant analysis.

We now turn to a description of the dominant clusters summarized in Figure 1. Table 1 provides a list of the variables on which this particular analysis was based.

Table 1
Variables in Hierarchical Clustering Analysis
to Define the Groups in Figure 1

1	Agency has written enforcement policy
2	Importance of law enforcement in agency functions
3	Education and persuasion regarded as more important than law enforcement in agency policy
4	Education and persuasion get more resources than law enforcement
5	Level of concern about fewer prosecutions this year compared to last
6	Agency engages in prosecution crackdowns on a particular aspect of the law
7	Agency engages in single showcase prosecutions with maximum publicity
8	Agency targets single repeat offenders
9	Adverse publicity directed at corporations an important part of regulatory strategy
10	Publicity about corporate malpractices used without naming companies

Table 1 (Cont.)
Variables in Hierarchical Clustering Analysis
to Define the Groups in Figure 1

11   Offenders named in annual reports
12   Goal is to get companies to do better than minimum required by law
13   Negotiating agreements with companies a part of regulatory strategy   .
14   Encouraging self-regulation part of regulatory strategy
15   Staff not discouraged from threatening prosecution with expectation that matters will be otherwise disposed of
16   Tacit or explicit head office approval of threatening to use powers the agency does not really have, i.e. bluff
17   Policy or philosophy on whether better to prosecute individual or company
18   Licences suspended or revoked
19   Injunctions sought in a court of law
20   Production in a plant or on a machine shut down until compliance achieved
21   Assets seized
22   Centralization of decision making authority over how 'problems' are dealt with. Whether policy is for most authority to be with inspectors in field, middle management, top management, political masters
23   Political masters involved in decisions to prosecute
24   Proactiveness–reactiveness. Percentage of enforcement actions triggered by active patrol or investigation versus reacting to complaints
25   Patrol normally without warning
Patrol normally with warning
Discretionary warning depending on circumstances
No active patrol
26   Systematic productivity monitoring of enforcement and investigation staff
27   Emphasis on co-operative relationship with industry
28   Percentage of inspection or investigation staff from industry backgrounds
29   Staff given criminal investigation training
30   Police personnel seconded to agency
31   Number of convictions past three years
32   Prosecution activity increased or declined over past decade
33   Average fines past three years
34   Proportion of prosecutions which result in convictions
35   Conditions of licence used as a regulatory tool
36   Special rules for a particular site used as a regulatory tool
37   Agency has enormous powers over the financial future of companies which it implicitly or explicitly threatens to use but never in fact uses
38   Inspections more oriented to checking compliance with rules or to diagnostic or technical assistance
39   Conciliation between conflicting private parties an important part of regulatory strategy.

Conciliators

The conciliators are agencies which overwhelmingly reject any kind of law enforcement model, relying instead on achieving regulatory goals by bringing conflicting parties together to resolve disputes. At the core of this group are all four anti-discrimination agencies in the study. As Chapter 11 shows, these agencies do not fundamentally see themselves as concerned with enforcing the law. Rather the emphasis is on reducing discrimination by assisting complainants to confront the company whose practices they see as the cause of their grievance. The Prices Surveillance Authority (Chapter 6) also eschews law enforcement, and makes recommendations on prices in a conciliatory, non-binding mode. Parties with different views on whether prices should be increased appear at public hearings.

The conciliators group was formed by a merging of the above five agencies with a second cluster consisting of the Queensland, Tasmanian, Australian Capital Territory, and Northern Territory consumer affairs agencies. Consumer affairs agencies are split into two equal groups in the typology. The remaining four, which are much more enforcement-oriented, are in the 'token enforcers' cluster. The four consumer affairs agencies in the present cluster are distinguished by the fact that while they prosecute from time to time, the prosecutions are almost exclusively for the 'technical' offence of failure to provide information to consumer affairs officers. Queensland, Tasmanian, Australian Capital Territory, and Northern Territory consumer affairs agencies very rarely prosecute for substantive offences; their predominant regulatory approach is conciliation between complainants and traders. The consumer affairs sub-group of the conciliators is distinguished from the other sub-group by their greater reliance on adverse publicity as a regulatory strategy.

Benign Big Guns

These are agencies which walk softly while carrying a very big stick. We have discussed earlier the enormous powers of many of the agencies in this cluster: the power of the Reserve Bank to take over banks, seize gold, increase reserve deposit ratios, etc.; the power of the Australian Broadcasting Tribunal or the Life Insurance Commissioner to take away licences; the power of the Victorian and Western Australian oil and gas regulators to shut down oil rigs; the de facto power of the Supervising Scientist to shut down the Ranger Uranium Mine; and the power of commonwealth drug and motor vehicle safety regulators to refuse to allow a product on the market which has cost a fortune in research and development. The core members of this cluster have such enormous powers, but never, or hardly ever, use them. The very fact that they have such draconian authority, however, means that business cannot ignore them. Thus, counsel for the Australian Consumers' Association in a recent Australian Broadcasting Tribunal television licence renewal hearing described the ABT approach as 'regulation by raised eyebrows', and the Reserve Bank strategy was described in Chapter 10 as 'regulation by vice-regal suasion'.

The inclusion of the Patents Office, the Northern Territory food inspectorate, the South Australian radiation safety, and the Australian Capital Territory and Northern Territory environmental agencies in this group does not make a great deal of theoretical sense. The 'benign big guns' was the most clearly defined factor in the 105-variable factor analysis, accounting for one-third of the total variance, with the Reserve Bank and Australian Broadcasting Tribunal having the highest loadings. The stronger predominance of this dimension in this analysis was undoubtedly due to the inclusion of legislative variables which captured more of the enormous powers of the benign big guns.

Figure 1 shows that at a lower level of similarity, the conciliator and benign big gun groups combine. This combined group is distinguished most from the rest of the agencies by its scores on variable 2 (Table 1): law enforcement is not regarded by these agencies as an important function.

Diagnostic Inspectorates
This group is distinguished by its policies concerning the nature of inspections. They are decentralized inspectorates where most decision making authority rests with well qualified inspectors who are trained to diagnose problems which could reduce safety. In short, they offer technical assistance to companies on improving safety rather than simply drawing the attention of management to specific violations of the regulations. Encouraging industry self-regulation is an important part of their regulatory strategy (variable 14) and they are concerned to maintain co-operative relationships with industry (variable 27).

All but one of the inspectorates in this group are radiation or mine safety inspectorates. Some of the small number of mine inspectorates which were not in this group in the hierarchical clustering analysis reported here, were added to it in other hierarchical clustering analyses. The only agency not concerned with radiation or mine safety — the National Biological Standards Laboratory — perfectly fits the model with its diagnostic approach to inspecting pharmaceutical manufacturing plants.

The diagnostic inspectorates give almost as low a priority to law enforcement as the conciliators and benign big guns. However, when they do prosecute, they are unusual in that they have a policy of prosecuting individual managers rather than the company (variable 17). While in the analysis reported here, the diagnostic inspectorates combine with the detached token enforcers at the next level of aggregation, in other analyses they joined the conciliators and benign big guns.

Detached Token Enforcers
This is by far the least stable of the groups across analyses. The group is distinguished from the previous three in that its members did not, in the course of our interviews, place great store on maintaining co-operative relationships with industry (variable 27). Fostering industry self-regulation (variable 14) and negotiating agreements with industry (variable 13) were not important parts of their regulatory strategy.

Detached Modest Enforcers
In some other analyses the distinction between this and the previous group is rather more blurred than Figure 1. The detached modest enforcers also do not include negotiating agreements with industry and fostering self-regulation as important in their regulatory strategy. While sharing the same arms-length approach to business as the last group, they are more rulebook oriented. They are also more inclined to provide criminal investigation training for their staff. They prosecute more, seize assets more, and are more inclined to target repeat offenders.

Token Enforcers
This group manifests the predominant style of Australian regulatory enforcement. It is the largest and most diverse group. Its members are more proactive on average than the other agencies; their inspections tend to be rulebook oriented rather than diagnostic; most of them initiate a steady flow of prosecutions (only the Australian Taxation Office and the Australian Customs Service among them have an unusually high level of prosecution), and these prosecutions produce derisory average penalties which can only be interpreted as a slap on the wrist.

Modest Enforcers
This group scores highly on all the enforcement related variables. Its members average more convictions than those of any other group. Among them, only the National Companies and Securities Commission does not use prosecution, and as we saw in Chapter 2, it is punitive in other ways. The average fines for this group are also much higher than for any other group, though much of this has to do with the unusually high fines of one agency, the Trade Practices Commission. These agencies also make greater use of alternative means of enforcement: licence suspensions, shutting down production, injunctions, and adverse publicity.

Conceptualizing the Typology
Even though the foregoing has summarized from one analysis only the most important of a larger number of differentiating variables across a larger number of analyses, it is sufficient to make clear that the most important general dimension which underpins the typology is the degree of emphasis on enforcement or punitiveness in regulatory strategy. Essentially, as one moves from the left to right on Figure 1, one is moving towards more enforcement oriented agencies.

  Secondly, across groups there is some important variation independent of enforcement orientation, according to whether agencies use command and control regulation at arms length from industry, or whether they put emphasis on co-operative relationships with industry so that self-regulation might be fostered. The three non-punitive groups on the left of Figure 1 are distinguished from the other agencies in this regard, and this 'arms length' issue is broadly the basis for the differentiation of the two detached enforcer groups from the other two enforcer groups.

A diagrammatic representation of these general bases for distinguishing the groups is presented in Figure 2. A third general basis for differentiation is also captured by Figure 2. This is that the four 'enforcer' groups in the top right quadrant are distinguished from the three 'persuader' groups, in that while the former are more rulebook oriented (legalistic, applying the universalistic rules codified in law), the 'persuader' groups are more particularistic, concerned to find the best solution to a particular problem irrespective of what the law says. Conciliation is of course a particularistic strategy *par excellence*, while the diagnostic inspectorates and the benign big guns both have low mean standard scores on variable 38 (−1.57 and −.72 respectively), which measures a policy emphasis on checking compliance with rules.

The two dimensional representation of types of regulatory agencies in Figure 2 affords a more sophisticated perception of regulatory variation than Reiss's (1984) unidimensional distinction between deterrence and compliance enforcement systems. At the same time, our data show that Reiss's simple model does not excessively distort reality because nearly all the variation in Figure 2 is confined within two quadrants. There are no detached non-enforcers, nor any groups defined by co-operative fostering of self-regulation and tough enforcement.

A single diagonal from particularistic non-enforcers who engage in co-operative fostering of self-regulation, to rulebook enforcers whose policy is detached command and control, would capture most of the variation in Figure 2.

If we are to adopt a two or three dimensional representation of regulatory variation, certainly Figure 2 provides a better guide in the Australian context that Frank's (1984) second dimension of centralized agencies with formal monitoring of inspectors versus decentralized informal agencies. Variables 22 and 26 (Table 1) did not prove to be important in discriminating between the groups and subgroups of similar agencies in our study, with the exception that diagnostic inspectorates tended to have more decentralized decision by making inspectors in the field than other agencies.

While the bottom right quadrant of Figure 2 is devoid of groups of agencies, some shifts are occuring into this quadrant. Tough enforcement under a particularistic self-regulatory regime is the suggestion of Braithwaite's (1982) 'enforced self-regulation' model. Under this model, companies write their own rules in ways which are tailor-made to their particular circumstances; these rules are ratified by the regulatory agency; the company sets up its own internal compliance group to privately enforce the rules; the regulatory agency audits this enforcement, and steps in with tough public enforcement where the private

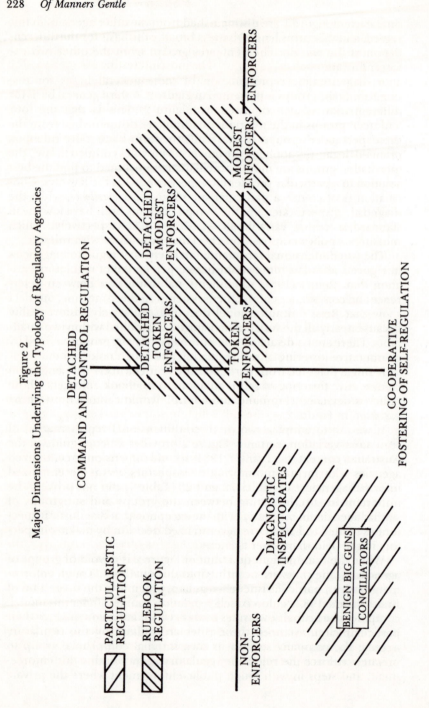

Figure 2
Major Dimensions Underlying the Typology of Regulatory Agencies

enforcement is weak. This book has shown that shifts in this direction have already occurred with the regulation of uranium mining in the Northern Territory (Chapters 3 and 5) and in some other areas of mining and aviation safety regulation. The most interesting prospective shift into particularistic self-regulation with tough enforcement may come as the New South Wales and South Australian Commissioners for Consumer Affairs experiment with co-regulation under their new commercial tribunals (Chapter 6). The commonwealth affirmative action legislation to be introduced in 1986 also seems likely to be based on principles of enforced self-regulation (Chapter 11). Another new area which also looks as if it may go the way of enforced self-regulation is the regulation of animal experimentation (Stewart, 1985).

From Typology to Theory

Typologies fulfil an important role in social science as frameworks on which theories can be constructed. Two of the types of agencies identified by our analysis are quite different from any suggested in the past: the conciliators and the benign big guns. The coherent clustering of these two groups should cause some rethinking of theories on regulatory behaviour.

Just as some shift toward enforced self-regulation is identifiable in Australia, a shift toward the conciliation model is also evident. The newest agency in our study — the Prices Surveillance Authority — which commenced operations in 1984, is a conciliator. In fact all nine conciliator agencies were established in the 1970s or 1980s. Occupational health and safety regulation in Australia is being reshaped at the moment by taking on board important elements of the conciliation model. Tripartite structures on which business, workers, and government are represented are being set up at all levels of occupational health and safety regulation, such that the inspector is becoming more a facilitator of workers acquiring an involvement in their own safety by electing safety representatives, and establishing safety committees to conciliate safety disputes. The intention in most states is that inspectors will spend less of their time reminding employers of the requirements of the rulebook, and more time explaining to workers how they can monitor the safety of their workplace and establish structures to ensure that grievances uncovered by this monitoring are addressed. Similarly, commercial tribunals and credit tribunals are being established by most consumer affairs agencies with tripartite representation of business, government, and consumer groups as a venue for conciliation rather than litigation of a wide variety of consumer grievances.

Conciliated regulation is less goal-directed than command and control regulation. We need theories which explain shifts to conciliated regulation, and which explain or contest the paradox that conciliation might better achieve regulatory goals than goal-directed regulation.

Existence of the benign big guns group demands a theory about the interactions among enormity of regulatory powers, punitiveness of regulatory enforcement, and corporate compliance. Can the benign big guns really change corporate behaviour with a raised eyebrow? If so, is this better for the economy than litigious regulation by agencies with pea-shooters? Indeed, if we asked them, would business tell us that they prefer to be regulated by agencies which walk softly with big sticks than by agencies which keep annoying them with fleabites?

On Painting Broad Canvases

This study has been unique in comprehensively painting the broad canvas of regulatory strategy in one country. But broad canvases can be very sketchy on detail, and that is certainly true of this one. We look forward to more scholars spending a year or two of fieldwork in one agency, or in a comparative study of two different agencies with a similar regulatory mission, to paint in the details of that corner of the canvas. As they do, the shallowness of some of the conclusions in our study will become apparent, and insights not possible under our macro-methodology will be grasped.

Our hope is that as this more important micro work is done, scholars in Australia will take the time to locate their study on our broad canvas. To illustrate why this is important, consider the studies cited in Chapter 6 on how and why the Trade Practices Commission is an impotent, even captured, regulatory agency. Andrew Hopkins is the author of the most sophisticated of this work. The present study has concluded that the Trade Practices Commission imposes the toughest enforcement of any agency in Australia, and spends more of its resources on litigation than any other.

Research which concludes that the Trade Practices Commission is impotent or captured might then be reinterpreted against the background of our canvas. Eckstein (1975) has distinguished five types of case studies in social science: configurative; idiographic; heuristic; plausibility probes; disciplined–configurative; and crucial case studies. The latter are the most useful kinds of case studies for testing theories. Crucial or least likely cases are those which can be expected to disconfirm a theory if any case can be expected to. Thus, if one wanted to test a theory of regulatory impotence, symbolic regulation or capture, the Trade Practices Commission can be identified from our study as the least likely case. If capture can be identified in the most punitive agency in the country, then the capture theory has crossed the biggest hurdle one could put in front of it. It is not within the purposes of this book to make a judgement on whether in fact the behaviour of the Trade Practices Commission sustains a capture or symbolic regulation thesis. We do not want to tell anyone how to do or how to interpret their case study research. We simply make the point that their work can take on new significance when it is located on the kind of broad canvas we have laboured to paint.

References

Braithwaite, John (1982), 'Enforced Self Regulation: A New Strategy for Corporate Crime Control', *Michigan Law Review*, 80, 1466-507.

Braithwaite, John, Walker, John, and Grabosky, Peter (1985), 'A Taxonomy of Regulatory Agencies', unpublished manuscript.

Cattell, Raymond B. (1952), *Factor Analysis*, Harper and Brothers, New York.

Eckstein, Harry (1975), 'Case Study and Theory in Political Science', in F. Greenstein and N. Polsby (eds), *Handbook of Political Science, Vol. 7: Strategies of Inquiry*, Addison-Wesley, Reading, Mass.

Frank, N. (1984) 'Policing Corporate Crime: A Typology of Enforcement Strategies', *Justice Quarterly*, 1, 235-51.

Reiss, Albert J. (1984) 'Selecting Strategies of Social Control over Organisational Life', K. Hawkins and J. Thomas (eds), *Enforcing Regulation*, Kluver-Nijhoff, Boston, 23-6.

Stewart, Hon. Kevin (1985), Opening Speech to Seminar on Animal Experimentation, University of New South Wales, Sydney, 8 July.

Veldman, Donald J. (1965), *Fortran Programming for the Behavioral Sciences*, Holt, Rinehart and Winston, New York.

Appendix
Regulatory Agencies Included
in the Data Analysis

CORPORATE AFFAIRS

New South Wales, Corporate Affairs Commission
Victoria, Corporate Affairs Office
Western Australia, Corporate Affairs Office
South Australia, Corporate Affairs Commission
Tasmania, Corporate Affairs Office
Australian Capital Territory, Corporate Affairs Commission
National Companies and Securities Commission

ENVIRONMENTAL PROTECTION

New South Wales, State Pollution Control Commission
New South Wales, Maritime Services Board
New South Wales, Department of Environment and Planning
New South Wales, Metropolitan Waste Disposal Authority
Victoria, Environment Protection Authority
Queensland, Beach Protection Authority
Western Australia, Department of Marine and Harbours,
    Shipping and Navigation Division
Western Australia, Department of Health and Medical Services,
    Clean Air Section
Western Australia, Department of Fisheries and Wildlife,
    Wildlife Conservator
South Australia, Department of Engineering and Water Supply,
    Water Quality Section
South Australia, Department of Marine and Harbours,
    Ports and Marine Operations
South Australia, Department of Environment and Planning
Tasmania, Department of the Environment
Northern Territory, Conservation Commission
Northern Territory, Department of Transport and Works,
    Water Division

Department of Territories, Environment Protection Section
(Australian Capital Territory)
Office of the Supervising Scientist for the Alligator Rivers Region
Commonwealth Department of Transport, Safety Operations
and Pollution Branch
Great Barrier Reef Marine Park Authority

OCCUPATIONAL HEALTH AND SAFETY

Victoria, Ministry of Employment and Training
Victoria, Department of Minerals and Energy, Mines Division
Victoria, Department of Minerals and Energy,
Oil and Gas Division
Queensland, Department of Employment and Industrial Affairs,
Occupational Safety Division
Queensland, Department of Employment and Industrial Affairs,
Industrial and Factories and Shops Inspectorate
Queensland, Chief Inspector of Coal Mines
Queensland, Chief Inspector of Explosives
Queensland, Chief Inspector of Metalliferous Mines
Queensland, Department of Health and Medical Services,
Division of Public Health Supervision
Western Australia, Department of Industrial Affairs
Western Australia, Department of Mines, Petroleum Division
Western Australia, Department of Mines, State Mining Engineer
South Australia, Department of Labour, Industrial Safety Division
South Australia, Department of Mines and Energy
Tasmania, Department of Labour and Industry
Tasmania, Department of Mines
Northern Territory, Department of Mines and Energy,
Industrial Safety Division
Northern Territory, Department of Mines and Energy,
Mining Division
Department of Territories, Technical Services Branch
(Australian Capital Territory)

RADIATION CONTROL

New South Wales, Department of Health, Radiation Health
Services Branch
Victoria, Health Commission
South Australia, Health Commission
Tasmania, Department of Health Services

CONSUMER AFFAIRS

New South Wales, Department of Consumer Affairs
Victoria, Ministry of Consumer Affairs

Queensland, Consumer Affairs Bureau
Western Australia, Department of Consumer Affairs
South Australia, Department of Public and Consumer Affairs
Tasmania, Consumer Affairs Council
Northern Territory, Commissioner of Consumer Affairs
Queensland, Chief Inspector of Weights and Measures
Australian Capital Territory, Consumer Affairs Bureau
Trade Practices Commission
Prices Surveillance Authority

FOOD STANDARDS

New South Wales, Department of Health, Chief Food Inspector
Victoria, Health Commission
Queensland, Department of Health and Medical Services,
    Chief Inspector of Food
Western Australia, Department of Health and Medical Services
South Australia, Health Commission,
    Chief Inspector of Food
Tasmania, Department of Health Services,
    Chief Inspector of Food
Northern Territory, Department of Health,
    Chief Inspector of Food
Australian Capital Territory Health Authority,
    Chief Inspector of Food
Melbourne City Council, Chief Health Surveyor
Gold Coast City Council, Health Surveyor
Commonwealth Department of Primary Industry,
    Export Inspection Service

DRUG AND MEDICAL DEVICE REGULATION

National Biological Standards Laboratory
Commonwealth Department of Health,
    Therapeutic Goods Branch
Commonwealth Department of Health,
    Pharmaceutical Benefits Branch

TRANSPORT SAFETY

Commonwealth Department of Transport, Office of Road Safety
Commonwealth Department of Transport, Ship Safety Branch
Commonwealth Department of Aviation, Flight Standards Division

PRUDENTIAL REGULATION

Reserve Bank of Australia
Insurance Commissioner
Life Insurance Commissioner

ANTI-DISCRIMINATION POLICY
New South Wales, Anti-Discrimination Board
Victoria, Commissioner for Equal Opportunity
South Australia, Commissioner for Equal Opportunity
Commonwealth Human Rights Commission

FRAUD AGAINST THE GOVERNMENT
Australian Taxation Office
Australian Customs Service
Commonwealth Department of Health, Surveillance
and Investigation Division

MISCELLANEOUS REGULATORY REGIMES
Australian Broadcasting Tribunal
Western Australia, Department of Fisheries and Wildlife,
Chief Fisheries Officer
South Australia, Department of Fisheries
Brisbane City Council, Building Surveyor
Gold Coast City Council, Surveyor of Buildings
Melbourne City Council, Buildings Division
Sydney City Council, Building Surveyor
Commonwealth Department of Employment and
Industrial Relations, Arbitration Inspectorate
Commonwealth Patent, Trademarks, and Designs Office

ADDITIONAL AGENCIES VISITED BUT NOT CODED
FOR PURPOSE OF QUANTITATIVE ANALYSIS
Western Australia, Department of Conservation and Environment
Western Australia, Department of Health and Medical Services
(Occupational Health)
Queensland, Department of Harbours and Marine
South Australia, Health Commission (Occupational Health)
Tasmania, Department of Health Services (Occupational Health)
Northern Territory, Department of Health (Occupational Health)
Australian Capital Territory Health Commission (Occupational
Health)
Northern Territory, Department of Health (Radiation Control)
Australian Atomic Energy Commission
Australian Atomic Energy Commission, Regulatory Bureau
Commonwealth Department of Health, Secretariat
to the Food Standards Committee of the National
Health and Medical Research Council
National Occupational Health and Safety Commission
Commonwealth Department of Arts, Heritage, and Environment,
Environmental Contaminants Division
Commonwealth Department of Arts, Heritage, and Environment,
Assessment Branch

Index